𝕸𝖎𝖘𝖈𝖊𝖑𝖑𝖆𝖓𝖊𝖆 𝕴𝖓𝖎

With a bibliography of Inverness

newspapers and periodicals

John Noble, John Whyte

Alpha Editions

This edition published in 2019

ISBN : 9789353952358

Design and Setting By
Alpha Editions
email - alphaedis@gmail.com

" Mr. Noble's Shop, where you can buy the Jacobite Pamphlets."—Andrew Lang.

PREFACE.

A NATIVE of Inverness, resident in it during the greater part of his life, and for many years engaged in the business of a bookseller and antiquarian collector, few men enjoyed better opportunities for acquiring and utilising the fugitive lore of the town and district than the late Mr. JOHN NOBLE. It was his intention to devote what leisure moments he could command from time to time to the preparation and publication of selections from his vast accumulations of local history and reminiscence. His lamented and unexpected death a few years ago, however, prevented the realisation of his purpose, beyond putting into printed form the following 184 pages of Miscellanea. In issuing these to the public, the present publisher has, with the permission of Mr. KENNETH MACDONALD, Inverness, for Mr. NOBLE's family, and of the Editor of "Scottish Notes and Queries," Aberdeen, added a Bibliography of Inverness Newspapers and Periodicals, which was contributed by Mr. NOBLE to that interesting serial, and which he intended to form portion of the present volume. The Bibliography referred to has been revised, and a few notes supplied to bring the information down to the present day.

INTRODUCTION.

THE papers forming the present Miscellanea, though thrown together without any special plan or method, will be read with interest by Invernessians at home and abroad, as affording vivid glimpses of their native spot, its people, and their habits, in times long gone by. With the appended "Bibliography of Inverness Newspapers and Periodicals," this volume will also form a not unimportant contribution to the existing, but altogether too meagre and fragmentary, works on local history. Readers familiar with the Inverness of to-day will find here matter for amusing and interesting comparison and contrast between the condition of society now and that which prevailed in what are called "the good old times." Great as the changes have been as regards the people and their habits, what Inverness owes to Nature—and it is admitted on all hands that she is liberally endowed in that respect—remains unchanged. The poetic tribute to the beauty of the town with which the volume opens is as appropriate now as when it came from the pen of its scholarly author, Dr. Arthur Johnston, of Aberdeen, more than two centuries ago; and every summer brings hundreds and thousands of visitors prepared to re-echo the poet's enthusiastic appreciation of the charms with which "Nature and the genius of the place" have conspired to grace the town. Nor has Inverness herself lacked for admiring citizens gifted with power to move the muses into rapture over her lordly river and her picturesque and beautiful Islands. In past years she could point to her Andrew Frasers, her "Jamie" Patersons, and her John Macraes, the specimens of whose rhyming effusions in the following pages prove their title to stand side by side with those who have maintained the apostolical succession of her bards down to our own day.

A valuable and instructive paper by John Anderson, W.S., on Macbeth's Castle leaves the question of the exact site of the building an open one, and the subject still continues to occupy the attention of our Scientific Society and Field Club, and of the more sanguine and less fastidious compilers of our tourist guides.

O

The references to the " Characters " of the town will recall
names, and perhaps faces, familiar to some of our oldest
citizens, while at the same time emphasizing the circumstance
that here, as elsewhere, these oddities of the population have all
disappeared, and have left no successors. Several causes,
which need not be here discussed, have contributed to the
extinction of this class; but none the less does their dis-
appearance excite emotions of regret, and their absence will
seriously impoverish the " Miscellanea " of future chroniclers.
Other social features of past times have also yielded to modern
arrangements. The billposter and the advertising columns of
the press have almost superseded the bellman ; and though we
can still improvise a political heckler on occasion, the ballot
box has destroyed much of what rendered memorable the
elections of which our fathers delighted to tell us. The
" fiddles " of our fathers' days have become " violins," and
superfine " artistes," who would shudder at the very mention
of " the waits " and " penny-weddings," have taken the place
of our lively and interesting old " fiddlers," of whom the last,
but certainly not the least, in Inverness was the well-known
" Allie Bo-Bo."

" Jamie " Paterson's poem and Mr. Noble's accompanying
observations on the Martinmas Market speak of a time when
home industries flourished without the patronage or help of
societies promoted by the wives and daughters of the landed
and titled aristocracy. All honour, we would say, to these
generous and exemplary ladies for their efforts to revive and
foster those old local industries which formed such a conspicuous and interesting feature of the Inverness Martinmas
Market. " Butter and cheese," says Mr. Noble, " was the
staple of the Fair, and from the top of Academy Street, near
Baron Taylor's Lane, to Rose Street we have seen the country
carts closely packed together on both sides of the street, laden
with butter in kegs and jars, and kebbocks or cheeses, the
produce from their crofts and small farms. The market
lasted for three days. As early as Wednesday afternoon
might be seen the signs of the approaching Fair—the arrivals
of country carts in town with their loads of produce. On the
Exchange or Plainstones in front of the old Town Hall, and

crowded round Clachnacuddin Stone, were seated old women
with rolls of plaiding, bundles of stockings, and homespun
thread, while crowds of thrifty housewives discussed the quality
and the price.   Friday was the chief day of the Fair, and on
which most business was done, and the attendance largest."
" Stents " or " petty customs " seem to have been a grievance
no less then than in the present time, as we are assured by
" Jamie " Paterson in his realistic poem on the Martinmas
Market :—

> " Frae ilka airt in crowds they thrang
>   On cairts stocked, heavy-laden
> Wi' butter kits, baith stout and strang,
>   An' fine-wove wabs o' plaidin' ;
> But they, puir sauls, aye think it wrang
>   The Custom Stents they've laid on
> Sic guids as come oor streets alang—
>   They think that they are played on,
>   On sic a day."

By the way, it seems strange that Paterson and Macrae
should have affected Lowland Scotch in their poetic effusions
—a dialect which is extremely little heard in the Highlands—
and it is further astonishing that they were able to use it with
such accuracy and so expressively.

In no department of our social economy has development
and improvement been more remarkable than in the Post
Office.   This is very strikingly brought out in the evidence led
in the curious Post Office dispute, Warrand against Falconer,
which occupies such a large space in the present volume.   One
can scarcely believe that at almost any period such primitive
and happy-go-lucky arrangements could prevail in a public
office as evidently obtained in the local Post Office of that
time, if Post Office the place could be called which consisted
simply of the postmaster's kitchen, the " dresser " being the
receptacle for letters going and coming, while the domestic servants and their gossiping visitors assumed the role of " sorters."
Nor did they confine themselves very strictly to the duties of
their office, for it came out in evidence that even the contents
of the letters did not always escape their prying curiosity.   The
letters were delivered by one old man, and after his decease,
or when he became infirm, by his wife, an old woman of
seventy-seven and quite illiterate.   From her own evidence,

we learn that when she received any foreign letters, or letters
with high postages to pay, she was instructed " to deliver them
to the merchants with her own hands, and that she commonly
put such letters into her breast." The other letters she kept
in a great pouch, dropping into some shop by the way, when
occasion required, to have the addresses on the letters read
out to her, that she might be able to deliver them to their
owners.   All this was about the year 1770; but it is not necessary to go so far back to show the immense strides which the
postal arrangements and equipment in Inverness have made.
The late Mr. Penrose Hay, who was postmaster of Inverness
for about fifty years prior to the year 1888, tells us in his
address to his employees, on the occasion of his retirement,
that about the time of Queen Victoria's coronation the dimen-
sions of the old Post Office, which stood in Church Street, at
the top of Bank Lane, were 110 square feet.   The Highland
Railway postal sorting-carriage which now runs daily to Perth
is nearly three times this area, while the spacious new Post
Office in Queensgate has an area of 15,300 square feet.   In
1839 the letters received in Inverness numbered only 2771,
while now they reach about 50,000 per month, in addition to
newspapers, book packets, and post cards.

The valuable and exhaustive Bibliography of Inverness
Newspapers and Periodicals which concludes this volume,
testifies to an amount of literary activity and journalistic
enterprise that would have done credit to towns of greater
pretensions, and possessed of much more ample facilities for
obtaining and dealing with local and foreign intelligence.
Financially, these journals may not have all been successful,
but of the press of Inverness it may, we believe, be affirmed
that its tone has in the main been wholesome; its influence in
the conserving of public morals has throughout been powerful
and constant.   And despite the fact that the daily papers from
the South arrive before breakfast is well over, Inverness is
still able to maintain its local papers on five days of the week
—the "Courier" on Tuesday and Friday, the "Northern
Chronicle" on Wednesday, the "Highland Times" on Thursday, and the "Highland News" on Saturday.

INVERNESS, Jan., 1902.   J. W.

CONTENTS.

ILLUSTRATIONS.

JOHN NOBLE'S SHOP, - - - Frontispiece.

PORTRAITS.

LIST OF SUBSCRIBERS.

Aitken, Mrs., Inverness.
Alexander, Samuel G., Inverness.
Anderson, Provost, Stornoway.
Andrew, Dr., Doune.

Bain, Wm., Lochmaddy.
Barron, James, Inverness.
Batchen, Mr., Inverness.
Beveridge, Erskine, Dunfermline.
Blair, A. S., W.S., Edinburgh.
Brown, Charles Marshall, Inverness.
Brown, C. M., Inverness.
Brown, Wm., Edinburgh.
Bulloch, John, Aberdeen.

Cameron, Dr. J. A., Nairn.
Cameron, John, Bookseller, Inverness.
Campbell, A. D., Komgha, Cape Colony.
Caruthers, W. L., Inverness.
Cook, W. B., Stirling.
Cran, John, Inverness.

Darwin, F., Muirtown.
Davy, Richard, Stirling.
Devavault, P., Inverness.
Drysdale, William, Stirling.

Forsyth, W. B., London.
Fraser, Alex., Solicitor, Inverness.
Fraser, D., Bridge of Allan.
Fraser, H. E., M.D., Dundee.
Fraser, J. Leslie, Castle Tolmie, Inverness.

Gossip, James A., Inverness.
Gray, George, Glasgow.
Graham, John, Inverness.
Grant, Lieut.-Colonel R. A. P., A.M.S., Inverness.

Holmes, Messrs W. & R., Glasgow.
Hutchison, Wm., Broughty-Ferry.

Jolly, William, Blantyre.
Johnstone, G. P., Bookseller, Edinburgh.
Johnstone, Miss, Bookseller, Inverness.

Kemble, Major, Broadford.

Logie, D. W., Stirling.

MacAndrew, Lady, Inverness.
MacBain, Alexander, M.A., LL.D.
MacBean, Andrew, Invergordon.
MacBean, George, Inverness.
MacBean, L., Kirkcaldy.
Macbean, Wm. M., New York.
MacCallum & Co., Glasgow.
Macdonald, Andrew, Inverness.
Macdonald, John, Inverness.
Macdonald, Kenneth, Inverness.
Macdonald, Rev. Mr., Killearnan.

Macdonald, T. D., Stirling.
MacGregor, James, Falkirk.
MacGregor, John, Partick.
MacKay, Alex., London.
MacKay, D. J., London.
MacKay, Donald, Inverness.
MacKay, James H., N.W. Territory, Canada.
Mackay, John, Stirling.
MacKay, Rev. G. S., Doune.
MacKay, William H., Johannesburg, Transvaal.
MacKay, William, Solicitor, Inverness.
MacKay, Wm., Bookseller, Inverness.
Mackie, J., Stirling.
MacKenzie, Miss, London.
MacKenzie, W., Elgin.
MacKintosh, Miss Fraser, London.
Mackintosh, Duncan, Inverness.
MacLaren, Thomas, Bookseller, Inverness.
MacLeod, Fred, Edinburgh.
MacLeod, John, Inverness.
MacLeod, Malcolm Chisholm, Dundee.
MacRitchie, Andrew, Inverness.
Mactavish, P. D., Inverness.
Matheson, Gilbert, Inverness.
Melven Brothers, Booksellers, Inverness.
Melven, Miss, Inverness.
Menzies & Co., John, Glasgow.
Mitchell, Alex., Inverness.
More, R., Glasgow.
Munro, Sir Hector, of Foulis.
Munro, Henry, Inverness.
Munro, J. J., Stirling.
Murdoch, John, Saltcoats.

Newlands, Mr., Inverness.
Noble, Mrs., Inverness.
Noble, Roderick, Inverness.

Paterson, Alex., Llanbryde.
Public Library, Dundee, per John MacLauchlan, Librarian.
Public Library, Inverness.

Reid, R., Stirling.
Ross, Alexander, LL.D., Inverness.
Ross, James, Inverness.

Small, James A., Denver, Colorada, U.S.A.
Smith, Dr., Sunderland.
Smith, John Rae, Aberdeen.
Smith, Robert, Dundee.

Wallace, T. D., Inverness.
Wallace, J. D., Inverness.
Watson, Adam, Stirling.
Williams, Rev. George, Thornhill, Stirling.
Wilson, P. G., Inverness.
Whyte, John, Inverness.
Wylie & Son, D., Aberdeen.

Young, W. H., Stirling.

Portrait and Signature of John Noble,

Bookseller, Inverness.

MISCELLANEA INVERNESSIANA.

EARLY POEM ADDRESSED TO INVERNESS.

THE following poem—the earliest we have met—written in praise of Inverness, is the composition of Arthur Johnston, an eminent Latin poet, a native of Aberdeenshire ; born in 1587, died in 1641. He was Physician-in-Ordinary to Charles I. He commemorated in his poetry many of the most notable families and the chief towns of Scotland.

The translation from the Latin is the work of the Rev. J. Barclay of Cruden, and first appeared in a work " Memorialls for the Government of Royall Burghs in Scotland" printed at Aberdeen in 1685 :—

DE INNERNESSA,
CARMEN ARCTURI JONSTONI.

URBS vicina freto, tu surgis in ubere campo,
Et prope Parrhasiae Virginis ora vides.
Atria te Regum decorant, et sanguine fuso,
Pictorum, toties qui rubuere lacus.
Vela ferens Nessus vitreis interluit undis
Et ratibus famulas applicat ille rates,
Non coit unda gelu, medio sed tempore brumae
Libera victrices in mare volvit aquas.

INVERNESS.

A TOWN not far from sea in fertile land,
Even near unto our northmost coast doth stand ;
With palaces of kings thou'rt garnished,
And lakes with blood of Pechts oft coloured.
With Ness pure stream thy borders watered be,
Where ships float and approach for serving thee ;
This rives freezeth not by winter cold,
Its waters to the sea flow uncontrol'd.
The earth doth plenteous harvests here dispense

1

Nec desunt gravidæ gelido sub sydere messes,
Nec minus, est famuli festilis unda freti.
Proxima re Thule vicinaque ditat Ierne,
Omnis et arctois insula septa vadis.
Abstulit imperii dudum Bodotria fasces,
Et Dominæ titulo cœpit Edina frui ;
Tu tamen emporium, regni diceris, honerem.
Hunc natura tibi dat geniusque loci.

In spite of northern stars' cold influence ;
Thule and Iernie which thy neighbours be,
And all the Northern Isles, send wealth to thee.
Forth long ago the chief command doth claim,
And Edinburgh yields not to thee the name
Of the chief city ; yet they ever shall
Thee an Emporium of this Kingdom call.
Both nature and the genius of the place
Have with this honour joynéd thee to grace.

THE SITE OF MACBETH'S CASTLE AT INVERNESS.

THE town of Inverness is situated on a plain, at a short dis-tance from the junction of the river Ness with the Murray Firth. The range of mountains, extending northwards from Loch-Ness gradually falls in elevation as it approaches the town, which is environed on the south by a rising ground of inconsiderable height. At its western extremity, this ridge towers abruptly over the river, which, half-a-mile further down, terminates its course. From this precipitous brow, a line of low-lying hills runs eastwards, immediately above the high road, broken occasionally by small lateral glens. The first of these occurs about four fur-longs to the eastward of Inverness, at the foot of the 'Crown Hill,' which forms the eastern, as the mount above the river does the western point of the whole eminence ; and it is through part of the latter that the approach to Dores, Fort-Augustus, etc., now called 'Castle Street,' has been cut.

From its commanding position over the narrow strait which separates Inverness from Ross, this eminence must at all times have been an object of great importance ; and appears from the emotest era, to have been crowned by a fortress.

In the year of Christ 565, Brudi II., son of Meilochon, held the sceptre of all the Picts.* His capital stood on the banks of the Ness; and thither Columba directed his steps from Iona across the hills of Drum-Albyn. The Pictish monarch, and most of the northern Picts, were converted to Christianity by the Saint; and the observations of the latter's biographer, Adomnan, seem to fix the court of the royal convert to have been on the height above the present town of Inverness, then graced also by the presence of a Scandinavian chief of Orkney.†

Supposing King Brudi's mansion to have adorned the hill in question, we have no means of ascertaining its exact site, whether toward the *western* or *eastern* slope. That, in after times, each of these promontories was surmounted by a *ballium*, or strength, is beyond a doubt; and it is from inattention to particulars that so many have jumbled 'Macbeth's Castle' with the 'Castle of Inverness.'

That Macbeth was Maormor of Ross by birth, and succeeded to that of Moray by marriage, cannot be gainsaid.‖ In his latter capacity, that ample region from the Spey to the Beauly, and extending westward to Argyll, fell under his domain. No spot could be more favourably chosen for the government of either principality than Inverness, dignified, as it had formerly been, by being the abode of royalty. The difference of our historians, in an important part of Macbeth's life, has, nevertheless, gone far to shake the truth of the great part he acted altogether.

Fordun, who flourished about 1380, is the first who details the means by which Macbeth obtained the crown.‡ Speaking of Duncan:—'Hic autem, pius Rex occisus est scelere, generis occi-' sorum tam avi quam proavi, quorum praecipuus erat, MACHA-' BEDA, filius Finele, a quo latenter apud Bothgofuane ‖‖ vulneratus ' ad mortem, et apud *Elgin* delatus, occubuit, et insula *Iona* se-' pultus est.' Boece, who gave his History and Chronicles of Scot land to the world in 1526, omits entirely all mention of *Both-gofuane;* stating that Macbeth was instigated by his wife to murder Duncan at *Inverness:* and that the King was buried at *Elgin*, but afterwards removed to *Icolmkill*.¶ The Chronicon Elegiacum,§

* Pinkerton's Enquiry into the History of Scotland, i. 282, 298.
† Caledonia, i. 262.   ‖ Caledonia, i. 405.   ‡ Lib. iv. c. 49.
‖‖ *Lochgosnane*, editio Hearnii.
¶ Lib. xii. c. 3.   § Pinkerton's Enquiry, App. vol. ii. p. 333.

says :—

> ' A Finleg natus percussit eum Maeabeta ;
> ' Vulnere lethali Rex apud *Elgin obit.*'

Adding—

> ' Hos in pace viros tenet insula *Iona* sepultos,
> ' In tumulo Regum judicis usque diem.'

Buchanan * joins in placing the murder at Inverness ; Hollinshed follows ; and Shakespeare closes the array.†

The difficulty consists, not in placing the King's death at Elgin, and subsequent removal to Iona ; but in assigning to Bothgofuane, or to Inverness, the infamy of the attempt upon his life.

The event which threw Duncan in the way of his murderer was produced by the refusal of Torfin, Jarl of Caithness, to render tribute to the Scottish Crown. In his progress to chastise that rebel, his Majesty was obliged to traverse the territories of Gruoch, and her husband Macbeth. The latter, who was allied to the royal family (being a son of Doada, daughter of Malcolm II.), saw in this circumstance a fitting opportunity of gratifying ambition, by the removal of a man who filled a throne,, to which his claim was novel.‡ The rights of hospitality had not, however, lost their force ; and a *smith's* dwelling (so Lord Hailes ‖ translates *Bothgouanan*)—not his Castle of Inverness— was chosen by Macbeth for the murder of his sovereign. There is nothing to imply this hovel was beside Elgin (not Inverness). What is there, in the *Chronicon Elegiacum* to sanction Mr Pinkerton's reading that Duncan was slain near Elgin ? It is his *death* alone which is fixed ' *apud Elgin :*'—*where* the ' mortal stroke ' was given, is not stated. By laying the scene in the palace, to which suspicion of treachery could least attach, Shakspeare added to the horror of the action, but departed not from the main features of the tragedy ; and the subsequent transfer of Duncan to Elgin has nothing in it to startle us. Possibly, some shrine stood there at which the dying Monarch wished to pay his last vows—a request his foeman (as believing it, in the spirit of the age, conducive to his soul's repose) might not refuse ; possibly the assassins fled, impressed with the belief of having slain their victim ; thereby affording his attendants an opportunity of escaping the more

---

* Book vii.   † See Malone's Shakspeare, iv. 266, 267.
‡ Pinkerton's Enquiry, ii. 196.   ‖ Annals, i. 1.

readily from the territories of Moray. Elgin was the last town, it will be remembered, on the confines of that province.

Whether it be an illusion, as Mr Chalmers * has so dogmatically stated it to be or not to talk of the walls of Macbeth's Castle at Inverness, 'where he never had a castle nor a residence,' we are now to consider.

The Statstical Account of Inverness says † that the 'Thane of Calder's Castle' was built on the *eastern* extremity of the hill which covers the town ; and that it was *razed to the ground* by Malcolm, in detestation of his father's murderer. 'The remembrance of the theatre of Macbeth's ambitious villainy is preserved, however, in the old charter names of the lands ‖ which belonged to it. The castle *near the river*, on the *western* extremity of the hill, was destroyed in the Rebellion of 1745. An ancient family, the Cuthberts of Castlehill, derive their designation from the site of '*Macbeth's* Castle.'

It is much to be regretted that the compilers of these particulars did not amass all the traditionary tales current respecting this *eastern* fortress at the period they wrote. These are now vague and unsatisfactory ; and I find on inquiry that they merely give a general support to the above statement.

There are, however, circumstances which materially aid the supposition of Macbeth's Castle having occupied the situation thus assigned to it; and of its having been a distinct structure from that vulgarly styled 'the Castle of Inverness.'

In an old MS. in the archives of the Society of Antiquaries of Scotland, relative to the above-mentioned family of Cuthbert, which bears date on the back 1635, I find this passage : 'In all 'their charters and old wryts they are called Cuthbert's of the '*Alde* Castlehill ; this castle *now* in being, being *then* the *new* 'castle ; and it was founded by King Eugenius the Second. 'There is yett some vestiges of their *old* castle to be seen.' Again, the *eastern* extremity of the hill which shields Inverness

---

* Caledonia, i. 405. † Vol. ix. p. 633.

‖ In an especial manner, in that of 'Auld Castlehill.' I had occasion to inspect a beautiful deed, dated at Inverness, in the Feast of the Epiphany of the Holy Cross, A.D. 1362, by which 'Robertus de Chesholme, miles, dominus ejusdem,' granted to the altars of the Holy Cross at Inverness, for the safety of his soul and those of his ancestors and successors, six acres of arable land within the lands of 'the *Old Castle* of Inverness.' These acres are to this day called Diriebught (*i.e.* the Poor's Lands), and run immediately under the supposed site of Macbeth's Castle, at the base of the Crown Hill.

has from time out of mind been known as 'the Crown.' To
have obtained this appellation of ' the Crown ' * a royal seat must
at one time have graced the mount, built or repaired by none more
likely than by that King, whose authority was here, perhaps, first
acknowledged ; and traditionary lore stamps the conjecture, by
embodying it with the history of Macbeth. Immediately opposite
to ' the Crown,' on a similar eminence, and separated from it by a
narrow valley, is a farm belonging to a gentleman of the name of
Welsh.¶ That part of the ascent to this farm next Viewfield, from
the great Highland Road, is called ' Banquo's Brae.' The whole
of the vicinity is rich in wild imagery. From the mouth of
the valley of Diriebught to King's Mills, thence by the road to
Viewfield, and down the gorge of Aultmuniack to the mail-road
along the sea shore, we compass a district celebrated in the
annals of *diablerie*. It was in this last glen, on the borders of the
rivulet Aultmuniack (or witches' burn) that withered beldames
joined in their unhallowed rites ; and it was upon the small
croft at the eastern extremity of Aultmuniack vale, that the last
witch was burnt in the commencement of the 18th century.†
George Cuthbert of Castlehill, sheriff depute of Inverness-shire,
under the too renowned Simon Lord Lovat, a notorious persecu-
tor of these victims to a degraded belief, met his death in the
year 1748, at the western extremity of Aultmuniack, by a fall
from his horse A smiddy now stands upon the spot ; remarkable
also, as being, in the traditionary belief of the country people,
" the pit or grave of King Duncan," and so named, *Slochd Dunache*.
With the characteristic weakness of popular superstition, Mr
Cuthbert's death was, and is, looked upon as the retributive act

* ' The lands and barony of *Auld Castlehill*, commonly called the CROWN,
' occur in the register of sasines for Inverness-shire, 25th November 1805.
' By the same record, sasine was given to the Hon. Colonel Archibald
' Fraser of Lovat, 8th February 1808, of the "lands and barony of Auld
' Castlehill, commonly called the CROWN, and long rig immediately around
' the *Crown*, called the AULD, or MACBETH's Castlehill." '

¶ Now (1892) occupied by the New Barracks, the depot of the 79th
(Cameron) Highlanders.

† The latest instance, according to general belief, of an execution for
witchcraft, occurred at Dornoch, in Sutherlandshire, in the year 1727,
when the sheriff-depute condemned a mother and daughter to the stake,
A gentleman of property in Ross-shire has repeated told me that his grandfather, who died in November 1800 at the age of 90 years, used to mention
to him his having seen, when a youth, an old feeble man burnt on the
Schoolhill of Aberdeen, as a wizard. He was pinioned down into a chair ;
and so placed upon the pile, which consumed him. In all probability he
was the last sufferer for the ' black art ' in Scotland.

of those ' weird sisters,' whose compatriots had suffered by his command.*

The town of Inverness is said to have anciently stood a little to the south of this 'Crown Hill,' about a mile from its present site in the plain ; and tradition still points out near *Kingsmills*, the *locale* of the burgh-cross. These mills may have been attached to the royal granary ; whilst the object of the townspeople by building there was to obtain protection from the fortress.‖ When it was demolished, their security ceased ; and hence the reason why the town took a *westerly* direction under the walls of the *New* Castle. If Malcolm Cean-Mhor was the founder of this second strength (as he is commonly reputed to have been), it is probable that the charter he granted to the town was dated in the same year in which the fortifications were commenced.

About the year 1802-3, whilst some labourers were trenching a portion of the adjacent farm of the late Bailie Wilson,§ on the eastern side of the Crown Hill, contiguous to Dickson's nursery grounds,‡ they met with a quantity of rubbish and the foundation of walls supposed to have belonged to the ancient castle. Mr Wilson removed the stones and partially built with them a cottage in the valley below the hill. One of the stones, remarkable for carved decorations, was given to the Honourable Colonel Fraser of Lovat : but every attempt to learn what became of it after his death has proved unsuccessful. I may also mention that traces of what has been an approach to a place of consequence are still discernible. This approach enters the lands of Diriebught from the present mail-road from Fort-George ; and, running through the valley, gradually ascends the bank of the Crown Hill ; and, the level attained, strikes again to the eastern point, where it terminates. Here the 'pleasant seat' is rumoured to have stood, facing the sea ; and singularly correct with respect

---

* See " Reminiscences of a Clachnacuddin Nonagenarian," 1886, and " The Witch of Inverness," 1892, for notices of 'Creibh Mhor' and her practices.

‖ See Dr Hibbert's Shetland, p. 256, for the connexion between the ancient *burgh* and the adjacent village, which in time acquired the same appellation.

§ Father of the late James Wilson, solicitor, and many years agent for the Commercial Bank of Scotland at Inverness.

‡ Dickson's nursery occupied grounds now partly built on, between the present Millburn Distillery and the recently formed road approaching to Victoria Terrace.

to the relative points of the compass will be found in the poet's disposal of the portal 'at the south entry.' I remember, when a
boy, to have heard that a drawwell which existed at this spot had
been filled up in the memory of persons then, or shortly before,
living, but such individuals as might have enabled me to check the
accuracy of this tale are unhappily dead. Dr Johnson, in his
Tour to the Western Isles, observes, that the walls of 'Macbeth's
Castle' were at that time standing ; but it is clear that both the
Doctor, and the Commentator who re-echoes him,* spoke of the
remains of the western peel.

The extreme accuracy with which Shakspeare has followed the
minutiæ of Macbeth's career has given rise to the opinion that he
himself visited those scenes which are immortalised by his pen.
The daring Gruoch, the daughter of Bodhe,† and wife of
Macbeth—

> ———'from the crown to th' toe, top full
> Of direst cruelty,'

was no fictitious personage. Boece tells us it was by her persuasion that her Lord was tempted to crime. Her wrongs 'un-
sexed' her.‡   Guthrie § first threw out the probability of
Shakspeare's having been in Scotland, and Sir John Sinclair followed.‖ It is certain that companies of English comedians tra-
versed this country towards the end of the 16th century   On the
23rd of June 1589,¶ a troop of players applied to the church-
consistory of Perth for a license ; and the minister and elders gave
license to play, with condition that no swearing, banning, nor onie
scurrility be spoken.' In the year following, King James desired
Queen Elizabeth to send him a company of comedians. She complied with his request ; and James gave them a license to act in his
capital, and before his court, to the great horror and in the face of
a fanatical faction of church zealots. This very company visited
Aberdeen, if not *Inverness* ; and it is by no means improbable that
Shakspeare was, by her Majesty's command. of the party. A passage in Mr Kennedy's Annals of Aberdeen corroborates this
conjecture :—' In the year 1601, James made ' an application to
' Queen Elizabeth for *her* company of comedians. to be sent down

---

* Steeven's on Shakspeare, vol. vii. p. 367.   † Chartulary of Dunfermline
   ‡ Caledonia, i.   § Statistical Account, vol. xx. p. 244.
‖ Statistical Account, vol. xviii. p. 522.   ¶ History of Scotland, viii. 358.

' to Scotland, which was readily complied with. And, after they
' had tired his Majesty and the people of Edinburgh with their
' entertainments, the King ordered them to repair to *Aberdeen* to
' amuse the citizens with the exhibition of their plays, comedies,
' and stage plays. They were recommended by his special letter
' addressed to the magistrates, and were under the management of
' Lawrence Fletcher, who, with the celebrated *William Shakspeare*,
' and others of their company, obtained the first license to perform
' plays in Britain. It was granted by King James within two months
' after he had ascended the throne of England.* The company of
' players who came to *Aberdeen* performed several times in the
' town ; and were presented by the magistrates with 32 merks for
' their services, besides being entertained with a supper on one
' of the nights of performance. At the same time, the freedom
' of the town was conferred upon Lawrence Fletcher the manager,
' and *each* of his company." †

Several passages of his works seem to demonstrate that Shakspeare had acquired a knowledge of the ballads and traditions of
Scotland, by a personal acquaintance with the country. The fine
old song in Othello, Act ii. of " Tak' your auld cloak about thee,"
is evidently Scotish.‡

With the exception of the foul act which won him a diadem,
Macbeth is by no means deserving of the opprobrium cast upon his
memory. Actuated by a spirit of piety or remorse, he visited Rome.
but the passage from Simeon of Durham and Roger Hoveden, on
which the incident rests, meets an assailant in Sir David Dalrymple,
and a defender in Mr Pinkerton. The Chronicon Elegiacum
says of Macbeth :—' In cujus regno fertile tempus erat ;' and

* The license alluded to by Kennedy was granted to *W. Shakspear*
and the players, his fellows, in 1603, ' to use and exercise the art and faculty
' of playing comedies, tragedies, histories, interludes, morals, pastorals,
' stage plaies, and such like.' See Percy's Reliques of Ancient Poetry, i. p.
261.
† Council Register, vol. xl. p. 210, 229. Kennedy, in saying *each* of the
comedians, has gone, it would appear, beyond his authority. Mr William
Robson, advocate, Aberdeen, was kind enough to consult the Council
Register at my request. He writes :—' I have searched the Council Regis-
' ter at the places you mention, but am sorry I cannot find Shakspeare's
' name. The minute, p. 210, mentions no names, and refers to a gratuity
' ordered to be paid by the Dean of Guild to the players then in Aberdeen.
' I send you prefixed a copy of the minute, p. 229.' In this last document,
' the only entry respecting *any* player admitted a burgess is ' Lawrence
' Fletcher, comediane, serviture to His Majestie.'
‡ Percy's Reliques of Ancient Poetry, i. 320.

2

Winton :—' All his tyme wes gret plente.'   He died at Lunfanan,
Aberdeenshire, after a reign of seventeen years.*   The events at
Dunsinnane are but the creations of the Poet.

It may be proper to say a few words, before I close, on the
Castle of Inverness.   It often received the sovereign within its
gates.   Thither James I. of Scotland summoned the Highland
Barons to a Parliament, and to the unusual spectacle of feudal
ferocity made subservient to the laws.   The unfortunate Mary met
insult and defiance at this very citadel from the adherents of
Huntly ; and the forces of the Pretender besieged, and blew it up
in 1746 †   Alexander, Earl of Huntly, Lord Gordon and Baid-
zenach, was created Sheriff of Inverness, and custodier of ' the
Castle' thereof, by King James IV.   By royal charter, dated 16th
January 1508, several lands are allocated to the support of the
Castle ; among others are the lands of Little Hilltown, Meikle
Hilltown, and Castletown, ' cum *piscaria sub muro* dicti castri, et
eidem pertinen.'   Geographical truth can only apply these words
to the river Ness, which washed the walls of the more modern
tower, since the elder strength is at a distance from any fishing
station.

[The writer of the preceding article was John Anderson, W.S.,
author of " The History of the Family of Fraser," and other
works on northern antiquities.   The Paper on " The Site of
Macbeth's Castle," was read at the Antiquarian Society in 1828.
It seems to have been hitherto unknown, or overlooked by all our
local historians.   Additions have been made to the notes and
references, so as to bring the information contained in the Paper
up to present date 1892]

* Reg. St And. ap. Hailes' Annals, i p. 3.
† In 1776, a Mr Godsman, factor to the Duke of Gordon at Inverness,
completed the work of destruction which the Highlanders had begun, by
removing the walls to build dykes.   He took away, much to the chagrin of
the gentlemen of the town (as a venerable lady resident there has informed
me) a carved stone bearing an inscription commemorative of the æra when
the Castle was erected.   My informant, when a little girl at school, was
often promised a reward by her father if she could discover this stone in
any of the dykes ; and many were the anxious and fruitless researches she
made in conquesence.   She never learnt that it was found.]

LOCAL CHARACTER.

JOHN STEPHEN,

HECKLER, BELLMAN, AND SEXTON.

TO the Clachnacuddin sexagenarian, whose recollection can go back over two score and
ten years, the local worthy whose name stands at the head of this article, must have been as well known as the town steeple.

John Stephen, or "Jock," as he was familiarly called at the period to which we refer, was the bellman or public crier of Inverness. He became lessee of this office in September 1842.

At this date he must from appearances have been between 60 and 70 years of age. The figure of "Jock" was peculiar, as he appeared invariably clad in summer and winter in a heavy, loose, long, brown greatcoat, with chimney-pot hat. The coat reached his heels, and to him might be applied the answer of the well-known school-boys' conundrum, "What two towns in France he reminded them of," when thus decked out in his ill-fitting inseparable garment—"Toulouse and Toulon" would be the reply.

Jock reminded one a good deal of the character in Lever's

" Harry Lorrequer," of that cross grained Irish servant, " Corney,"
only this Clachnacuddin worthy was not quite so short in the
temper or grain, or sc ill natured as his Irish compeer.

" Jock," when in full feather was a fellow of a merry mood—
with a twinkle in his eye that bespoke the pawky humour which
permeated him ; and when an audience used to gather round him
as he daily performed his public duties—as " Jamie Paterson,"
one of our local poets, wrote of our hero in his poem, " Inverness Martinmas Market "—

> " And Jock wi' vigour rings his bell,
> Auld guids for sale reportin'. "

On these occasions he did not confine himself to the mere call, but
bandied his joke with the crowd, and most frequently had the
best of it.   Many used purposely to make a set on Jock, as if to
make him the butt of their fancied smartness, but the bellman was
more than a match for them, as he generally by his keen sallies
and mother wit turned the laugh of the crowd against his
opponents.

The high festival days in the bellman's professional career was
when he appeared as the town drummer.   That was part of the
town crier's duty.   When Government announcements and official
business had to be made by tuck of drum, Jock was in state
at these times, and was always accompanied by Sergt. Alexander
Giant—" Supple Sandie."   As representative of town officialism
" Supple" carried the important document to be proclaimed by
Jock, and when the latter had, by a prolonged beat on the rather
woody instrument, completed the preliminaries, " Supple," with
great gravity, presented to Jock the document, when the latter
proceeded to cry the announcement.   This performance always
commanded a large audience of the boys and lassies of the town,
and on the finish of the call Jock was always received with loud
hurrahs by the boys.   The town-officer then proceeded to clear the
way for the crier by waving his stick and giving a fling to his legs,
to maintain, we presume, his name of " Supple."   A passage was
made, and they proceeded to the next point of call.

John Stephen was a native of the town ; in fact a pure " Clachnacuddin boy," and in it spent all his life.   In his younger years he
was noted for his boyish frolics and his odd tricks ; and, as was usual

in those days before the new police was heard of or invented, he was the hero of many of the street fights and sqabbles that used to be indulged in by the boys of the various quarters of the town.

These were the days of the stone-fights between the boys of Rose Street and Petty Street, or those of the Big Green against the Merkinch, or in the nomenclature of the boys—" The Marknish." These fights were not always bloodless, and many of those youthful warriors in later years carried to more bloody scenes, where the " red heckle " and the " thin red line " stood on the fields of the Crimea, the prowess that many of them in their juvenile days displayed on the banks of the Ness.

When Jock grew up to manhood, he learnt the trade of a heckler—at that time a business of some standing—it was driven out by the invention of machinery that superseded the manual worker. When heckling became used up, and work at the ' Sconce " slackened and moved off to Dundee, Jock for a time acted as sexton in the Chapel-yard, and filled up the time when not engaged in the sad duty of burying the dead, with catching the living—not of human kind, but birds. He was locally famous as a bird-catcher. Many a time in our youthful days have we seen Jock dressed in the usual surtout and tall hat wending his way in the early morning to the " Ramparts," carrying the cage with his " cock-calling bird." This decoy bird was nearly as famous among the Chapel Street boys, where he had his residence, as Jock himself.

The " Ramparts," where he exercised bird catching, was the eastern bastion of the remains of Cromwell's Fort, now known as the Citadel At that time it was thickly grown over with wild rose bushes, and was frequented by rose linnets, who were easily attracted by the syren strains of Jock's cock-calling bird, and got themselves caught on his limed twigs. The birds thus captured were sold, and many a house among the poorer townsmen was enlivened by the singing of these victims. We have heard it whispered, but do not warrant the insinuation, that our bird-catching worthy was not above imposing a hen bird on the unlearned fancier, even to touching up the colours of the plummage of the feathered articles of his calling.

The " Ramparts " were not alone Jock's happy hunting grounds —Shepperd's Nursery, at Ballifeary, where now stands Mr Charles

Innes's house, was a famous place for goldfinches ; while the woods at Culloden were also visited for blackbirds, mavises, &c.

In the more distant expeditions he was frequently accompanied by Sandie Gordon, a shoemaker who lived in Shuttle Lane, Maggot, and who was a bird fancier and a dealer, not in so large a way as Stephen.   On one of these expeditions to Culloden, a story has been told that Jock was chaffing Gordon, and said to him while hearing the birds singing, that their melody in Gaelic said— " *Gordonich dhu ! Gordonich dhu ! fag a choille,*" (" Black Gordon ! Black Gordon ! leave the wood "), when Gordon answered, " Not so ; it is saying— *Iain a chluig ! Iain a chluig ! tha 'm peathair a tighinn !*' ('John of the Bell John of the Bell ! the forester is coming.')"

We do not know if it was while acting as sexton that Jock took to snuffing.   But when we first made his acquaintance he was a great snuffer.   He always carried a box in those days, but we suspect he had another store of the pungent " Taddy " somewhere about the brown coat, for he applied it so frequently to his nose. He was, as appearances went, well provided by nature with a receptacle for the dust, and although he carried a large turkey-red handkerchief, a lot of the "Taddy " generally clung to the conduit from his nose and the lappet of his brown overall would have supplied an ordinary snuffer with sufficient for his wants for days.

To his other accomplishments Jock added that of a good singer of the old ballads—" Sir James the Rose," " The Bonnie House of Airlie," and the " Haughs of Cromdale," were favourites, and were in request in the companies he frequented. To these he added some power in story-telling—possessing as he did a fund of racy anecdote and wit—also old stories of Clachnacuddin and her citizens, which if some *Seneachie* had taken down would have been of much interest now, descriptive as they were of local worthies and old times and manners passed away.

In the happy go lucky sort of life he led for many years, it will not surprise any one who knows the drinking habits of those days that he was not fond of water when the native beverage could be had cheap.

With fine Highland malt whisky at threepence per gill, and in some places at less price, and with " *Tomhais Mhor* " (or big measure) served out, it is no wonder that Jock sometimes indulged overmuch in the barley bree. In one of those years we heard on a Martinmas market an English Cheap Jack, who was holding forth his wares to the gaping rustics on the High Street of Inverness, give vent to his feelings on the quality and cheapness of whisky—" A glorious country this, my friends, where a man can get drunk for a shilling ! " But Jock became an abstainer in his latter years. It fell out that he was seen drunk on duty as town bellman ; the magistrates' attention was called to his conduct, and the bellman was warned that if it occurred again he would be deprived of his public office.

Jock was thus induced early in the history of teetotalism in Inverness to take the pledge. The change in his habits was such a wonder that it was talked of among his " drouthy " chums as if the sky was about to fall. Jock himself a week after he took the pledge was heard to say joyfully that " It was the first week that passed over his head for fifty years in which he had not indulged in liquor."

Living in the period of the struggle for the great Reform Bill. it is needless to say that as one of the People he was a Reformer. He is said to have taken part and voted in the first Parliamentary election after the passing of the Reform Act 1832. If so it must have been as a non-elector, because from a printed roll of those who voted in the contest, the name of John Stephen does not appear. The " List of the Electors of the Burghs of Inverness, Forres, Nairn, and Fortrose," exhibiting the manner in which they exercised the franchise at the election, December 1832, Accurately compiled from the original Poll Book,—*Inverness : printed by R. Carruthers, and sold by the booksellers*, 1832,—is now before us, and, as we have said, the name of John Stephen does not occur as exercising the franchise on that occasion ; but in the first municipal election 1833-34, we find another printed " List of of Voters within the Royalty of Inverness for the election of Town Councillors," and his name is entered in the Third Ward—" John Stephen, flaxdresser," as an elector.

The first Reform Election in the Inverness District of Burghs was a keenly contested one. There appeared four candidates for the seat, viz. :—Major Charles Lennox Cumming Bruce of Roseisle and Kinnaird ; Colonel John Baillie of Leys ; John Stewart, Esq. of Belladrum ; and Robert Fraser Esq. of Torbreck. Major

Cumming Bruce and Colonel Baillie were the Tory candidates;
while Stewart of Belladrum and Fraser of Torbreck were the
Reformers.   The latter was out of the running from the first—
he only polled six votes.   The contest really lay between Colonel
Baillie and Mr Stewart of Belladrum.   The polling lasted for two
days, and on the second day (21st December 1832), Stewart of
Belladrum, the popular candidate, was two ahead after all Colonel
Baillie's supporters had voted.   At this crisis, and within a short
time of the close of the poll, an arrangement had been come to
between the agent of Major Cumming Bruce and Colonel Baillie
by which nine supporters of the Major's unpolled came forward
and recorded their votes for Colonel Baillie, and thus the scale
was turned by a majority of seven in favour of the latter, who
secured the seat.

We have said that Belladrum was the popular candidate, while
Cumming Bruce was the unpopular one ; but Colonel Baillie, as a
local man, stood well with the populace.   We remember a rhyme
that the boys of that day and their successors used to chant for
many years after the remains of that hot contest: —

> " Skin a louse for Cumming Bruce,
> Cook a goose for Stewart."

Nor were the "nine" who had given their suffrages to turn the
scale in favour of Colonel Baillie forgotten ; for, at after Parliamentary and municipal elections, when any of them appeared on
the hustings or at the polling booths, they were reminded of the
part they played in the contest following on the great Reform Bill.

TO THE NESS ISLANDS.*

YE beautiful ! ye hermit Isles ! of the loved and lovely Ness
    Which moans beneath your flowery smiles like beauty in distress,
    It sighs to leave you evermore like lovers loath to sever,
And clings a moment by your shore then *waves* adieu forever.
Oh ! wafts it not to a distant land remembrances of you ?
Some floweret from your sparkling strand, a branchlet from your yew ?
Some Crystal lighter than the rest to float on the billowy stream
And glitter on some foreign breast—a Nessian beauty·gem ?

Twin sisters of the summer hours ! sweet Nature loves to stray,
And loiter in your islet bowers—an everlasting May !
Warbling the richness of her song far o'er the outspread vale,
Like voice of Heaven poured along the balmy evening gale.
Within that high and lengthened grove where never fiery sun
Pierced the deep shade around, above, in sultriness of noon,
There I would lay me down and dream of Islands far away
Blooming beneath the golden beam that lights the southern sea.

Give me to watch the king-fisher sport thro' your mazes wild,
A lovely flitting fairy thing—your *monarch* feathered child !
Like Iris gleaming on the sight or momentary flash
Of heaven's pure and purple light ere bursts the thunder crash.
O how I like thy forest moan, thou melancholy bird
That would like me be all alone, as if of kindred tired ;
I too ; blue cushat of the shade ! would court thy solitude
And be with thee serenely sad, a wanderer of the wood.

Isles of that water on whose sides angelic woman moves,
Gazing at beauty in its tide where smiles a thousand loves ;
As if the blue streams had embraced a seraph wandering near.
One holy moment as it passed and left her with a tear.
Islets of beauty ! must I leave your peaceful bowers again ?
Again the stormy billows cleave, again sigh o'er the main
A blessing from my severed heart, ye foliaged twins ! for you
A lowly song when far apart—adieu ye Isles ! adieu !

The subjects of the preceding verses are the most prominent
feature of the River Ness. At present they form a group of three
unequally-sized islets, beautifully wooded and laid out with
walks and bridges—two light aerial structures being laid as con-

* For a notice of Andrew Fraser, author of this Poem, see "Recollections of Inverness, by an Invernessian," 1870 ; and "The Witch of Inverness and Fairies of Tomnahurich," 1891.

necting approaches from the roadways on each side of the river, while the small centre island is joined to the others by wooden erections.

Many years ago there was a very lucrative salmon fishery carried on at this point of the Ness by means of *cruives*, or salmon traps, that were placed in the streams which divided the islets, and were a pretty effectual method of intercepting the progress of the fish to the upper stretches of the river; the proprietors along the banks toward Loch Ness were compelled in self-defence to raise an action and had these obstructions removed by law.

Seventy years or more ago it used to be the custom of the inhabitants of Inverness in dry seasons, when the river fell much below its ordinary level, to resort to the west bank on the romantic walk from the turnstile at Ballifeary to watch the beautiful fish as they proceeded up the shallow waters of the stream towards the cruives, which on certain days were left open. The salmon were often seen making a clean spring from one pool to another in order to avoid the "pitiless pelting" of some town urchins concealed among the hazel underwood on either side. Nor did the aquatic wanderers always escape the missiles thus thrown at them by their assailants, —there were few of the boys who did not succeed in capturing one or more fish, which they concealed in some stray corner. But though the cruives are long down, and the river has frequently become as low as at the time alluded to, the fish, comparatively speaking, are gone,—neither salmon, grilse, nor large trout are now to be seen floundering half out of the water in the nearly dried-up stream. The desolating cause of this change is ascribed to the proximity of the Caledonian Canal, which is said not only to have disturbed the old-established spawning banks, but affords a ready though ultimately more dangerous channel to the fish, in their passage to and from the sea.

But another cause, of a maledictory nature, is assigned for this change. Prior to the time of the removal of the cruives, a most unfortunate affair occurred in connection with them. A townsman was detected one morning lifting the entrapped fish out of one of these cruives with a clip and placing them in a large sack which was by his side. While thus engaged he was fired at from the opposite bank by a man who was superintendent over the salmon fishery in the Ness. The poacher was killed, and his body fell into the river. The party who fired the fatal shot escaped punishment; but the local opinion is that the malediction of the unfortunate man's widow and orphans fell upon the waters, and the fish in large numbers fled the stream so wantonly polluted by human gore. Be this as it may, we only give the local tradition, and it is certain that the yearly product of the River Ness has declined since that period.

In the early part of the 18th century the magistrates of Inverness were in the habit of entertaining illustrious strangers—more especially the Lords of Justiciary on Circuit—in the Islands; and beneath the umbrageous canopy of the spreading beech trees a place is still pointed out where these burghal entertainments were held, and high jinks indulged in. At what date the city worthies ceased to entertain strangers in this lovely spot is not specified, but the following ludicrous occurrence is said to have been the immediate occasion of the discontinuance of these civic festivals.

Before bridges were built the Islands were approached by boats, and it occurred to some practical joker on the last of these occasions when the Judge and magistrates were partaking of the banquet—which banquet consisted largely of salmon from the Ness—to cut adrift the whole flotilla of the boats, which drifted down the stream long before the dilemma in which thereby the provost and magistrates were placed was discovered. It would take hours before the boats could be brought to the rescue, and to add to the disagreeable position in which the party were placed a drenching shower of rain came on. The Provost suggested that their important guest should be placed on the broad shoulders of Archie Fraser, a then well-known character, who from his habits of rod-fishing in the Ness, knew almost every stone, pool, and ford from Loch-Ness to the mouth of the river near Kessock. Archie being duly primed with a stiff beaker of brandy by his acquaintance the Provost, undertook the task to carry his Lordship, and set out with his trembling charge to cross the river. He proceeded safely till about the centre of the stream, when he came to a dead halt, and, turning up his face to his Judgeship, addressed him thus—

"They tell me your Honour was deevilish hard yesterday on the poor souls who broke the nets at Beauly."

"Ah, my good fellow," replied his Lordship, "they were a bad lot, and poaching must be kept under.   Pray go on."

"Imph !" growled Archie, "Keep't under, is't you say?"

"Go on !" roared the Provost from the wooded bank, who had seen the hesitation of the burden bearer, '' what makes you stick there, Archie ?   Do ye not know who's above you ?"

Archie replied from mid-stream, "I ken fine, Provost, but don't be confusing me wi' your bawling."

Archie had only moved on a few steps, when suddenly slipping backwards he fell over his Lordship into the stream amidst a storm of screams and howlings of the most discordant sounds from the spectators that were ever heard on the banks of the peaceful Ness. The Judge, however, was soon rescued by a rush of willing hands from his watery situation, and on getting to dry land expressed his fears that the Provost might undergo a like unpleasant experience ; but that worthy functionary, who stood high and dry beside him, said in a high voice—

"De'il the fears of that, the rascal would shoulder me over the *Mussel Scaup* without as much as wetting my big toe."

This is the tradition set down, as related to us by a Clachnacuddin citizen many years ago, as the chief reason why the junketings on the Ness Islands came to an end.

CAPTAIN BURT.

THE author of the "Letters from a Gentleman in the North of Scotland to a friend in London, containing a description of a capital town [Inverness] in that Northern Country," etc., 2 vols., 1754, was one Burt, an understrapper commissary, who, as is natural to such people, was, in his own opinion, a man of great consequence, Major Hepburn of Aldercro's regiment, mentioned at Madras an anecdote of Burt, which I think happened at Inverness. Burt, giving himself some consequential airs, said *he represented His Majesty.* Upon which a dry Scot replied, "Hoot mon ! *you represent His Majesty !— He*, God bless him, is muckle better represented on a bawbee."

——o——

THE TRIAL OF JOHN GRANT, SHERIFF-CLERK DEPUTE OF THE SHIRE OF INVERNESS,

Before the Circuit Court of Justiciary there on 1st May 1793, for Forgery.

THE case of John Grant, Sheriff-Clerk Depute of Inverness-shire, is one that possesses considerable interest. At one time the writer held the opinion that Grant had been hardly dealt with, that the verdict in his case should have been one of " Not Proven," if not one of " Not Guilty," but that opinion has been considerably modified since the confirmation of the justness of the verdict by one of the jurymen, who, as will appear from the letter that follows, written more than sixty years after the trial, confirms his previous judgment in the case of this unfortunate man, and in which he clearly shows that he had no doubt in his mind as to the guilt of the Sheriff-Clerk Depute.

The trial is interesting from various other circumstances. It presents a striking instance of the change for the better that has taken place in the character and administration of the Criminal Law of our country, in its greater mildness and humanity toward the criminal ; while it appears to us that the ends of justice are better secured by our modern practice in this respect than in the harsh treatment of a past age. The evidence produced at the trial also affords a curious picture of the habits, hard drinking customs, and the manners that prevailed to a great extent one hundred years ago in these northern parts.

A noteworthy fact in connection with this case is that one of the jurymen, who sat on the Assize for the trial of Grant in 1793, was living as late as the year 1859. The late Isaac Forsyth, book-seller, Elgin, is the juryman to whom we allude—in many respects a remarkable man—for half-a century one of the most enterprising booksellers north of Edinburgh. Three years before his death Mr Forsyth had an opportunity of a perusal of the copy of the report of John Grant's trial, from which these notes are reprinted. A copy of the published report was sent to him by a then well-

known citizen of Inverness—the late Alexander Forbes, chemist
and for many years Treasurer of the Northern Infirmary.

Here follows Mr Forsyth's reply after perusal of the case :—

ELGIN, 15th March, 1855.

DEAR SIR,—I return your kindness with my best thanks for a perusal
of this remembrance of a passage in my early life, which it has renewed in
all its original vividness. I was then a youngster of twenty-five, and ever
ready, and often employed, in helping forward public matters, hence my
official connection with this unfortunate trial. This account of it, however,
as might be naturally expected from the hand of its victim, is sadly garbled
and one-sided. There was not a shadow of doubt on the minds of the jury
of the truth of the crime committed. He has purposely omitted the
dignified, solemn, and most impressive charge of Lord Henderland. I have
never in all my long life heard anything of the kind that I could compare
to it ! When I look over the list of this jury, I feel as if I was standing
alone of the generation that then existed. Not one of the fifteen that sat
on it, whom I personally knew, is now alive ; and, except myself, perhaps
all are gone !

As the law and practice then stood, our verdict must have deprived the
poor unfortunate youth of his life. The idea of which cost me a sleepless
and miserable night ; that my hand, as well as my vote, should have been
visible in such an event. I believe a little *private*, but powerful influence,
exercised that night by the amiable and much respected *Head* of the clan,
softened the Judges, who, awaiting of a legal loophole, got death turned
into banishment. If the poor unfortunate returned to this country, or died
in despair, I never heard, and would gladly know if it happens to be in your
power to say.

I admire, and fully agree, with all your remarks on the mildness of our
present administration of the Criminal Law of this country. The system
that hanged a man for stealing 1s 6d in England, or a sheep in Scotland,
was certainly most barbarous ! I hope the temperance habits of our
lower classes will yet be improved. At present they are surely the source
of misery and crime, as they were in 1793. Forbes Mackenzie's Act, if
continued to be *acted* on, in the same spirit of vigilance by our police as
of late, has done, and will do much more good. But, like the damming up
of water, there must be *perseverance* in that vigilance, before old habits
are restrained. That, and a *right* system of education, so universal as to
include all, even the most destitute, may, and I trust, under Providence,
will create a blessed revolution in their habits.

Again, returning my warm thanks for your kind attention, and offering
any services I could render you in this quarter.—I remain, dear sir,
very respectfully, yours,   ISAAC FORSYTH.

A Forbes, Esq.

Lord Henderland was the presiding Judge at the trial, John
Burnett being Advocate-Depute. The prisoner was defended by
James Grant of Corriemonie, advocate, a well known Highlander,
and author of " The Origin and Descent of the Scottish Gael."

INDICTMENT.

JOHN GRANT, Sheriff-Clerk Depute of the shire of Inverness, you are indicted and accused at the instance of Robert Dundas, Esq. of Arniston, his Majesty's Advocate, for his Majesty's interest, that albeit, by the laws of this and every other well-governed realm, Forgery, as also, the feloniously uttering and using any forged writing, more particularly the feloniously forging, or feloniously procuring to be forged, the subscription of any person as indorsee of any Bill or Draft : as also, the feloniously uttering and using any such Bill with a forged subscription thereon, or causing the same to be uttered, used, or discounted, knowing the subscriptions thereon to be forged, as crimes of an heinous nature, and severely punishable ; yet true it is, and of verity, that you, the said John Grant, have presumed to commit, and are guilty actor, art and part, of the foresaid crime, in so far as you, the said John Grant, having drawn a Bill or Draft, bearing date the 21st day of July 1792, for Twenty Pounds Sterling, addressed to Donald M'Gilvray in Tullich of Strathdearn, and accepted, or pretended to be accepted, by him, of which the tenor follows, viz. :—£20 Sterling. ' In-' verness, 21st July 1792.   Three months after date, pay to me, or my ' order, within the Post-Office here, the sum of Twenty Pounds Sterling ' for value of (signed) John Grant.   To Mr Donald M'Gilvray, in Tullich ' of Strathdearn. (Signed) Donald M'Gilvray.' You attempted to get said Bill discounted at the Office of the Branch of the Royal Bank, established at Inverness ; and the managers of said Bank having refused to discount said Bill, you, the said John Grant, did, at Inverness, or elsewhere, in the County of Inverness, upon one or other of the days of the month of July 1792, or of August immediately following, falsely and feloniously forge, or feloniously procure to be forged, the subscription of Angus M'Edward, drover in Balnespick, in Badenoch, upon the back of said Bill, as second indorser thereof, thus, ' Angus M'Edward ; ' and upon one or other of the days of the month of July, 1792, or of August or September immediately following, you, the said John Grant, gave the said Bill, with the forged subscription thereon, as a true and genuine Bill, and as being truly signed by the said Angus M'Edward, as indorser, to John Miller, merchant in Inverness, in partial or full payment of a debt, which you owed to the said John Miller ; and the said John Miller received the same as a true and genuine Bill, and as being truly signed by the persons whose subscriptions were adhibited thereto, although the name of the said Angus M'Edward, as indorser of said Bill, is false and forged, and was falsely and feloniously forged by you the said John Grant, at least, known by you when you used and uttered the same, by giving it to the said John Miller, in payment of the debt you owed him, to be false and forged; and you, the said John Grant, having been brought before Simon Fraser, Esq., Advocate, Sheriff-Depute of the shire of Inverness, upon the 31st day of December, 1792, did emit and sign a Declaration, which was also subscribed by the said Simon Fraser, Esq., which Declaration, together with the Bill particularly described and recited above ; as also another Bill, dated, Forres, 19th May, 1792, for £100 Sterling, at six months, drawn by John Gordon, and accepted by the said Angus M'Edward, which Bill is marked, No. 1018 ; as also,

another Bill, dated Forres, the 11th August, 1791, for £100 Sterling, at
three months date, drawn by John Gordon, and accepted by Angus M'Edward, which Bill is marked, No. 2126 : as also, a Letter, wrote by the said
Angus M'Edward, dated Balldow, the 28th day of December, 1791, addressed
on the back to ' Mr Alexander Cameron, taylor at Alvie ; being all to be
used in evidence against you the said John Grant, will, for that purpose,
be lodged with the Clerk of the Circuit Court of Justiciary, before which
you are to be tried, that you may have an opportunity of seeing the same.
At least, time and place foresaid, the subscription of the said Angus
M'Edward was feloniously forged, and the Bill above recited, having the
said forged subscription thereon, was feloniously uttered, used, and passed,
by a person knowing the pretended subscription of Angus M'Edward
thereon to be false and forged, and you, the said John Grant, are guilty of
the foresaid crimes, or one or other of them. All which, or part thereof,
being found proven by the verdict of an assize, &c.

(Signed)   JOHN BURNETT, A.D.

To this indictment Grant pleaded " NOT GUILTY."

The following jury were empannelled to try the case :—

1. Arthur Forbes, Esq. of Culloden.
   General Charles Ross of Morringie
   Allan Cameron, Esq. of Tyrish
   George Munro of Culrain
5. Charles Munro, of Allan
   John M'Kinnon, merchant in Tain
   Peter Rose Watson, Esq. of Coltfield
   Henry Andrews, merchant in Inverness
   John Hoyes, merchant in Forres
10. Alexander Urquhart, merchant there
   Captain John Ross, of Castle Craigs
   Hugh Ross, younger of Gladfield
   Alexander Tulloch, merchant in Campbelton
   Mr Isaac Forsyth, stationer in Elgin
15. James Miln, Esq. of Bishopmiln

No objection having been made to any of the Jury, the Counsel
for the Crown now proceeded to call the witnesses.

ANGUS M'EDWARD.*

The Counsel for the Panel objected to this witness, observing
that he had a manifest interest in the cause, and consequently

* It is well here to note that the report of Grant's trial published in
1793 was issued by the prisoner or some of his friends, as a defence against
the justice of the verdict in his case, protesting his innocency, and " throw-

could not be admitted ; that moreover, he was conscious the Prosecution was carried on wantonly and maliciously by the Pannel's enemies, and the benefactors of the witness. The Judge however repelled the objection, observing that, in cases of this nature, the testimony of the Private Prosecutor was the most essential that could be adduced ; he was therefore clearly of opinion, that the witness should be called, but directed the Jury to lay such stress on his evidence as they thought it really merited ; and accordingly he was called.

Angus M'Edward depones that he was in company with the Pannel and James Davidson, *alias* M'Kay, drover in Moymore of Strathdearn, on the night of the 21st of July last, in the house of William Porterfield, vintner in Inverness, where they drank freely, though not so much as to be intoxicated, but had no conversation relative to Bills of any kind ; that he never saw the Pannel before but once, which was between Blair in Athol and Dalwhinnie, in August 1790, when the Pannel was on his way from England : and the Pannel having learned that he was from Badenoch, he ordered the chaise driver to give him a horse, which followed the chaise (otherwise termed a return horse), but, from that time until the 21st July last, he never saw him ; that, on Sunday morning the 22d of July, after breakfast, the Pannel went home, but in a short time thereafter called, as he understood, for some of his clients at the house of Alexander Clunas, vintner in Inverness, where he then was ; that, to his knowledge, fourteen half mutchkins of spirits was drank, besides two bottles given by him and the Pannel : That, about one o'clock, they left the house of Alexander Clunas for their respective places of abode, and, about two miles distant from Inverness, the Pannel, who was escorting his father, overtook them ; that, after some persuasion, the Pannel and his father, with two of the Pannel's

ing himself on the protection of the public." The reflections on witnesses and officials concerned in his case must therefore be taken *cum grano salis*, as may be seen from Mr Forsyth's observations in his letter. It may be here stated that Angus M'Edward, the chief witness, lived and died much respected among his countrymen. His death occurred in 1812, and the following obituary notice of him appeared in the "Inverness Journal" of the 24th July :—"Died at Beauly on Thursday the 16th curt., Mr Angus M'Edward, tacksman of Kerrowmeanach, in Badenoch, in the 44th year of his age, after a short illness brought on by fatigue in the prosecution of his business as a drover. He was an honest, industrious, and useful member of society, and his loss will long be felt by his friends and acquaintances."

4

Clerks, accompanied them into the house of Donald Rose, vintner in the Park of Inches, where a considerable quantity of spirits was drank ; that the name of Donald M'Gilvray was introduced, as being left behind, when the Pannel enquired if he was acquainted with M'Gilvray, and if he was in good circumstances, his answer was in the affirmative : That the Bill now shown to him, bearing his indorsation, was never signed by him, nor was he asked to sign it.

Interrogate for the Pannel—Q. Was you drunk when in Rose's ? A. No.

Q. What quantity of spirits was then drank ?   A. Better than two bottles ; besides porter.

Q. Did you call for pen and ink ?   A. Yes

Q. For what purpose ?   A. To write my address.

Q. To what end ?   A. The Pannel wished to correspond with me ; as I was going to Falkirk Tryst he seemed anxious to know how cattle sold.

Q And did you write your address ?   A. Yes.

Q. In what manner !   A. " Angus M'Edward, drover in Balnespick, Badenoch."

Q. Upon what paper did you write ; was it a Bill ?   A. *Not that I know of.*

Q. If the Pannel was to write you at Falkirk why give him your address iu Badenoch ?   A. I do not know.

Q. What size was the paper you wrote on ?   A. Much about the size of a Bill.

Q. Who gave you the paper that you wrote on ? A. The Pannel.

Q. Did you write your name more than once ?   A. Yes.

Q. Was it at the desire of the Pannel ?   A. No ; but merely to please myself.

Q. Did you always write on the same paper?   A. No.

Q. What other paper did you write on ?   A. A letter which I had in my own pocket.

Interrogate by the Judge—Q. Do you always sign your name in the same manner ?   A. No.

Q. How do you sign in general ?   A. Sometimes " Angus. M'Edwards," " Angus Mac Edward," and at other times " A. Mac Edward."

The witness during his examination spoke so low and indistinctly that his Lordship repeatedly threatened to have him set upon the Court table.

JOHN SMITH depones that he was employed by John Miller, merchant in Inverness, the latter end of October last to raise diligence on a bill drawn by the Pannel, accepted by Donald M'Gilvray, and indorsed by Angus M'Edward ; and that accordingly he raised horning thereon, and upon the 17th November last served the Pannel and M'Gilvray with copies thereof in presence of each other.

Interrogate for the Pannel—Q. When did you charge M'Edward ? A. On the 27th December last.

Q. Why delay him so long? A. Because M'Gilvray the acceptor promised to see M'Edward and settle it ; however, he failed in his promise, and as I had no other business in Badenoch where M'Edward resided, I declined going on purpose, as it was my intention to go to Edinburgh in December, and in passing through Badenoch I meant to charge him, which I did.

Q. Did you see the Pannel frequently in the intermediate period ? A. I had occasion to see him daily in his office.

Q. Did you see him when on your way to charge M'Edward ? A. Yes ; I was a night with him at Corryburgh Inn, on his way from the country to Inverness.

Q. Did he dissuade you from charging M'Edward ? A. No ; on the contrary, he advised me to it, and desired I would send the caption to Mr Miller from Edinburgh as soon as possible. I gave him a second copy of charge, and told him I meant to give M'Gilvray one also, in order to save two executions.

Q. Did you tell Mr Miller that the Pannel had the Bill now in question, previous to its being indorsed to him ? A. Yes.

Q. How did you know ? A. M'Gilvray the acceptor told me that he had granted such, and that he had a balance to get after paying the Pannel anything he owed him, and that how soon he discounted it he would pay him.

Q. Did you send the letter to M'Edward which Miller gave you notifying to M'Edward that the Bill was dishonoured ? A. I put it into the Post-Office myself.

Q. Did you see M'Edward when you went to the house to charge him ? A. No ; but I saw his father, who told me he knew there was such a Bill, but did not think it would come the length of a horning.

JOHN MILLER depones that the Pannel upon the 25th day of

July 1792, gave him a Bill for £20 Sterling, accepted by Donald M'Gilvray, and indorsed by Angus M'Edward, which he discounted, and gave the Pannel £9, not having more cash then by him ; he also gave the Pannel a letter, acknowledging to have got the Bill, and obliging himself to pay the balance ; that he was informed by John Smith the messenger, that M'Gilvray had granted his acceptance to the Pannel to the amount of £20, but did not know it was indorsed by M'Edward until he saw it, nor would he place any dependence on his indorsation, being utterly unacquainted with him ; that he would discount the Bill as soon without as with the name of M'Edward ; that it was on the faith of M'Gilvray and the Pannel's signatures he discounted the Bill ; that he offered to the Pannel to take his own acceptance sometime before the horning was executed, which he declined, and desired that he would use all diligence ; that he wrote both M'Gilvray and M'Edward before any diligence was used, notifying his intention of raising horning on the Bill unless it was paid, but received no answer.

JAMES GORDON, examined in the Gaelic language by the Sheriff of Inverness, depones that the subscription of Angus M'Edward, adhibited to the Bill now shown him, does not appear to be the writing of M'Edward.

Q. How do you think it is not his writing ? A. I seldom or ever saw him write so large—the two Bills mentioned in the indictment being shown to him, and asked if he thought they were M'Edward's subscriptions?   A. I believe they are more like than the other.

Q. Are you in the habit of corresponding with M'Edward ? A. No.

Q. And how did you become acquainted with his writing ?   A. I was at the school with him when he was writing text copies.

Q. Did you ever see him sign his name when he was drunk ? A. No.

DONALD M'GILVRAY, examined in the Gaelic language by the Sheriff, depones that the name Donald M'Gilvray, adhibited to the Bill now shown is his writing, that he has no knowledge of the writing of M'Edward ; that he had a conversation with M'Edward relative to the Bill in question ; that he told him he did not recollect to have indorsed it ; that he wrote his address on a blank piece of paper in the house of Donald Rose, smith in Leys, but did not think it was a Bill.

MARY GRANT, examined in the Gaelic by the Sheriff, depones that on the Sunday subsequent to the last July market, the Pannel and several others came to her house and called for some spirits and porter ; that M'Edward called for a whole bottle, and mixed it with some milk, and, to the best of her remembrance, he drank it all off.

Q. Was any in the company drunk when they went to your house ?   A. Several of them.

Q. Was M'Edward drunk ?   A. I really think he was.

Q. What quantity of spirits was drunk in your house ?   A. Better than two bottles, besides porter.

Q. Who paid the reckoning ?   A. The Pannel.

Q. Did you see any person writing ?   A. No ; but I heard pen and ink called for.

Q. By whom ?   A. I am not very certain ; but I think it was by M'Edward.

JAMES DAVIDSON, examined in the Gaelic language by the Sheriff, depones that on Saturday the 21st July last, he was in company with the Pannel and Angus M'Edward, in the house of William Porterfield, vintner in Inverness, where they staid all night ; that they drank very freely, and were rather intoxicated than otherwise ; that after breakfast, on Sunday morning the 22nd July, the Pannel left them, but soon after joined them in the house of Alexander Clunas, vintner in Inverness, where there was a good number of people ; that, to the best of his knowledge, about fourteen half mutchkins of spirits, besides two bottles given by the Pannel and M'Edward, was drank ; that several of the company, who intended to leave town, were obliged to go to bed ; that he, M'Edward, and some others left Inverness about one o'clock, and, about two miles from town, the Pannel, who was escorting his father, overtook them about two miles distant from Inverness, whom they entreated to accompany them into the house of Donald Rose, vintner in the Park of Inches, which they did ; that a considerable quantity of spirits was drank, besides porter : that M'Edward was very much intoxicated, but did not see him write any, though he heard him call for pen and ink ; that he was so deeply engaged in conversation with one of the

Pannel's clerks, a deal might be wrote during the time without his knowledge ; that towards the evening they proceeded on their journey till they arrived at the house of Alexander Fraser, vintner in Faillie, three miles distant from the house of Donald Rose ; that M'Edward, on his arrival, was so very much in liquor, that he fell off his chair ; that there was no house betwixt Rose's and Fraser's ; that they all remained in Fraser's for the night, and M'Edward, from his intoxication, slept on the kitchen floor with the greyhound ; that he heard the Pannel and M'Edward converse about M'Gilvray, while in the house of Donald Rose.

DONALD GRANT depones that he is clerk to the Pannel, and, on Sunday the 22nd of July last, in the house of Alexander Clunas, vintner in the Castle Street, Inverness, where he happened to call for some of his friends from the country, whom he found engaged with the Pannel, he saw M'Edward, M'Gilvray, and several others there drinking ; that he saw about fourteen half mutchkins of spirits, besides two bottles, given by the Pannel and M'Edward, drank ; that Mr Grant, the Pannel's father, was then waiting for his son as he was leaving town ; that the Pannel sent him with an apology, that he was engaged, but would soon wait on him, and, accordingly, about one o'clock, he came, when Mr Grant left town, and William Mackintosh, another of the Pannel's clerks, accompanied them out of town, and about two miles distant they fell in with Angus M'Edward, and several others, who entreated the Pannel and his father to accompany them into the house of Donald Rose, vintner in the Park of Inches, which they did ; that a good deal of spirits was drank. and the company in general was intoxicated, except Mr Grant the Pannel's father ; that he heard the Pannel and M'Edward converse about M'Gilvray, and saw the Pannel taking a small paper from his pocket book which he presented to M'Edward, who immediately called for pen and ink, and wrote his name upon the paper, which appeared to him to be a Bill, but. being at some little distance, could not distinguish the stamp ; that M'Edward was very familiar with the Pannel, and had his arm round his waist, or somewhat higher.

WILLIAM MACKINTOSH depones that he is clerk to the Pannel ; that on Sunday the 22nd of July last he was in the house of Alexander Clunas, vintner in Inverness, where he saw Angus M'Edward and several others.

This witness concurs with the preceding witness as to what happened in the house of Alexander Clunas ; but having the charge of the Pannel's father's horse, he did not see anything that passed in Rose's.

Captain JOHN M'PHERSON depones that the subscription to the Bill now shown to him, drawn by the Pannel, and accepted by Donald M'Gilvray, and apparently indorsed by M'Edward, does not appear to him to be the signature of M·Edward ; that he seldom or ever saw him write in such a large character ; that the two other Bills shown to him, as mentioned in the indictment, appears to be the writing of M'Edward, but that he never saw him subscribe his name ; that he corresponded with the Sheriff of Inverness about the Bill in question, and examined several witnesses thereanent.

JOHN ROSS depones that the Pannel, in the month of July last, inclosed him a Bill for £20, to be discounted ; that it was accepted by Donald M'Gilvray, and, as his constituents were not in town, he could not take upon himself to transmit any business, otherwise that he would have been glad to serve the Pannel, and to that effect returned the Pannel a letter ; did not examine if it was indorsed, not having it in his power to discount it.

WILLIAM FRASER depones that the Bill now shown him, drawn by the Pannel, accepted by Donald M'Gilvray, aud indorsed by M'Edward, is the very identical Bill given to him by John Smith, previous to his setting off for Edinburgh, to be given to either of the parties who paid him the money.

PROOF IN EXCULPATION.

DONALD M'KAY depones that, on Monday the 31st December last, he met with Angus M'Edward in Inverness, and on the following day proceeded on their journey to Badenoch together ; that their conversation principally turned about the Pannel, when M'Edward told him that he had signed a paper for the Pannel in the house of Donald Rose, vintner at the Park of Inches, on Sunday the 22nd July last, but to the best of his knowledge it was not a bill ; yet, when he saw the Bill in the hands of the Sheriff, he could not positively deny but it was his writing, and that nothing led him to think otherwise, but that he was informed a Sheriff-Clerk could write all manner of hands.

ALEXANDER MACKINTOSH depones that he heard Angus M'Edward acknowledge to have called for pen and ink in the house of Donald Rose, vintner in the Park of Inches, in order to write his name, by way of address for the Pannel, which he wrote on a slip of paper, but did not recollect what paper it was.

The other witnesses cited in exculpation (except Alexander M'Pherson and Lachlan M'Kenzie, who were prevented by sinister means from attending), having been examined by the Crown, and interrogate for the Pannel, it was not thought necessary by his Counsel to call them, as he considered the Pannel sufficiently acquitted, and declared his proof ended.

The Counsel for the Crown then addressed the Jury in a few words, and told them that, as his Lordship had taken down full notes of the evidence it would be unnecessary for him to comment on that evidence, as his Lordship with his usual accuracy, in summing up the whole, would point out to them whether or not the Pannel was guilty, and that they would return a verdict agreeable to the dictates of their own conscience.

The Counsel for the Pannel then addressed the Jury to the following effect :—

Gentlemen of the Jury,—The business, which has occupied your time and attention this day, is now concluded, and the witnesses for the Crown have so fully demonstrated the innocence of my client, that I thought it unnecessary to call any more witnesses in exculpation. There are two of the Pannel's most material witnesses, Alexander M'Pherson vintner in Corryburgh, and Lachlan M'Kenzie, post, Pitmain, Badenoch, who have been regularly cited, but, from motives best known to themselves, did not attend ; the post is more excuseable, as his business is urgent, but if my client should unfortunately, and most unexpectedly be found guilty, from their non-attendance, I for ever will lament it ; however, the all-wise Providence will direct the Jury, in whose hands the fate of the Pannel must rest ; and, from the evidence that has been adduced against him, I think, in my own opinion, there is no ground of conviction. The first witness that was called is Angus M'Edward the private prosecutor ; and to his testimony I objected, as he has a manifest interest in the cause ; but his Lordship was pleased to repel the objection, and, with his usual candour, directed you, gentlemen of the Jury, to lay such stress on his evidence as you think it really merits, and in my opinion that is none at all. He says he wrote his address on a small slip of paper, but not a bill ; he also says he wrote his name more than once, and for what purpose ? Merely to please himself. He says that the paper on which he wrote, at the desire of the Pannel, had no writing on it when he signed his name ; it is well known that the drawer of a bill seldom indorses his name on the back until he is discounting it or paying it away ; and it must be known to you, gentlemen of the Jury, from the evidence you have heard, that the paper on which he wrote, at the desire of the Pannel, was the Bill in question. Donald Grant, another witness examined in this cause, tells you that he saw the Pannel take a small paper from his pocket-book, and presenting it to M'Edward, who called for pen and ink, and wrote his name on it. Can there be more circumstantial evidence? I think not. And, after what that witness has said, I will not trouble you by commenting on the rest of the evidence ; indeed, I do not consider it necessary. You, gentlemen of the Jury, must be sensible that the testimony of Alexander Cameron and James Gordon, two illiterate men, cannot be paid any regard to ; they cannot read the English language ; they have been examined in the Gaelic, and surely that being the case, they cannot be supposed to be competent judges of writing ; it is morally impossible. Another evidence, Captain John Macpherson of Invereshie, in examining the Bill in question, and comparing it with the Bills mentioned in the indict-ment, he says that the subscription adhibited to the Bill challenged is not like M'Edward's ; that he seldom or ever saw any of his write in such large characters. The Advocate-Depute was pleased to ask this witness if he ever saw M'Edward subscribe his name ? and he told, he never did. From the whole of the gentleman's evidence, however respectable he may be, I am clearly of opinion it must pass for nothing. And, as for the Bills lodged in Court for comparison, ought to have no weight on your minds, as it is well known that when a man is drunk, he cannot sign so exactly as if he was sober : Moreover, M'Edward tells you that he signs his name three different ways. James M'Kay tells you that M'Edward was drunk ; you cannot therefore have any hesitation in returning a verdict finding my client not guilty.

5

I have observed some of the gentlemen of the Jury taking down full notes of the evidence, which renders my task less arduous; and to God and you I commit the life of my client.

The Court retired at half-past seven o'clock at night, and met again the following day at ten o'clock in the morning, when the Jury returned the verdict :—

At Inverness, the Second day of May, One Thousand Seven Hundred and Ninety Three Years.

The above assize, having inclosed, made choice of the said Arthur Forbes, Esq. of Culloden, to be their Chancellor, and the said Mr Isaac Forsyth to be their Clerk ; and, having considered the criminal libel, raised and pursued at the instance of His Majesty's Advocate for His Majesty's interest, against John Grant, Pannel, and the interlocutor of relevancy pronounced thereupon by the Court, the evidence adduced in proof of the libel, and evidence in exculpation, with the witnesses produced in the course of the trial, they all, in one voice, find the Pannel GUILTY : In witness whereof, their said Chancellor and Clerk have subscribed these presents, in their name, and by their appointment, place and date foresaid.   (Signed)   ARTHUR FORBES, *Chan.*
ISAAC FORSYTH, *Clerk.*

The Clerk had no sooner read the verdict, than Arthur Forbes, Esq. of Culloden, Chancellor, presented a letter to his Lordship, of the tenor following, viz. :—

Inverness, 2nd May, 1793.

MY LORD,—' Though the Jury have found themselves under ' the disagreeable necessity of returning an unanimous verdict, ' finding the unfortunate prisoner at your bar guilty, solely in- ' fluenced by motives of humanity, and also taking under their ' consideration the time of life of the unhappy young man, they, ' with the same unanimity and greatest submission, recommend ' him to the mercy of this Court, in full reliance (if admissible), ' that your Lordship will be pleased to pay attention to the above ' recommendation.   ' I have the honour, in name of the gentle- men of the Jury, to subscribe myself, my Lord, your Lordship's most obedient humble servant,

(Signed)   ARTHUR FORBES.
" Addressed to the Right Honourable Lord Henderland."

His Lordship upon reading the above letter (privately), assured the gentlemen of the Jury, that every attention should be paid to their recommendation : That he would lay the whole case, with their letter, before the Court ; and, in the meantime, grant warrant for transmitting the Panel to Edinburgh, to have his sentence pronounced the 3rd day of June.

In terms of, and conform to warrant, the said John Grant was on the 7th day of May, sent off from Inverness jail, and was delivered in the jail of Edinburgh on the 15th of said month. And, on the 3rd day of June, he was called to their Lordship's bar, when Lord Henderland reported to the Court that, after the verdict had been returned at Inverness, he had received a letter from Mr Forbes of Culloden (of which a copy is already given); that the Counsel for the Panel had likewise represented that, in cases of forgery the Court had not gone the length of a capital punishment, and therefore he had remitted the consideration of this case, the Pannel being very young, to their Lordships' consideration, that they might either pronounce a capital sentence against the Pannel, and transmit the recommendation of the Jury to be laid before His Majesty, or inflict a punishment less than death, as they should think proper.

Lord Justice Clerk, Lord Henderland, Lord Abercromby, and Lord Dunsinnan, came to Court precisely at eleven o'clock in the forenoon of the 3rd day of June.

J. Montgommery, Esq., Counsel for the Crown. William Honneyman, Esq., James Grant, Esq., for the Pannel.

But, as nothing remained to determine the fate of the unfortunate Pannel but their Lordships' sentence, the Counsel on both sides had nothing to say.

Lord HENDERLAND then addressed their Lordships in the following manner :—

MY LORDS,—I have before me the substance of the evidence, adduced against the unfortunate Pannel at your Lordships' bar on his trial at Inverness ; and I think it would be unnecessary for me to recapitulate that evidence, as it induced the Jury to return a verdict of guilt against the unhappy Pannel. It only remains for your Lordships to determine what punishment ought to be inflicted. I have produced a letter of recommendation from Mr Forbes of Culloden, in favour of the Pannel, to this Court. Mr Forbes is a gentleman of great reputation, and I trust your Lordships will pay every attention to it.

LORD JUSTICE CLERK.—I feel for the unhappy young man at

the bar, but the crime for which he is convicted is of so henious a nature, that, unless a severe punishment was inflieted, in all probability such causes would be before us every day. I do not know any erime that is more dangerous ; highway robbery is not near so dangerous, for, in the latter case, a man has a chance of guarding himself, but in cases of forgery a man cannot keep his money safe in the most secure corner of his house. My Lord Henderland has very properly remitted the case to this Court ; and, had I presided as Judge on the trial of this unfortunate young man, I would have done the same ; and, my Lords, the Court of Session is the most competent Court for trying cases of this kind in the first instance ; I wish from my heart that the Pannel's case had come before that Court : And, as that Court often passes sentence without a remit to this High Court, I am clearly of opinion, that we may do so in this case, that that sentence may be less than death ; as I have no doubt were we to pass the sentence of death upon the unhappy Pannel at the bar, but he would obtain a pardon ; I therefore think, that transportation for life ought to be the sentence of this Court.

LORD HENDERLAND.—I am clearly of your Lordships' opinion.

LORD DUNSINNAN.—I agree with your Lordships.

LORD ABERCROMBY—I perfectly agree with your Lordships in the sentence pronounced.

The sentence was then recorded as follows :—

" Order and adjudge, that the said John Grant be transported beyond seas, to such place as His Majesty, with the advice of his Privy Council, shall declare and appoint, and that for all the days of his life ; with certification to the said John Grant, if, after being so transported, he shall ever return to, and be found at large within, any part of Great Britain, without some lawful cause, and being thereof lawfully convicted, he shall suffer death, as in case of felony, without the benefit of clergy, by the law of Eng-land. And ordain the said John Grant to be carried back to prison, therein to be detained till he is delivered over for being so transported, for which this shall be to all concerned a sufficient warrant. " (Signed) ROBERT M'QUEEN, J.P.D."

DEFENCE APPENDED BY THE PRISONER TO REPORT OF TRIAL.

I have now furnished the public with the grounds of my unfortunate trial, and the evidence as taken down in Court If I have erred I solemnly declare, it is not voluntarily, and as I have not been induced to lay my case before you from vain or idle curiosity, I trust it will meet with your approbation. I am actuated to lay it before you to contradict some base insinuations propagated against me of having been guilty of similar crimes, in answer to which I shall only say, that it is, in one word, false, equally false, base and atrocious, with M'Edward's accusation, and if he will but examine his own heart, he must join me in saying that I am innocent—innocent I say, because I am conscious of being so, as much so of the crimes laid to my charge as the angels that surround the throne of glory.   But it is evident that the prosecution has been wantonly and maliciously set on foot by my enemies, who have been too, too successful in their designs ; to their machinations I attribute all my sufferings ; I have not the officers of the Crown to blame for those sufferings, they did their duty. But let M'Edward, and some other witnesses adduced against me, remember, that they must one day appear before the awful tribunal of God, that upright Judge, whose presence none can avoid, where no corrupt evidence will be received, and where no excuse will be admitted.   There and then will their conduct towards me fly in their face : May they meet with forgiveness is my earnest wish ; I have a consolation under my sufferings, which they have not, and that consolation will be my companion through life.   I can appeal to the Almighty with a clear conscience that I am innocent.

It cannot be supposed for a moment that had I been conscious of having acted wrong, I would have staid in the country until this bill fell due, far less until horning was raised on it, and especially when on the 17th of November I was charged by virtue of that horning ; and surely had I any thing to dread I would have fled. Every man possessed of common reason would have done it ; this is not all , six weeks elapsed afterwards, and nothing further was heard or done relative to the bill, and had I been afraid of any danger, I had time enough to make my escape.   I was not in custody ; and on the 26th December, I was on my returu from the country to Inverness, when I met the messenger at Coryburgh on his way to charge M'Edward ; and in order to save two executions, I got a second copy of charge ; and so far from dissuading the messenger to execute the horning against M'Edward, that I positively desired him to put it in force, and send the caption to Mr Miller with all convenient speed. Armed with an innocent conscience I went home to Inverness ; and on Monday following the 31st December, I was informed by Wm. Kennedy, servant to Alexander M'Pherson in Coryburgh, that M'Edward was come to town, and denied his subscription, to which I could give no credit. This happened about eleven o'clock A.M., and about six in the evening I was called before the Sheriff for examination, when I not only gave pointed and accurate answers to every question that was put to me, but gave up all the names of the witnesses present at the transaction, and cited against me, but helped the Sheriff to discover where the bill lay ; yet it is believed that men in general know, that, however prudent it may be for an innocent person to answer any question fairly, it may be otherwise for a person conscious of guilt ; I acted upon the principle of an innocent person, expecting it would have due weight ; had that not been the case, I was not bound to say who held the bill. It would have been my province to conceal it and get it settled ; but I wished to let my base accuser see it, supposing it impossible for him to deny his own hand writing. The reverse was the case, and with the utmost effrontery he declared that it was not his writing ; a warrant of commitment was in consequence granted, and I was thrown into a horrible dungeon, to await the event of a precognition of the witnesses on whom I condescended. It was afterwards sent to the Crown agent, and a long delay being made in returning it, I applied for letters of intimation against the procurator fiscals and private party, to fix a diet for my trial, which I obtained and executed ; and upon the very day the time, limited by the Act of Parliament, was expired, that day I was served with an indictment, from the High Court of Justiciary, to stand trial fifteen days thereafter.

Soon after my incarceration, I applied to the Sheriff to be admitted to bail, which he refused, though in similar cases, he had granted it to others. What his reason was in refusing me is best known to himself.

What I have since suffered may be conceived, but cannot well be expressed, what I even suffered coming from Inverness to the jail of Edinburgh, is punishment enough for almost any crime ; but in order that you may judge, I will here insert it for your perusal.

Upon the 7th day of May I was politely escorted by the Sheriff of Inverness, to the end of the town, my hands bound in irons, a party of soldiers with screwed bayonets, and a Sheriff-Officer attending me with a horse and cart to carry my baggage, and if I inclined to sit in it when fatigued, this party conducted me to the town of Nairn, the next county town, sixteen miles distant from Inverness, when I was thrown into jail; when delivered to the Substitute Sheriff there, he caused his officers to search not only myself but my trunk, fearful I had any dangerous weapons, but found none.   I was then thrown into a miserable dungeon, still in irons, some straw given me for a bed ; yet they were so destitute of humanity, that they would not allow me to take off my clothes—I was fed like a child—I could not feed myself—I threw myself amongst the straw—what I suffered that night I leave every feeling heart to judge.   I was sent in the same manner to Elgin, under the escort of twelve soldiers and eighteen men chosen by the Sheriff, but to their praise they took off my handcuffs until we arrived near the town, when they were obliged, consistent with their orders, to replace them, I was received there in the same manner, thrown into a wretched dungeon, and both my legs fastened in irons, well supplied with a straw bed.   The next stage was Banff, where I was conducted in the same manner, and where I was still worse used (if worse usage was possible).   I was sent off about 2 o'clock in the morning, escorted by thirty men, some armed with swords, some with bludgeons, some with guns, and others with rusty swords, both my legs fixed in irons by a blacksmith, and exhibited like a puppet show, through the streets of Aberdeen, on the top of a cart, when hundreds of people assembled to see me.   By this time I thought I had arrived in a Christian place, as one messenger and three men were my only attendants ; they delivered me in Stonehive jail, where none was but myself : From thence I was sent to Forfar, escorted by thirty-five old and young men, with my hands tied with cords behind my back, and in the same manner from Forfar to Perth.   But it was there that I found

myself amongst Christians; the Honourable Sheriff (Mr Smith)
was shocked at the inhumanity I was treated with, and the manner
in which I was sent, observing that my situation in life entitled
me to a carriage, and he accordingly sent me to Edinburgh in a
carriage with a messenger and two men only. Had I been
riotous, or had I wished to escape, I would consider this treatment as deserving; but I challenge my attendants to say, that
ever I expressed a wish to avoid my fate; on the oontrary, I was
determined to attend the bar of the High Court of Justiciary, and
receive my sentence; and if that sentence had been death, I would
mount the scaffold in the most serene manner.   No punishment
can daunt the innocent heart: God, who knows my innocence,
'supported me through those sufferings, and whatever they may
yet be. I trust God will grant me grace to support them.

[Some years ago a gentleman interested in matters connected
with Inverness, had a perusal of Grant's trial from the writer.
This gentleman had spent some years of his life in Australia.
When returning the copy of the trial, he appended a note in connection with John Grant, which we here give, as it carries the
convict's narrative to a later period than in the published report.
The story of Grant of Norfolk Island is given—it is at least
curious :—

"John Grant was conveyed on board the 'Royal George,'
Excise yacht, on 15th October 1793, lying in Leith Roads, for
London.

" Immediately on the arrival of the prisoners in the Thames,
they were put on board the hulks, and, after a long detention,
transported to New South Wales.

" I was in Sydney in 1858, and have a recollection of hearing a
story from one of the " Execution Guard" of a noted Grant from
Norfolk Island, who cast lots with a fellow convict who should
kill, or be killed, but do not remember if the name was *John*."]

FIDDLERS.

—o—

FIFTY years ago there was quite a colony of fiddlers in Inverness who found ready employment for their musical talents on three or four nights of every week during the greater portion of the year when out-door sport could not be indulged in. In those days the public-houses were frequently open to all hours, and at certain houses all night if the state of trade demanded it ; but the Forbes Mackenzie Act seems to have almost killed the race.

Penny reels, penny weddings, shoemakers' balls, apprentice footings, brotherings, &c., were the multitudinous opportunities that were made and taken advantage of to keep up the frolic and spree, with dancing, to the earliest hours. The frequenters of these rather noisy scenes were seldom cleared out before dawn, and may be said to have only gone "home with the milk in the morning." At Halloween, Christmas, and New Year's time, there was a fortnight or three weeks of this species of merrymaking indulged in.

The quantity drank at this time of the Highland beverage, as may be supposed, was great, "from early morn to dewy eve," it was nothing but tasting—the said tasting going to several glasses at a time. Whisky was cheap—a gill (three dram glasses) was to be had for threepence, while a bottle of the best malt could be had for a shilling. The young fellows of these days must have been a strong-headed, hardy race, to cope with the quantity of liquor consumed ; but as one man, we have heard say, who went in frequently for these frolics—"The whisky was not 'doctored' like what is sold now."

"ABERFOYLE."

But to come to our local fiddlers of those past days. The earliest of our recollection goes back to old lame "Aberfoyle." We could not have been more than eight years old when we had our attention first attracted to this Orpheus. On Lower

6

Kessock Street, one summer evening in the early " forties," with other neighbour bairns, we found ourselves following a rushing crowd to see what was the attraction. It turned out to be poor " Aberfoyle" He was rolling about outside of " Muirhead's" public-house at top of Lower Kessock Street, next door to the ' Deer's Head." He was considerably elevated, and had his violin slung in a green bag over his arm. The landlord (Muirhead) was standing outside the door defending the entrance against the attacks of the fiddler. Muirhead was a jolly, florid little man with a wooden leg, and the struggle between Muirhead with his wooden leg, and " Aberfoyle." with his lame limb, was a source of great amusement to the spectators. We have heard the cause of " Aberfoyle's" lameness from an old Invernessian who had seen him carried to the Northern Infirmary :—One night when he was crossing Kessock Ferry after performing at a wedding party— happy as usual, and with more sail than he could safely carry —he came to grief, and had his leg broken between the pier and the boat.

He was called " Aberfoyle" from the district in Perthshire from which he came originally to Inverness. He chiefly worked at Kessock Ferry playing in the boats, and receiving doles from the passengers ; he was also considered as fiddler to the " Sconcers," who used to be kind to him while work was plentiful at the Citadel. His favourite reel was "Delvinside," and the children of the town when they saw " Aberfoyle" pass along would call after him to give them " Delvinside." He obliged them occasionally if he was in the humour, especially if the boys, with a cheer, gave him " Aberfoyle for ever." He lived in his latter days in a lodging in Chapel Street.

JOHN FOWLER.

John Fowler was a player at raffles, and a favourite place where he was to be found playing was a barn in Davis' Square. He got paid by " penny reels." This was the sum paid by the young lads and workmen who attended the dance—hence the name, and by this means in a few years he succeeded in accumulating sufficient money to establish himself in a public-house which stood at the junction of Young Street with King Street. Fowler the fiddler's daughter, who generally played the " cello," only died a few years past in Inverness. By the way, Davis' Square, it may be here mentioned, was so called as it was built by Davis, a Welshman of that name, who worked several small contracts during the construction of the Caledonian Canal, and had made some money over them.

"BLIND WILLIE."

William Macgillivray, or "Blind Willie," was also a player at "penny reel" entertainments. Although blind, he was said to be a good judge of horses, and his services in this capacity were in request at the Inverness Horse Markets." We have heard a story of "Blind Willie's" expertness in this way in judging a horse. His method was by passing his hand all over the animal from the tips of his ears to the tail and his legs. On completing his feeling examination of the beast, on one occasion being asked for his opinion, he said—"Aye, he is half like myself, although not blin' of his two eyes, he is blin' in the left one." His musical talents were chiefly confined to Inverness and to his native district, Strathnairn.

"Blind Willie" is said to be the composer of some Gaelic songs. We have heard repeated several verses of one of these, which was characterised by a coarse freedom that quite unfit them to a place here. This worthy used to be led about in his wanderings by "Dunca' Phailaa"—a simpleton who became attracted to him by the charms of his playing, and whom he trained to accompany him on the "cello." A faithful attendant was "Tenor," as he was called by the country people, from his bass performances. "Tenor," while accompanying "Willie" at dances, was very apt to indulge in too much liquor if the parties present were over kind. On one of these occasions the blind leader gave the hint to their employer that "Dunca" was not to receive any drink. When blind "Willie" was treated, "Tenor" was passed over—thus occurred once or twice during the evening, and he evidently felt the slight. When his leader, a little after, requested him to rosin' his bow well, "Tenor" replied—"Rosin' your throat, you greedy fellow." We think it was of "Blind Willie" we heard a story in which Jock Stephen and another heckler played off a trick on this poor fiddler. At one of these dances, and at an interval in the evening performance, "Blind Willie" was asked to take some refreshment, and retiring to a side room, he left his fiddle and bow on the chair where he had been seated—a rostrum elevated on the top of a table. Jock and his friend saw their opportunity, and, having provided themselves with a piece of soap, they seized the bow of the violinist and greased or soaped it most carefully, and then replaced it on the chair. The fiddler soon returned to his elevated position, and the company having formed to dance a reel, the musician attempted to begin, but not a sound could he get out of the catgut. Again and again he essayed to start ; at last he divined the situation and the trick played upon him, passing his fingers over the hair of the bow, and throwing the violin down, he, with an oath in the Gaelic, exclaimed—" *Droch diabhol cha thig glic mach es.*" (" Bad luck to it ; a squeak won't come out of it.")

" CORN IN EGYPT."

" Corn in Egypt" was a fiddler whose real name was John Macrae, but he was always called by the boys by his sobriquet. This generally made the man very angry. He was nimble and swift of foot, and many a chase the Merkinch youths had when they roused him by calling his nickname, and if he caught any of his tormentors they received a good clouting from this fiddler of irascible temper. At his public performances " Corn" was always accompanied by his daughter performing on the "bass fiddle," as it was called. The last time the writer of these notes heard Macrae play was in an old hostelrie kept by a youngish buxom, " Luckie," that stood on Grant Street, near the wooden Bridge. It was on the occasion of a raffle for a watch, and there was a good deal of " throwing" about the dice for the prize. The raffle was on this wise :—Each subscriber of sixpence had so many " throws" of the dice for his money, and he who scored highest ultimately got the watch. The game was continued for hours till the value of the watch was got, and ties were finally adjusted. One could subscribe more than once, and by this means get several " chances" of securing the prize. These subscription raffles were got up for behoof of some unfortunate fellow-workman, or widow, but they were the occasion of much drunkenness and riot. After the first spell of " throwing," which, generally began about 8 P.M., and lasted for two hours

"Corn," in full fig at ten o'clock, led off the dancing with his "foursome" and full "bass" accompaniment. Macrae was an old beau, and on all occasions was rather smartly dressed. We have never seen this old fiddler without being done up in full swallow-tailed coat with brass buttons, chimney-pot hat, and sporting a rather loud neckcloth—red being his favourite colour —he had evidently, poor old chap, a weakness in that direction.

"WATERLOO."

Another fiddler, John Mackay ("Waterloo,") was a brave soldier who had served his country through the chief battles of the Peninsula, and finally was one of those who stood in the British squares at Quatre Bras and Waterloo. He served in the 79th Regiment or Cameron Highlanders ; was present at Badajoz, Corunna, and Toulouse, at which latter he was wounded in the shoulder, and finally at Quatre Bras and Waterloo, where he was shot in the ankle. Hence the name "Waterloo," by which he was best known to us boys of the Merkinch. What a host of Peninsular heroes there were residing in that district in those days—men who had passed through the well-fought campaigns of the Napoleonic wars in Spain, Portugal, Belgium, &c. They lived so much in the neighbourhood that the thoroughfare now called Upper Kessock Street was then locally known as "Veteran Row," and formed the subject of a song by John Macrae, a versifier of whom we shall have something to say in a future page. The song was sung to the old Scottish air—" Fye, let us a' to the bridal." We here insert the first verse :—

> " Frae tented field free, and frae barrack,
>   As brethren united and free ;
> Wha oft bore the musket and wallet
>   When foreign faes victors wad be ;
> You'll find our lads happy and cheery
>   A' strangers to sorrow or woe ;
> Where ilka ane now guards his deary
>   An' bairnies, in Veteran Row.
> Chorus—Then here's to the lads wha hae conquered,
>   Then here's to the brave and the free ;
> Lang life to them a' wha hae ventur'd
>   To guard us by land and by sea."

These veterans lived worthily and much respected. We would mention with honour Angus Ross (who was minus a leg), a godly elder in the "Chapel of Ease" (now Free East Church). Sergeant Mackintosh, whose sword and scarf we boys used to look up to with awe as it hung over his mantelpiece in Grant Street. Donald Mackay, a brother of "Waterloo's," who lost a leg at the memorable retreat of Corunna, and other heroes.

But to return to Mackay, who was in better circumstances than others of his fellow-soldiers, and farmed some acres of land behind the present Barracks on Telford Road ; and whose horses, when not engaged on the land, were employed in carting jobs. The playing at weddings was supplemental to his other employments, and perhaps only for amusement. While " Waterloo's" crop on the lands he farmed were ripening, he watched with great care the inroad the boys of the neighbourhood made on his fields of wheat and turnips. In this he was aided by his dog—a brindled mongrel—which was the terror of all the prowlers on his pre-serves. One episode in which the writer took his part, and the dog did his, may be recounted. A few Merkinch boys (boy like), as Halloween approached, agreed to make a raid on " Waterloo's" turnip field to provide themselves with lanterns for the forth-coming festival, but they did not succeed in attaining their object. As they approached the land they began to suspect that a figure they saw against the light, near the hedge that bounded one side of the field, was old Mackay. One of the boys gave a howl, and cried " Waterloo," and they all took to their heels ; as they ran, they heard the old soldier urge on his dog in pursuit, and it was not long before the animal had one of the raiders by the leg of his nether garment, and held him fast until his master arrived, and then to find out who the youth was, as he would give no reply to enquiries as to his name and parentage, he denuded him of his cap and jacket ; in this plight on returning home he had to tell his story. But it was the next day, and after a journey to Madras Street before the articles were recovered, and then only on the youngster promising that he would never—no, never !—go near any of " Waterloo's " fields again.

Our recollection of " Waterloo's" fiddling is that it was not in so much demand as the others who preceded him in this notice of Inverness fiddlers. The writer heard him on two or three occasions, and his impression is that " Waterloo" had been self-taught and played by the ear. His playing of Strath-speys and reels had not the true "ceoil" of some of his contemporaries, such as Fowler, or " Corn in Egypt." Mackay was accompanied on the " bass" by his daughter, Nell, who was lame. The young lads, however, used to enjoy asking Nell to dance, and she entered into it, notwithstanding her lameness, with great spirit, but when getting exhausted with the excitement of the prolonged reel, she usually on these occasions cried out to the fiddler—" Cut it short, father ! cut it short ! "

DONALD DAVIDSON.

There was another fiddler, whose name was quite familiar to us, and of whom we have stories to tell, but it was never our luck to know his personal appearance. We have known those who were associated with him in many a bout, but the nearest that we ever came to him was that we heard him nearly fifty years ago on a Christmas morning. We had an opportunity of seeing Donald Davidson on that occasion, but we neglected it, and only heard his music at a little distance ; and although our boyish curiosity was excited. we did not follow it up. On that busy occasion full of youth, and on pleasure bent, we were more interested in contributing our share to the noise and turmoil that distinguished the streets of Inverness "on a cold and frosty Christmas morning," than the attractions of " Morair Sheim," or the " Flowers of Edinburgh," however feelingly or sprightly played.

Donald Davidson's musical talents were in great demand among the gentry and at country dances. Accompanied by his nephew, Sandie Cameron (" Allie Bo-Bo "), who played the " cello," he was known to the uttermost corner of Inverness-shire. Like all the others of this race of Invernessians, he was rather given to worship at the shrine of Bacchus, and many a story we have been told of his adventures. We will only give one that we have heard the late Dr John Inglis Nicol repeat. himself a performer on the violin of no mean order, and a physician of the first standing of his day in Inverness. The doctor was possessed of a fine old violin, and for a special occasion Donald Davidson borrowed it ; he was going to Moyhall to play at a ball. Returning next day by mail coach Donald had got on the driver's seat ; not very steady after his night's playing, and from what he had imbibed, unfortunately the violin, in the green bag, fell from him while near Daviot Bridge, and getting under the coach wheels, was crushed to pieces, and in this condition was taken home by Davidson. For some time Dr Nicol heard nothing of his fiddle, and Davidson was evidently keeping out of his way. At last the doctor called on Donald, and insisted on him returning the instrument, when Davidson had at last to confess the mishap that had befallen it. He produced the bag with all the fragments, when the doctor got angry over the ruins of his favourite violin. Davidson, putting the best face on the matter, said—" Never fear, doctor, I will make it better than ever it was." " How that ?" enquired Nicol. " By putting it together again," replied the fiddler. " Pooh ! pooh !—nonsense !" said the owner—" ridiculous ! " " Ridiculous here, or ridiculous there, wait till you see." The doctor did wait, as he could do nothing better, and in a few weeks after Donald Davidson appeared with the damaged violin neatly repaired, and done " maist as new," or rather better, as the doctor always declared " the tone was vastly improved, and the jointing better sent out of Donald Davidson's Hospital than any ever sent out of a medical one."

Donald Davidson and his nephew Cameron did good business as that of " waits." Soon after Halloween they began, to leave off only after the New Year was in, playing in the early morning at the best houses. And when Christmas day came they called on that forenoon, or on New Year's Day, at the various houses to get their " boxes " for the music supplied. They were out as early as four o'clock A.M., and for two hours or more they went round the town playing at selected points. They generally began with a slow measure, and finished up with a quick time, and then a salute of " Good morning to Mr and Mrs ——, a fine frosty morning," or as the weather might be. There was a jocular story among the boys that at one of the houses thus visited resided a Mr Bird, and that the musicians salute to them was— " Good morning to Mr and Mrs Bird ; I hope you are quite well, and all the little Birds ! " *

* A friendly correspondent who has seen the article " Fiddlers " in proof adds the following with respect to Donald Davidson :—" Recollect him well. Latterly, from age and so obstinate, Lowe could no longer employ him. He it was who played the ' Reel of Tulloch '—' Huilichan,' properly speaking—with variations I never heard since. In truth he was a very prince at Reels and Strathspeys."

"JOCKIE CUMMING."

John Cumming— or "Jockie" Cumming, as the name he was best known by—was a contemporary of Donald Davidson, and survived him for many years. "Jockie" had early joined the Inverness Militia, in which he served for a long period, having risen to the rank of Sergeant, and passed ultimately into the band. Our earliest recollections of him was performing on the trombone in the procession of the Justiciary Lords on Circuit, from the Caledonian Hotel to the Castle. "Jockie" was not in such repute as Davidson, and others, we have mentioned, as a player at dances, but he always played in the orchestra at the Northern Meeting Balls, while the music was in charge of Mr Joseph Lowe, dancing master of Edinburgh, Inverness, &c. Cumming was a composer of Reels and Strathspeys, and some of them have been found worthy of a place in Lowe's Collections, notably "Cutty Sark." The origin of this Strathspey was curious, and we give it as repeated to us by a son of the composer :—Passing down one day the Old Meal Market Close, off the High Street, "Jockie" witnessed a quarrel of words and blows between two noted characters who resided in the close—viz., Nannie Kennedy, and another called Mary Fraser—"Mary Cod." Kennedy was the mother of a local character, "Willie" Thompson, who used to serve as porter to Donald Fraser. ironmonger, and others —the lady with the fishy cognomen acted as fish carrier to several of the houses of the neighbouring gentry Cumming, as we have said, witnessing the fight between these worthies, and the vocable squabble carried on in Gaelic, was so tickled with the scene and sounds that immediately on getting to his home a few doors further down the same thoroughfare, he noted down a musical imitation of the strange scene he had seen, and the Gaelic expletives which he had listened to, and "Cutty Sark" was the result. "Cromarty Janet" and "Half Moon" are other composi-tions of his, which found some local fame among players.

Mr Joseph Lowe, who was teacher of Highland dancing to the Royal Family, thought so much of Cumming's playing of Reels and Strathspeys, that "Jockie" got an invitation to play at Buckingham Palace. Proceeding to London, which he did by sea, he arrived in the great City, but failed to report himself.

Poor Cumming had got entangled among some boon companions
in the purlicus of Drury Lane, from which he never emerged
until he was literally cleaned out of every article that could be
turned into money. Without experience, and a simplicity of
character that rendered him a fit object for the imposition of the
worthless characters that he had fallen amongst, he was cast out
to wander for weeks homeless and penniless through the wilderness
of London.   Driven to great straits—even to wanting a bed—
for some weeks sleeping in Hyde Park, he met at last one day a
former Inverness acquaintance who got his story, and provided
him with some means to tide over for a few days. This friend
brought Cumming's case before some countrymen, who provided
the necessary funds to pay his return fare by the " Duchess of
Sutherland" steamer to Inverness.

" Jockie " returned to Inverness, broken in body and health
only to die.   He lived for five weeks after his return, suffering,
no doubt, from the effect of exposure and the want of food
in his London experiences.

The last time we heard "Jockie" Cumming play was in the
orchestra of the Theatre in Lowe's Hall, Church Street, when
J. W. Anson, late stage manager of the Adelphi, London, and
Secretary of the Royal Dramatic College, was lessee of Lowe's
Hall. On that evening " Jockie" had three times to play '· Morar
Sheim " in response to the repeated calls of " Geordie Bean," *
who led the " Gods."   " Jockie" had his reward in the loud ap-
plause and " well played" ejaculations of his aerial admirers.

There are several others of these fiddlers of a past generation
who deserve notice, and we may return at a later time to the
chronicling of kindly " Kenny " Clark, old soldier, barber, and
musician.   Sandie Cameron, nephew of Donald Davidson, and
who only passed away a few years ago ; and also his frequent
leader in latter days, as Cameron called him—" The *Chappie*
M'Callum ;" and finally, James Mackenzie, who spent many of
his early years as a workman in the house of Broadwood, famous

* George Macbean—a well-known citizen—who for over fifteen years was
Sub-Inspector of Poor and a prominent member of the Inverness Tem-
perance Society. We have heard George at an earlier period, as a pronounced
Radical, " heckle," with considerable smartness and effect, candidates for
Parliamentary and Municipal honours, both at the hustings and public
meetings.

pianoforte-makers, London.   Mackenzie was a skilful piano-tuner,
and also a maker of violins.   Many specimens of his deft work-
manship still occasionally are found among local violin players.
Of all these worthies we will only say in the words of the local
poet, Macrae :—

> " For mirth and glee I do repeat,
> A nobler band ne'er took a seat ;
> In posture, easy, manly, neat,
>   They drew the bow.
> While keen before them mony a foot
>   Strathspeys gae'd through.'

THE BATTLE OF DRUIMASHIE.

OSSIAN, and the literary controversy that followed on the
publication of Macpherson's volumes, we have no desire to
enter on in this work ; the battle still rages, and the fight may be
prolonged for an indefinite period.   We simply are chroniclers
of the local traditions which still lingers in these northern parts.

"The Battle of Druimashie and the Castle of Dunrichath " still
forms part of the talk of the common people of the district
round their firesides of a winter evening ; and even finds mention
among the learned members of the Inverness Field Club, as we
found when on a pleasant excursion in the summer of 1882
we spent with them a day exploring the antiquities and the
archæological remains of Loch-Ashie, Duntelchaig, Achnabat, etc.

The local tradition as to this Fingalian fight, is that Fingal,
when a very young man, fought a desperate battle with the
restless piratical Danes, in which the latter were defeated on the
banks of the streamlet, a few miles south of the town of Inverness,
named " Alt an-arn," so called from the number of alder bushes

which line the margin of the stream.   The Danish or Norwegian leader is said to have been Ashie. the son of the King of Denmark and Norway—hence Druimashie, or the *Hill of Ashie*.   It is also said that near here Fingal established one of his duns, or round towers, which was named " Dunrichath, or *Castle of the King of War*.   There are several cairns in the neighbourhood which are supposed to be remains of this early period. The following poem, founded on this tradition, is from the MS. collection of Andrew Fraser :—

BATTLE OF DRUIMASHIE.

PART I.

THE COMING OF THE DANES—SONG OF LOCHLIN.

Sons of the wild and icy North ! why have you left your land ?
Why men of Lochlin, wander forth to darken Albyn's strand ?
Why restless as the streamy light which o'er you flit on high,
Are ye, red wanderers of the night, beneath your own stern sky ?

Your gallies on the snow-fraught breeze hath spread their daring wings,
And dash along the boiling seas whilst the old Norsman sings,
" All hail to thee, thou glittering star ! thou beamest on the shore
Where Albyn's warrior sleep afar, and Albyn's waters roar.

" Wake to the rushing of your streams, sons of the waving heath !
Wake to yon little stars bright beams before ye sleep in death,
Waken, oh wake ! to Cona's song, the soul of all your hills,
Ere your red blood is carried on the white foam of your rills.

" The King of Lochlin strikes his shield, hark ! dread ye not the sound,
There is not one small speck will yield in all its ample round ;
Its surface is the lightning's flare when the black clouds are driven
In wild commotion thro' the air and Morven's rocks are riven.

" The King of Lochlin lifts his spear like Loda in his might,
Hurling his stormborn meteor thro' the vaulted gloom of night,
Fate bears it on its awful force, it never sped in vain ;
A thousand deaths is on its course, a thousand ghosts its train !

" The King of Lochlin wields his sword, destruction strews the waste,
Dark Odin gives the fearful word, his voice is on the blast :
The spirit of the tempest sweeps the thistle down away,
And all the world submissive creeps beneath its boundless sway.

" The King of Lochlin on his head the crested helmet rears,
Ha ! spirits of the warrior-dead ! why thus renew your fears ?
Doth pity move each phantom-breast for the pale coming dead ?
Or shrink'st in terror at the crest 'neath which your spirits fled ?

" The King of Lochlin on thy strand hath sprung with panther-bound,
Fair Albyn ; mighty is the band which girds thy spirit round ;
Never again shall Morven's King the note of war proclaim,
Blood-clotted is his broken wing, he falls without a name, "

PART II.

DUNRICHATH—FINGAL ALONE ON THE HEATH.

The oakbeam in Dunrichath hall had sped its mighty flame,
Scarce showing on the trophied wall the spoils of war or game ;
There lay the spear of Lochlin's sires, there hung the battle beam,
And the shield threw out its sparkling fires from many a native gem.

Slumber had shed its balmy wings on each tall chief around,
While in his dream the deerhound springs with wild and fancied bound
Across the dashing mountain-stream and up the wooded vales,
Scarce lighted by the solar beam or rustled by the gales.

Deep on the silence of the night across the stilly heath,
Sounded the shield of Trenmore's might the note of coming death,
It fell upon each warrior's ear and in his slumber deep,
He eager grasped his battle-spear and shook it in his sleep

Louder again the sound had broke on clouded vale and wood,
Startling old echo from its rock in gloomiest solitude,
And ringing on the midnight hour so loud, so long, and dread,
As seemed within Dunrichath's tower a warning from the dead.

Loud, and more loud, again it shook the solemn gloom of night,
Each warrior from his slumber broke, and armed him for the fight,
'Tis Trenmore's shield, said Cona's voice, struck by great Fingal spear, ·
" To warn the children of the *ice* we mark their coming war."

Fingal by some bright spirit warned had sought the breezy hill,
Near where the *first* green wreath he earned by Arno's blood-soiled rill,
When the Sea-King and island-band had closed their dark career,
And Fingal through the rescued land hailed youthful *King of War*.

There, where the silence was unbroken, save by the brawling stream,
Where seldom sleepy echo woke but by the eagle's scream,
Stood mighty Trenmore's mightier son amid the starless gloom,
As if he would oppose alone the invaders of his home.

Why starts he ? ha ! yon cloud has driven with wild and fearful crash,
Blazing athwart the impurpled heaven a momentary flash,
Which for an instant had revealed the deeply varnished glow
Darting from spear, and sword, and shield, of Albyn's coming foe.

PART III.

THE BATTLE—COMBAT BETWEEN FINGAL AND THE KING OF LOCHLIN.

Warriors of Morven ! round your King a thousand swords had beamed,
A thousand ravens on the wing long ere the morning gleamed,
Long ere the earliest streak of light had tinged the eastern sky,
Closed in the shroud of endless night was many a gallant eye

Not thine, thou torn and clotted heath, that reeking coat of red,
That is the hue which covers death when laid on glory's bed ;
Not that the plover whistling by on strong and fearless wing,
'Tis but the voice of agony—the souls keen harrowing.

Dreadful contest ! man and horse, and sword and helm, were hewn,
The streams had changed their wonted course, the " peaceful ridge" was
        strewn
With limbs which lately strong in life had chased the bounding deer,
And hearts which gloried in the strife of desolating war.

Like rush of tempests on the wing, or mighty billows shock,
The war-cry wild of either King on either army broke,
They meet as meet the rushing floods the conflicts of the gale
When whirling o'er the groaning woods in dark Strathfarar's vale.

Both hosts had paused for now were weighed in Fate's unerring scale
The destiny of either side—the glorious rise or fall ;
This struggled for his own brown land against the invader's power,
And that had left his stormy strand to win a milder shore.

Eagle of Albyn ! prize thy wing, scream from thy rock afar,
The plumage of thy stately king waves foremost in the war ;
The ringing of his mighty blade resounds from hill to dale,
And dale, and hill, and greenwood shade, re-echoes Lochlin wail.

Morven ! its done, that glittering shield ne'er framed by mortal hand,
Lies shivered on the reeking field far from its own dark land ;
That helmets towering crest is cleft, and bleeding, pale, and low,
Of sword, and shield, and helm bereft, lies Albyn's mightiest foe.

Full many a hundred times the heath hath cast its purple bloom,
Druimashie ! since thy ridge of death became wild Lochlin's tomb,
And but traditions simple note you might have passed that moor
Without distinguishing the spot where stood Dunrichath's tower.

INVERNESS POST-OFFICE.

—o—

CURIOUS CASE.—WARRAND *V.* FALCONER.

IN that unsatisfactory " dry-as-dust" work, " Freemasonry in Inverness," compiled from the minute books of the Lodges, by Alexander Ross, F.G.S., F.S A.Scot, &c., we first' came across the *cause célèbre* that follows. The minutes of St John's and St Andrew's Lodges, in the hands of a congenial editor, could have been made a volume of most pleasant reading, containing as they do passing glimpses of men who played no inconsiderable part in northern society and politics of their day.

Among the early brethren of St John's are to be found the names of Macgillivray of Dumnaglass, who led the Clan Mackintosh at Culloden, and fell on that fatal day ; Gillies Macbean, tacksman, of Bunachton, who also fought in the ranks of Clan Chattan, and performed deeds of heroism (as mentioned by Chambers in his History of the " Forty-five"), a man of prodigious bodily strength, who stood 6 feet 4 inches and a quarter high— who, when hard pressed, stood with his back against a wall, and, single handed, opposed the onset of a party of dragoons, and was not overpowered till thirteen of his foes lay dead at his feet. There was also George Cuthbert of Castlehill, a kinsman of Colbert, the celebrated Minister of Louis XIV., of France, who was for some years R.W.M. ; and Lauchlan Mackintosh, merchant in Inverness, one of the earliest members of the old St John's Kilwinning Lodge, and to this gentleman is addressed the long letter from a Brother member of Grand Lodge, printed on the first page of " Freemasonry in Inverness." Lauchlan Mackintosh was a most enthusiastic Jacobite, and in 1745 deserted his business and joined the ranks of Prince Charles, as recorded in the MS. letters of an Inverness merchant, now before us. This merchant, in writing to his correspondent in Holland on 17th December 1745, says:—" Your friend, Lauchlan Mackintosh, who came with you to my house, has given over our trade, and taken another by the hand ; he is now with the Highland army fighting for Prince Charles." Mackintosh was wounded at Culloden, but after escaped to France.

But to come to the law case—Warrand v. Falconer—we have said it first met us in the published volume we have above mentioned. Under date of minutes on 5th June, 1770, we find as follows :—

" The Lodge having taken into consideration how obnoxious Robert Warrand, the present Postmaster, is to them, and several others, and how neeessary it is that that office should be filled by a man of fair character, and one who possesses the confidence and esteem of his neighbours, resolved, and agreed, on an application to the Grand Master, to have him removed from that employment, and that in conjunction with the sister lodge."

We have recently come across the full report of the action which followed on this minute, and the other steps taken by the opponents of the obnoxious Robert Warrand, and which fully explains the unusual proceedings of a Lodge devoted to the cultivation of works of brotherly love and charity, attacking the character of a public official.

The case is one possessing considerable interest from the light thrown on the state of the postal service in the North of Scotland in the years following the rebellion of 1745, and the manners and mode of Inverness during that period. It would appear that for more than a generation the duties of Postmaster or Postmistress of Inverness were discharged by Helen M'Culloch, who was appointed to that office in 1737 by Archibald Douglas, the then Postmaster-General of Scotland. In course of time she married Robert Warrand, who was shortly afterwards appointed to act with her as Postmaster. The office was a somewhat important one, as the Postmaster of Inverness was responsible for all letters posted to the North of the Firth of Forth ; but Warrand seems to have been an irascible and overbearing man, who did not get on very well with his neighbours, and complaints and quarrels became frequent. One would fancy that in view of the bloodthirsty manner in which the Government troops stamped out the rebellion, no public man would have dared to offend the Commander of the Royal forces ; but in 1746 General Husk, who served under the Duke of Cumberland, was so angry at the manner in which important letters were transmitted, that he threatened to have the matter reported to the Postmaster-General. This storm seems to have blown easily past ; but some interference with a love affair brought the Inverness Postmaster far more trouble than the wrath of the victors of Culloden.

In the year 1765, one of the officers at Fort-George was a certain Captain Walcoat, who sometimes visited Inverness, and was received into the social circles of the Highland capital. This officer fell a victim to the charms of Miss Betty Fraser, one of the daughters of Mr William Fraser of Bught, writer and Town Clerk. A clandestine correspondence was carried on between the lovers for some time, until the lady's cousin, Francis Knowles, who happened to be Postmaster at Fort-George, began to scent something wrong. He accordingly wrote to his friend and colleague, the Postmaster at Inverness, that letters for Miss Fraser should be delivered not to herself but to her father, or some other friend. How Mr Knowles ever came to know about it is a mystery, seeing that, as it came out in the evidence, the lovers were so very careful that Miss Fraser would not allow her own handwriting to go on letters sent to the Fort, but got her father's clerk to direct the letters. Anyhow, the result of Mr Knowles interference was that the next letter addressed to Miss Fraser was delivered to that young lady's father, who opened it, and found there such facts as led him to communicate with Captain Walcoat, and in a wonderfully short time the lovers were married, and, as one of the document puts it, the Town-Clerk had very soon both a son-in-law and a grandchild. This affair caused some gossip in Inverness, and there were not wanting people who denounced the Postmaster for his share in the matter, even going the length of saying that he had opened some of the lovers' letters. Probably the Postmaster became obnoxious on some other grounds, for it became a practice with gentlemen when playing cards to refer to the knaves as " Postmasters," or " Warrands," and sometimes " Robbie Warrands."

Public feeling was in this state when Hugh Falconer,* a merchant

* Hugh Falconer was also proprietor of Drakies, in the neighbourhood of Inverness. He died very soon after this case. His burying-ground is in the old Greyfriars at Inverness, near the north wall and close to the

in Inverness, began to suspect the Postmaster of dealing unfairly by himself. He, therefore, went boldly to the Post-Office to demand his letters, and on their being refused him, a brawl ensued, which led to a criminal case, which came to nothing. Both parties, however, wrote to the Postmaster-General on the subject, Mr Falconer's letter being dated 28th February 1770 and reading as follows :—

INVERNESS, 28th February, 1770.

SIR,—Though I have not the honour of your acquaintance, yet I am forced to trouble you with this letter, and in justice to you and myself, I must enter a complaint to you against your deputy, Robert Warrand, who is Postmaster in this town. I know that complaints have been made against him to the Commander-in-Chief of His Majesty's Forces in Scotland, and to others of the first rank ; but I think you are the person to whom his conduct should be represented. I am a merchant here who have suffered greatly by the bad behaviour of your deputy. I have the most convincing proof of his keeping up my letters, and have great reason to fear that he may greatly hurt my interest by such practices. It could likewise be proven that he detained letters for others in this town, and that he opened and read them. That I may not trouble you with a long letter, I beg leave to refer to the enclosed proof, which I was obliged to take before our Sheriff in vindication of my conduct towards Robert Warrand, who (as I'm informed) has entered a complaint against me to you, with an intention to screen himself under your protection, and to instigate you to distress me. All that was competent for me to do at this time, and, indeed, all that our Sheriff would allow me to bring a proof of, was only in my own exculpation of the charge laid against me by Robert Warrand, and as I could not learn what that charge was, I thought it sufficient at this time to prove in general that I had done nothing amiss ; but was it necessary to bring a further proof of what I allege, it can easily be done.—I am, sir, your most obedient servant,

HUGH FALCONER.

The Postmaster-General sent a copy of this letter back to Mr

entrance-gate. The following monumental inscription to his memory is affixed in the wall :—

" CONSIDERATE OBSERVER ! | PLACE NOT THY CONFIDENCE IN | VIGOUR, HEALTH, OR KNOWLEDGE : | FOR NEAR THEE LIE IN DUST THE REMAINS OF | HUGH FALCONAR OF DRAKIES ; | WHO, WITHOUT PAIN OR COM-PLAINT, | WAS BY THE SUDDEN STROKE OF DEATH UNTIMELY CUT OFF | ON THE 3RD DAY OF JULY 1775, | AGED 42 YEARS. | LIKEWISE THE REMAINS OF MARY, | ELDEST DAUGHTER OF HUGH FALCONER, | AND JEAN DUFF, HIS WIFE, | WHO DIED ON THE 5TH DAY OF JUNE 1832, | AGED 56 YEARS. | " IN RESPECT FOR THE MEMORIES OF HIS FATHER AND SISTER | THIS TABLET IS INSCRIBED BY | JOHN FALCONAR, | CONSUL FROM GEORGE IV., KING OF GREAT BRITAIN | TO LEOPOLD II., GRAND DUKE OF TUSCANY."

Warrand, who thereupon raised an action of damages in the Court of Session against Mr Falconer, concluding for £500.

The evidence was taken by commission in Inverness, and it was marked by several violent scenes and interference with the witnesses.

FRANKING LETTERS.

One of the overments made by some of the witnesses was that the Postmaster, in order to get merchants to send their goods by a ship in which he was interested (the " Peace" of Elgin), sometimes franked their letters.

SHARP PRACTICE.

Donald M'Intosh, master of the ship " Nancy " in the Russia trade, depones—That twenty years ago, he had the command of a vessel belonging to Provost Hossack and Bailie Inglis,* called "The Pledger," with which he plied generally in the London trade betwixt Inverness and London ; and that at said time, the pursuer, Mr Warrand, had a vessel called, as he believes, "The Peace" of Elgin, and afterwards "The Charming Helen" of Inverness, which vessel of the pursuer's came to London much about the time the deponent and his vessel were ready to return from London, and believes she was to have carried goods from London to Inverness, and was to succeed his ship as next upon the berth : That Mrs Warrand was then Postmistress, but believes when Mr Warrand was in town he acted in the above capacity for her. Depones—That he was in use always before he left Inverness for London to solicit the merchants of Inverness for having any goods they were to have from London set aboard his vessel to load the same, and particularly did solicit them (but not more so than formerly) at the time he saw Mr Warrand's vessel at London as above ; and that at the above time, severals of the merchants of

---

* Hugh Inglis of Kingsmills, owner of "The Pledger," seems to have sailed his own vessel in 1746, as we find from the manuscript letter-book of Duncan Grant, another Inverness merchant, who, in writing to his correspondent in London, says, "I now send by Captain Hugh Inglis of "The Pledger" four porter hogsheads, marked "D + G," which, with four others, you are to buy for me, making in all eight. You will please fill with your very best porter, which, if it is not very good, cannot sell here at present, as we have an army with us who are very good judges ! Order them quite full (for I never get them so), and as free of dreg as possible."

Inverness, and particularly John Willison, merchant there promised to send their goods on board the deponent's vessel. And being interrogate—If or if not, at the above period of his being at London he saw goods put on board Mr Warrand's ship "The Peace," having Mr Willison's mark ? Depones—That he did not, but that his mate told him he saw goods with the above mark put on board Mr Warrand's vessel. To which the deponent said that it mattered not, as all the goods being a chest of oranges, half a chest Florence oil, and a pair bellows, as his mate told him, were all directed to "The Peace." Interrogate—Whether or not the deponent thereupon went to the shipping factor to know the reason of Mr Willison's goods being put on board "The Peace?" Depones—That he did go to the shipping factor, who was George Forbes. Interrogate—What did Mr Forbes say to the deponent at that time and at that period ? Depones—That he (Mr Forbes) said, he had orders to ship the above goods on board "The Peace." Interrogate—Did Mr Forbes acquaint him in what way the orders to ship the goods on board "The Peace" were given, and whether these orders were in the body or on the back of a letter ? Depones—That he told him in his own compting-house, that he supposed they expected he sailed, as they had contradicted the orders in the body of the letter, and showed him the letter, on the outside of which was wrote under the wafer the words, " On board The Peace ;" and believes the writing was of Donald Ritchie's handwriting, then Bulkmaster at Inverness ; but did not tell him whether the said letter was from John Willison or not, as he did not show me the contents of it ; but that the factor told him, that he looked on the writing on the back of the said letter as the last order. Interrogate—Whether, on his arrival at Inverness from London at that time he had any conversation with Mr Willison or others, on the subject of their goods being shipped on board Mr Warrand's ship, notwithstanding of their having promised to put them on board " The Pledger." Depones—That upon his arrival at Inverness, he called upon Mr John Willison for the freight of what goods he carried home for him. That Mr Willison declined paying him because he had not received all his goods ; on which the deponent told him that he had got all that he had ordered by him, on which Mr Willison told the deponent he was mistaken as he had only received of his last order a pair of bellows, and as the other goods were perishable he would make him, the deponent, accountable for them. That the deponent to this replied, that the direction of the bellows which he saw was directed to be put on board " The Peace," and that his mate told him the other goods were directed in the same way. Upon which the deponent asked him, If he had a copy of his letter ordering these goods? That he answered that he had, showing him at the same time a copy of his letter to Mr Forbes, wherein he desired to ship the goods on board the deponent's ship " The Pledger." Upon which the deponent further asked him, If he had Mr Forbes's answer? Whereupon Mr Willison, being in a passion, showed him at the same time Mr Forbes's answer, importing, that in consequence of his last order, he had shipped the goods on board " The Peace ;" and that at that time Mr Willison denied that he gave any such orders to ship them on board " The Peace."

PURSUER'S POWERFUL FAMILY CONNECTIONS.

One of the complainers against the Postmaster was John Hay, a hirer in Inverness, but he got little encouragement, poor man. Hay was at the time a "burgh officer ;" but the Postmaster (Warrand) was a member of the Town Council and Treasurer of the Burgh. Moreover, Mrs Warrand was a niece of Provost Hossack, and a daughter of Provost Hossack had been married to Provost William Mackintosh,* and afterwards to his cousin Provost Phineas Mackintosh.† Another daughter was married to the Rev. Murdoch Mackenzie,‡ one of the ministers of the town. Here was a pretty strong family combination, as John Hay could well see. One day John Denoon, a messenger in the town, brought John a letter from the Post-Office, and Hay said—"Look, John,

* William Mackintosh, 1st of Easter Ballifeary, eldest son of William Mackintosh, senior bailie of Inverness.

† Provost Phineas, son of Angus Mackintosh of Drummond, junior merchant and bailie of Inverness ; and William, senior, and Angus, junior brothers, sons of John Mackintosh, commonly called of Lynvuilg, Badenoch This John was brother to William, 3rd of Borlum.

‡ Rev. Murdoch Mackenzie was translated to Inverness from Dingwall, and admitted to the *third charge* on 13th July 1741. He was translated to the *second charge* on the 5th February 1751. He was translated from the second charge to the *first*, and was admitted on 2nd May 1763. He died on 9th April 1774, aged 74.

Mr Mackenzie's daughter was married to William Fraser, merchant in Inverness, parents of Mrs Hugh Miller, wife of the eminent geologist.

has not that letter been opened ? " Denoon said—" You block-
head, the letter has certainly been opened, for there is a wet wafer
on it." Hay said he would complain to the Provost, but Denoon
said—" You know your friends and your foes, and if you
do complain, poor man, you will be turned out of your jacket."
Hay took this as an allusion to the red coat he wore as burgh
officer.

DEFENDER'S CONNECTIONS.

One witness deponed that he knows William Duff, Esq. of
Muirtown is father-in-law to the defender ; Captain Alex. Duff * is
brother-in-law ; Major Alex. Duff, first cousin to Mrs Falconer
and married to her sister, and that William Cuthbert was a
relation.

Another witness deponed that Captain Forbes of New's son is
married to a daughter of Mr Duff of Muirtown. And further, he
depones that Captain Forbes of New told him that he and some
others of defender's friends would join their purses and interest to
ruin the pursuer ; that the conference with Mr Forbes of New
took place near to the market-place.

It came ont in evidence that before this action was raised an
attack on Mr Warrand, Postmaster, had been made by Hugh
Falconer the defender and his brother-in-law (Captain Alex. Duff,
younger of Muirtown), and, in consequence, a lawborrows had
been taken out.

POSTAL ARRANGEMENTS IN 1772.

Both Robert Oliphant, of Rossie, the Deputy Postmaster-
General for Scotland, and Mr Ker, the Surveyor of the General
Post-Office, Edinburgh, were examined in the case, and gave a
description of the working of the postal system of the day. Mr
Ker said :—" Mr Warrand is employed to ride the mail by the
General Post-Office from Nairn to Inverness, and from Inverness
to Nairn, and he is allowed for so doing threepence a mile for
every time he rides it, including both the going and the returning,
which is the usual rate over Scotland—a few instances excepted—
by which means a stage of twelve miles carrying and returning
amounts to £23 8s sterling per annum. It is the practice in
the Post-Office in Edinburgh to send way-bills from Edinburgh
to the different deputies as far as Inverness—that is, the way-bill

* Father of Hugh Robert Duff, editor of " The Culloden Papers " 1815.

from Edinburgh goes to Aberdeen, and returns to Edinburgh, and a new way-bill is dispatched from Aberdeen and goes to Inverness and returns from Inverness to Aberdeen ; and such way-bills as go from Aberdeen to Inverness and return there, remain at Aberdeen in case they should be occasionally called for by the Postmaster here. It is the duty of the different deputies to mark on these way-bills the arrival and dispatch of the post. The deputies sometimes neglect to mark such bills regularly, and mistakes of this kind happen all over the country, and in England as well as Scotland, and sometimes it happens that the way-bills are lost altogether, though more frequently in England than in Scotland, though it likewise sometimes happens here. Witness sometimes heard of altercations between the different deputies about the way-bills being misdated, or their attempting to cut one another short in time ; but this particularly happened between Berwick and Haddington, and between Linlithgow, Falkirk, and Glasgow, and though it might have happened in other quarters, he does not remember to have heard of it. In the different departments of the Post-Office it is a general rule, in case the post arrives at an unreasonable hour, that the deputies should not wait in the Post-Offices at the end of the route—such as at Aberdeen or Inverness—in order to give out letters or forward the post northwards beyond Inverness, at which place is branched out in these different quarters—1st, Fort-Augustus and Fort-William. 2nd, Dingwall, Invergordon, Parkhill, Tain, Dornoch, Dunbaith, Wick, Auchennorice, Thurso, and Kirkwall. 3rd, To Fortrose and Cromarty. 4th, To Lochcarron, Dunveggan, Sconcer, in the Isle of Skye, and Stornoway, in the Isle of Lewis ; and 5th, To Ruthven, of Badenoch, the south-west of Inverness —the two last of which are weekly posts—the rest thrice a week, and all of them are dispatched by runners. The general directions to deputies are to dispatch business as soon as possible, consistent with their duty ; but he remembers of no particular directions being given to Mr Warrand on that head. He has received different letters from Mr Warrand in vindication of himself, and has likewise seen letters to Mr Oliphant on that subject. The general rule for riding the post is about five measured miles in an hour, or four computed, but the rule in general is never kept up. The deputy

of Inverness had no authority from the Post-Office here to employ
a carrier to deliver letters, having no allowance or payment for
the delivering of letters in general, though such a practice for
the accommodation of the lieges crept in to the most of the
towns in Scotland his opinion all deputies are bound to keep such
letters as he is desired to keep till called for, unless where
there is a letter carrier established and paid by Government."

SITUATION OF POST-OFFICE.

One witness depones "that it is a foreshop or cellar to the
street, and stands on the west side of the Church Street of
Inverness" (north corner of Bank Lane and Church Street).

OBJECTIONS TO WITNESSES.

Some of the objections stated against the evidence of witnesses
being received were very odd. One was objected to because he
was "in extreme low circumstances—not worth the King's
unlaw;" a young woman was objected to because she had an
illegitimate child, and accused the wrong party; several Free-
masons because they signed a petition against the Postmaster and
others, on the general ground of alleged personal malice.

GAELIC.

Most of the witnesses in the case, belonging to the well-to-do
classes, were able to give their evidence in English, but two or
three—notably the postrunners to Tain—had to be examined

through an interpreter, as they spoke " Earse." In spite of this, however, one of these runners confessed in Court that when he was refused his letters late at night by Mr Warrand's maid-servants, he was able to rate them soundly as bitches that tried to stop a man in the public service.

THE POSTMAN.

It appears from the evidence of several of the witnesses that in those days letters were delivered in Inverness by a postman. Angus Shaw, merchant, thus described the process :—" Ever since the deponent commenced trade there was an old man who—while he was able to go about—carried the letters through the town, and after his decease, or when he became infirm, his wife continued to do so ; but the deponent does not know whether that was before or after the year 1770, but knows he received his letters from both. Interrogate whether the said old man and woman demanded and exacted for these letters more than the postage of them, and how much ? Depones—They always did demand a halfpenny more than the postage. That very fre-quently they took the advantage of the deponent's boy and his wife, and they exacted and received a halfpenny for each letter, but that the deponent himself put them off for a halfpenny for his whole letters when he happened to be in the shop. That this induced the deponent frequently to speak to Mr Warrand and complain of it to him as an expense quite unnecessary, for the deponent had a boy who would always call at the office for his letters, and that at these times the deponent strictly forbad Mr Warrand to give any of his letters to the said woman. That sometimes Mr Warrand promised to keep the deponent's letters till called for by the boy. That accordingly the boy was in use to call at the Post-Office, but the deponent does not remember above two or three instances of his ever getting the letters at the Post-Office or any other channel, but in and through the woman or her husband. That the deponent himself has at other times gone into the Post-Office, and remaining there during the whole time of Mr Warrand's sorting the letters ; has begged of Mr Warrand to give him his letters in the office, and Mr Warrand has oft refused what his deponent thought so very reasonable, and he has been obliged to dog the woman through the town till she came to some house or shop where there might be

.9

light for him to find out his letters, and pay the woman. That there has, indeed, been some few instances, and these but lately, when Mr Warrand would, if he (the deponent) happened to be in the office give him his letters there ; and further depones that frequently after the deponent had spoken to Mr Warrand, and forbidding him to give any of his letters to the woman, finding that what he had requested of Mr Warrand had not been complied with, he then determined not to pay one fraction over the postage to the woman, thinking thereby that she would not take them out of the Office—but the cure turned worse than the disease. The woman took his letters, and, upon his refusing to pay what she demanded, kept them up and would not deliver them though she showed them to the deponent, unless she was paid the extraordinary halfpenny. That the deponent vexed at this, has sometimes wanted his letters over night rather than comply, though he afterwards found it his interest to follow the general rule rather than be disappointed in his correspondence."

THE POSTWOMAN'S STORY.

The evidence of the female letter-carrier may be reproduced almost entire :—" Margaret Robertson, aged seventy-seven years or thereby, being sworn and interrogate if or not she remembers how long she and her husband have been in the practice of taking out from the Post-Office here and delivering letters to those who do not call for the same regularly after the letters are sorted at the said Office ? Depones—That she and her husband have been so employed for about fifteen years back. Interrogate—How long is it since her husband died, and if or not he was not an Elgin post-runner for some time ? Depones— That it is five years since her husband's death, and that he was the post from here to Elgin for a short time before he was letter-carrier. Interrogate if or not the door of the Post-Office is kept shut when the letters are sorting ? Depones— That the door is kept shut when the letters are sorting, but that there will be enough in for all that. Interrogate—If or not the moment the letters are sorted the door is opened ? Depones— That it is. Interrogate—If or not she (the deponent) is dispatched with the letters delivered her as soon as the door of the Post-Office is opened ? Depones—That she is dispatched with the letters delivered her as soon as the door of the Post-Office is opened. Interrogate—If or not any letters are delivered out to the inhabitants of the town before the door is opened and she dispatched? Depones—That no letters are delivered to the inhabitants until she is first dispatched. Interrogate—If or not she receives particular orders from Mr Warrand as to any foreign letters she gets to deliver, or letters with high postages for the merchants, and what are that orders? Depones—That when she received any such letters Mr Warrand desired her to keep these by themselves, and to deliver them to the merchants with her own hand, and that she commonly put such letters into her breast, and delivered them accordingly to her directions from Mr Warrand as above, and that she kept the other letters in a great pouch. Interrogate—If or not there is a great hurry and confusion at the Post-Office when the letters are sorted? Depones—That there is; and that if everybody was allowed to come in there would be no standing in the Office. Interrogate—If or not she knows or remembers that in the hurry and confusion she some times receives letters for several persons who usually send for their letters, and if or not she knows or remembers who these persons are? Depones—That she does not remember to have received any such letters. Interrogate—If or not she knows any merchants who send their servants to the Post Office to receive their letters? Depones—That she knows several that does so—such as Bailie Andrew Murray, Mr Hugh Inglis, Mr Alexander Murray, Bailie John Mackintosh, and Mr Hugh Fraser."

THE POSTWOMAN AND THE GUAGERS.

Alexander Grigor, who was a merchant in Inverness from 1760 to 1767, said that he and other merchants suspected that their letters were shown by the letter-carrier to, and inspected by, some of the officers of the Revenue before they got their letters delivered to them, and that particularly it was alleged that the said letter-carrier was in use to go into the house of William Scott, Supervisor of the Excise, then in town, with the whole letters she brought from the office, and that it was alleged that she was hired weekly to do so by the said William Scott, and that prior to the year 1770. Interrogate—If he knows whether the said carrier could read the directions of letters? Depones— That he knows that neither the woman, the present letter-carrier or her husband, the preceding letter carrier, could read the directions of letters. Interrogate—Whether or not did the deponent himself suspect, or did he hear other merchants suspect that they suffered by such practice of the carrier? Depones—That he did himself suspect, and he believes others too did suspect, that Mr Scott's making so many seizures might be owing to his having seen their letters in the above manner by the letter-carrier.

.   .   .   .

He heard a horn blow, which was a sign by which he understood that the letters were sorted and the letter-carrier dispatched, and he, being anxious for a letter or letters which he expected by that post, he went to see and met the letter-carrier, and held down the Church Street until he came opposite to the Post-Office, but did not meet the letter-carrier, on which he returned, and in passing by John Grant's Close,* within which Mr Scott lodged, he discovered the letter-carrier with a lanthorn and candle in her hand coming out of said close, of whom he asked where she had been. That she answered that she was at Mr Scott's with a letter for him. That on this he asked the letter-carrier if Mr Scott had seen the rest of the letters she had, she answered not ; but that the deponent told her at the time that he had seen the whole letters as she could not know or distinguish his letters from any of the rest. That he does not remember what answer she made him at the time but that the deponent could get none of his letters from her until they had come up the length of George Schevize's shop, where the directions of the letters were called, and the deponent got his letter or letters.

LETTER-DELIVERY EXTRAORDINARY.

Sometimes, however, letters were delivered by others than by the professional postwoman. As already noted, a letter was delivered to John Hay by Angus M'Kinnon, burgh-officer. Hay's own account of the matter is worth reproducing :—" Upon his asking Angus M'Kinnon, he told him that he got it from Mr Warrand over the counter immediately before then, and that he had fourpence of postage to pay for it, to which he answered that he would get that and a bottle of ale. Interrogate—Did he, on getting possession of the letter, observe that the same had been

---

* John Grant's Close : Now known as Grant's Close, High Street, fifty years ago as Dr Grant's Close.

opened? Depones—He did. Interrogate—What did you say to
M'Kinnon upon observing that the letter had been opened? Depones—That he was not well pleased, and threatened to complain
to Provost Fraser who was then on the street, on account whether
M'Kinnon had opened the letter or Mr Warrand. That on this
they grappled, and tumbled into Mrs M·Leod's house below
" The Goat." Interrogate—Did M'Kinnon at that time tell the deponent that he had delivered the letter in the same way as he received it from Warrand? Depones—That he did with an oath.
Had that letter the appearance or mark of having been once
sealed with wax or a wafer? Depones—That it had the appearance
of being first sealed with wax. Interrogate—Had it the appearance of being recently or newly sealed with a wafer? Depones—
That there was a fresh wafer upon the seal, and betwixt it and the
broken part of the paper. Did the deponent refuse to pay postage
for that letter, or did he ever pay postage for it? Depones—That
he refused to pay any postage for it, nor was there any postage
demanded for it after that day, and if there had he knew what
answer to make. Interrogate—Did he, the night before receiving
the said letter, attend at the Post-Office upon the arrival of the
South post? Depones—He did till it was ten of the clock at night.
Had the post arrived before that time? Depones—He had. Did he
ask at the Post-Office if there were any letters for him, and what
answer did he receive? Depones—That he went into the office,
that is, the Post-Office, when the country posts were going in to receive their bags, when he asked Mr Warrand if there were any
letters for him (the deponent)? to which Mr Warrand answered,
Had he (Mr Warrand) nothing more to do than to look out letters
for him? therefore desired him to go out of the office until the other
posts were dismissed, and to call another time, for had he a letter
he would not then have given it him."

SUNDAY DELIVERY.

Captain Simon Fraser of Fanellan said he " never had any difference with the Postmaster but once, and that happened at or
about the time of the establishment of the riding post to Inverness that comes three times a-week. The occasion of the difference was this : Sunday was one of the days appointed for the
arrival of the post at Inverness, and the deponent sent his servant
to the Post-Office of a Sunday, but Mr Warrand told his servant

that he would not give out the letters on Sunday. The servant was sent to the Post-Office twice of that day, and received the same answer. Thereafter deponent wrote to Mr Jackson or Mr Bennet of the General Post-Office, and some time afterwards he received his letters regularly on Sundays as well as other post days. Interrogate—Had the deponent or not occasion to know, that notwithstanding the pursuer refused him his letters on a Sunday as above, yet he (the pursuer) gave out letters and newspapers to others in the town between whom and the pursuer there was either a close intimacy or family connection, and if the pursuer did so the deponent will please condescend and say who such persons were? Depones—That it is not consistent with his knowledge that he gave out a letter or letters to any person upon the Sunday at the above time, but upon recollection is certain that he received his letters out one Sunday after the establishment of the post as above, and that he thinks the Sunday that the servant was refused his letters was either the second or the third Sunday after the said establishment."

THE DINNER HOUR.

Northern society must have dined somewhat earlier 130 years than is fashionable now. Sir John Gordon of Invergordon, one of the witnesses in the case, stated that in April 1768, the year of the General Election, he was posting north, and came to the house of Kilraick between four and five o'clock, " before they had risen from the dinner table."

"THE MONTHLY MAGAZINES."

Donald Fraser, a former post between Nairn and Inverness deponed—That sometimes the South mail was heavier than the mail from Inverness to the South—particularly on some Thursdays, when the monthly magazines are sent north.

THE TOWN'S COMMON PASTURE.

Donald Fraser, gardener, Inverness, mentioned in course of his evidence that to the east of the town, near the sea, there was a " common pasture of the town, called the Links, and carse grounds, belonging to the town." A public high-road which led to these lands was called the " Scapegate," * and the

---

* Scapegate : A continuation of Rose Street, and now known as Longman Road. Mr Warrand's and Mr Falconer's lands were on the east side of the road, and nearest to the Firth, as shown on the Plan of Inverness and Lands adjacent, by John Home, 1774, which accompanies the " Transactions of the Inverness Scientific Society and Field Club, vol. II., 1880-83."

poiners * and those who kept cows and horses possessed these carse lands, and drove their horses and cows to the said Links and carse grounds. By this road, in fact, all the inhabitants of the town who had horses and cows used it. Sometimes these cattle strayed on to the fields of Mr Warrand and were poinded (that is, impounded and kept as a pledge for payment of the damage done). Mr Falconer, whose fields adjoined, also did a little in the way of poinding. ·

THE WARRAND-FALCONER FEUD

seems to have commenced in connection with this practice, Mr Warrand's cow having been several times poinded by Mr Falconer. Some of the witnesses declared that the poor animal was imprisoned in this way for days, and got nothing to eat but peats. Shortly thereafter Mr Falconer's servants noticed a footpath through his field, evidently made by Mr Warrand and his servants, and Mr Falconer, on being told of it, said the next time they saw Warrand passing that way they should take his hat off! One day soon afterwards Warrand was going through the field as usual, when one of Falconer's men-servants stepped up to him, coolly took off his hat and carried it away, and gave it to another man. Warrand went and asked his hat, but was told that he would not get it without Mr Falconer's orders. Mr Warrand accordingly walked bareheaded, and the hat was brought to Mr Falconer, who gave his servant 5s for bringing it. The hat, according to one of the witnesses, was taken to the stable and hung up "on a nail where horses' graith used to be hung, and there it remained all the summer. So far from apologising, Falconer told his servants that the next time Warrand passed through the field they were to take his coat off, and he would give them half-a-guinea.

LETTERS IN THE POSTMASTER'S KITCHEN.

It was stated in the proof that there was a hole in the Inverness Post-Office window into which people could slip letters intended for the post, but from the evidence given by the

---

* Poiners : One who gains a livelihood by digging feal, *divots*, or clay, and sells them for covering houses and for other purposes.

Jamieson's Scottish Dictionary (Supplement, vol. II. p. 228) says this word is peculiar to Inverness, and gives the following example : " Her father said that the people she saw were not tenants on the Green of Muirtown, but were *poiners*, or carters, from Inverness, who used to come there for materials " (Case of Duff of Muirtown 1806).

Postmaster's domestic servants it would seem that this mode of posting letters was little taken advantage of. People who came before office hours stepped round to the kitehen and handed the letters to any of the servants, who put them "on the table or dresser in the kitchen until the office was opened." The Postmaster had a man servant named William Clark who could read a little, and this man, being acquainted with the servants, used to step into the kitchen and while away his time by reading "the directions on the back of the letters." This sometimes yielded the servants some entertainment, and so William was encouraged to go further; and, in one case at least, he opened and read one of the letters and closed it again. This was the more interesting as the letter proved to be from a young man to his sweetheart.

ALARMING RESULTS OF THE KITCHEN POST-OFFICE SYSTEM.

William Munro, postman between Tain and Inverness, was one of the witnesses sworn in Gaelic, and he gave a lively account of using the kitchen dresser as a post-office. He said that James Robertson in Culcairn delivered to him a letter containing three £10 bank-notes from Culcairn to be put into the Post-Office of Inverness for Mr Falconer of Nairn. That he accordingly carried the said letter to Inverness, and finding Mr Warrand not then in the house, called upon both the maid-servants there to go up-stairs with him to see him deliver the said letter to Mrs Warrand. That the maids first declined going with him, but on his insisting a little further with them they complied, and accompanied him up-stairs, where, at their sight, he delivered the said letter to Mrs Warrand, telling, at the same time, that the same conveyed £30 in the three £10 bank-notes from Culcairn to Mr Falconer. That at about the distance of fifteen days afterwards, as he was on his way to Inverness, calling as usual at James Robertson's, the said James challenged and asked him what became of the foresaid letter and notes, for that Culcairn had a letter since craving the money, and that if he (William) had been any other than the man he was he would have been put up in the prison of Dingwall. Upon which the deponent turned in a degree of delirium swearing that he would get the money before he would return from Inverness, or otherwise that he would put the pursuer's house on fire if the letter and notes were not got. That he proceeded, and upon arrival at Mr Warrand's he neither then found him in the house, but, calling upon the maids, asked them whether or not they saw him deliver such a letter to Mrs Warrand? which they acknowledged to him. And then he requested them to go up-stairs to bear that testimony, which they did; —he being in such a frenzy that he took the kitchen tongs with a coal of fire in it, threatening to burn the house, driving the maids before him. And upon his appearance Mrs Warrand appeared surprised, her colour changing, and rising up out of her chair asked what was the matter? and he having asked what became of the letter delivered, as before deponed? and Mrs Warrand having appeared as if she forgot the maids testified that they saw him deliver the said letter—whereupon she drew out one drawer after another of two rows of drawers, in the lowest of which she found the letter, and with which she immediately went down to the Post-Office."

MARKS ON PARTICULAR LETTERS.

The same witness described how he distinguished valuable letters in those days and the means which he adopted. He said he was in the use of "putting a particular cross or mark on letters that are particularly recommended to his care, which he keeps sometimes separate from his other letters, that he may know them the better at his delivery; and that sometimes he makes others—the persons that deliver the letters to him—put such marks on them for the same purpose." As this postman could not read or write, he used in the same way to put some private marks on letters to remind him whom they were for.

THE KITCHEN-MAID'S ACCOUNT OF THE POST-OFFICE SYSTEM.

Margaret Baillie, spouse to William Troup, vintner in Inverness, deponed—That she served in Mr Warrand's family for the space of one year and a-half; that she remembers letters that were brought to go by the mail to the South were frequently brought into Mr Warrand's house, and were given to the Pursuer himself when at hand, and at other times left on the dresser or table in the kitchen, till they were sent out to the shop, or Post-Office. She remembers one William Clark served the Pursuer

10

when she was in his service ; that the said William Clark could read some writ ; does not know whether he could write or not ; that she had seen the said Clark pretty often, or oft enough, look at the directions on the letters left on the dresser in the kitchen ; that she never saw Clark open or read any of those letters, but heard the servants talk in the kitchen that he had opened a letter which had come from some lass's sweetheart. Deponed—That she had heard Margery Baillie (another witness), who was a co-servant with her, speaking with the said William Clark about the letter, and making their diversion of it. Mr Warrand and his wife enjoined the deponent and other servants to carry out the letters as above to the Post-Office when the same was opened.

MR FALCONER'S LANDS AT THE LONGMAN.

Paul Ross, gardener in Inverness, deponed—That Mr Warrand is proprietor of grounds to the eastward of the town, and more distant from the town than Mr Falconer's ground. Mr Falconer, some years ago, began enclosing his ground, and is enclosing them yearly. That Mr Falconer employed one Donald Mackenzie in making dykes and in leading stones for the said dykes from the sea-shore. He remembers that some years ago Mr Falconer's enclosures were damaged. He also knows that there was a process between Mr Falconer and Mr Warrand respecting the damage ; that the witness, along with Donald Fraser, gardener, was employed to comprise the said damage ; that he heard by common clatter that Mr Warrand's beasts or cattle had done the damage ; that the comprising made by himself and Donald Fraser was reduced into writing, and was signed by both of them. Knows that Mr Falconer's enclosures were among the first improvements, if not the first, on the grounds between the the town of Invernesss and the sea. Witness knows a road called the Scapegate that leads from the town of Inverness to the sea ; that by the said road access is had to both Mr Falconer's and Mr Warrand's grounds without passing over or through either of their grounds, as their properties lie upon the east side of said road. That the grounds belonging to Defender were enclosed upon three sides by a stone dyke, and on the fourth side, which is next to Mr Warrand's ground there was a dyke or ditch thrown up in order to be faced with stone. That

Mr Falconer's grounds were divided by a paling of wood from south to north ; and at the time that damage happened to his enclosures there was only a part finished with stone.

Deponent remembers that a row of trees and a row of quickset were planted round as far as the said stone dyke was finished, and the paling went no further. Deponent does not remember whether the trees were planted the year before the damage happened or that same year. Deponent knows that a number of other cattle, belonging to the poiners and others, go by the the Scapegate by Mr Falconer's park towards the sea ; it is a common road for all cattle where they pass and repass every day in the year. It was Mr Falconer that sent the deponent and Donald Fraser to make the comprisement.

THE FREEMASON SECRET.—THE RIGHT-WORSHIPFUL'S EVIDENCE.

Lieut. John Gregor* depones—That he was Master Mason of Old St Andrew's Kilwinning Lodge at Inverness upon 5th June 1770. He remembers there was a deputation sent from the sister Lodge to them on the said day. He also remembers that there was a motion made respecting an application to General Oughton, the Grand Master Mason of Scotland, for obtaining the removal of the Pursuer from his employment of Postmaster of Inverness, and that there was also a paper from the sister Lodge for the same purpose, and to be presented by him to the Lodge of which he was Master. He does not remember who the members of the other Lodge were who sent the said paper, nor by whom it was sent to the deponent. He remembers that the message wrote him with the paper was desiring him to lay it before his Lodge, and requesting their concurrence therein if they thought proper. Depones, That in consequence of the resolution or in consequence of the message from the sister Lodge, a writing was produced to the members present containing complaints against Pursuer with regard

* Lieut. John Gregor was an officer in the 42nd or Royal Highland Regiment. He was a native of Inverness, and returned to the North from service circa 1760. He was an ardent Free Mason, and in 1764 was elected R. W. Master of St Andrew's Kilwinning Lodge, and for the long period of ten years he continued to be elected annually to that most honourable position. In 1774, on his retirement from office, the Brethren presented him with a most flattering diploma for his services in building up and strengthening the Lodge.

to his management of the Post-Office, addressed to the Grand Master, to have him removed from that employ. In consequence of the way the complaint from the sister Lodge was worded, they desired that another paper should be made out, which was accordingly done to their own liking and of which they approved, and it was signed by the deponent and several other members, excepting two or three of those then present. and that one of those came next day in order to sign it. That William Welsh tanner, and John Gilzean were the two that he remembers did not sign, and John Gilzean spoke to him next day in order to sign it. He depones that he had a conference with Captain Duff (the Defender's brother-in-law) respecting the application to General Oughton, the import of which was, that it was told to the Defender that if the Lodges applied to the General there would be no doubt that Mr Warrand would be turned out of office

Deponent states that he, in company with Captain Duff, went to Cradlehall, and applied to Mr Baillie of Dochfour as Master Mason of the new Lodge to see if he would come to Inverness and wait on General Oughton with the Lodges ; and it was told Mr Baillie what the intention of the Lodges was. Mr Baillie replied that he was not for it—they might do as they pleased—and if the General did not arrive before the following day, he would do himself the pleasure to wait on General Oughton with the Lodges. The General, however, arrived that evening, and they were deprived of Mr Baillie's company when waiting on the General. This happened about the time of the first review which the General made at Fort-George.

The deponent admits, when interrogated as to his assisting in procuring evidence for the defence, that he has been in company and conversed with witnesses in Defender's presence when drinking a glass, and that oftener than once, but never suggested any witness, and he knew them himself. In reply to interrogations he answered that he did not furnish any cards or jotters respecting the process, but admitted that he was often in company with Mr Falconer and his friends when talking overly on the subject-matter of this complaint, and that the Defender did read paragraphs of letters from his agent at Edinburgh respecting the case.

The deponent, interrogated, replied that he was acquainted

with Captain Thomas Walcoat of the 12th Regiment, now at Gibraltar, who commanded a detachment of that regiment from Fort-George at Inverness. That, some time after he commanded at Inverness, Captain Walcoat was married to Miss Betsy Fraser, daughter of William Fraser, Town-Clerk. That he had occasion, before and after the marriage, to be often in Captain Walcoat's company, and has seen the Defender also in the Captain's company. That he never heard that Mr Warrand got himself acquainted with the Captain and Miss Fraser's correspondence by undue freedom with their letters; but that one day, being with Captain Walcoat going down the Church Street, Mr Warrand was at the time coming up the said street towards the Cross, Captain Walcoat said to him, on seeing Mr Warrand, " Damn that fellow," or " scoundrel ; " " if it was not for his connection with the honest Doctor " whom the deponent understood to be Dr Munro, " he would give him a drubbing." He asked Mr Walcoat what harm the Pursuer had done him for his expressing himself so against him ? That the Captain answered him that he had used freedom with a letter, or letters, of his— but which of the two he could not with certainty say, nor had he ever any further word with the Captain on that head.

William Welsh,* tanner in Inverness, depones—That he knows Mr Warrand since he came to this country in 1763, but had little or no intimacy with him or his family till 1765 or 1766, and during the above time he acted as Deputy-Postmaster of Inverness ; that he had no cause of complaint with regard to his letters ; Mr Warrand was not obnoxious to the deponent ; that in every transaction he acted fairly and honestly. He was present at a Mason meeting of the Old Lodge of Inverness, held on the 5th day of June 1770, when mention was made of Mr Warrand and his character as Postmaster of Inverness ; that he does not recollect of a deputation from the sister Lodge, but remembered well that a paper or memorial was presented by the Master, Lieutenant John Gregor ; that this paper, as first presented, contained many complaints of

* Father of the late William Alves Welsh of Millburn, and grandfather of Dr George Forbes, the donor of the handsome fountain that now covers the honoured remains of Clachnacuddin on the Exchange.

misconduct in Mr Warrand ; that the Master told the Lodge that the paper was put into his hands, and which he either read himself or gave to Mr Duncan Grant, writer in Inverness, or Thomas Young, secretary to the Lodge, to be read. The Master said that they behoved to support a brother, and that the paper was made out with a view to get Mr Warrand turned out of office. The brother who wanted to be supported was Mr Hugh Falconer, the present defender. The Master said so without reserve. The paper was to be addressed to General Oughton, as his interest was required for that purpose. The Master desired the members present to sign the paper after it was read. That several of the Lodge seemed to approve thereof and others to disapprove ; and thereafter it was moved to soften some of the expressions therein, to reconcile those who opposed subscribing. The Deponent absolutely refused to subscribe it. His reason for refusing was, that Mr Warrand had never injured him in any particular, and because he looked upon it as a most un-Masonlike request. He remembers the general scope of the writing to General Oughton was the setting forth of Mr Warrand's repeated misconduct in office as Postmaster made it necessary to have him turned out, and craving the General's interest for that purpose. He remembers that General Oughton was then Grand Master Mason of Scotland.

The deponent did not know till of late that there was any notice taken of the transaction in the minute-book of the Lodge. He also remembers there were present the Master (Lieut. John Gregor) ; William Cumming, glazier ; Duncan Fraser, merchant ; Duncan Grant, writer ; Thomas Young, tanner ; John Gilzean, maltster ; John Noble, merchant ; William Henderson,* bleacher ; the deponent himself, and several others whose names he is not particularly certain of. That the Master declared his willingness to subscribe. It was then offered to William Cumming and Duncan Fraser, who positively refused to sign it as it then stood. Thereupon a motion was made to new model the paper somewhat. This was accordingly done by Duncan Grant, when those two gentlemen were prevailed upon to subscribe. Deponent still refused to subscribe to this rectified copy.

* Mr Henderson's bleaching-field was at the Bught. His daughter became the second wife of Sir Hector Mackenzie of Gairloch ; and the late Provost John Mackenzie of Eilcanach was her son. William Henderson survived till 1816, and died aged 97.

William Inglis,* merchant in Inverness, depones, That he was
Secretary to the new Mason Lodge of Inverness upon the 5th of
June 1770. A meeting of the Lodge was held on that date, and
at the said meeting a minute was entered on the record of the
Lodge relative to the Pursuer and his character as Postmaster.
The extract of minute produced is an exact copy. The members
then present, so far as he can recollect, were Captain William
Macgillivray of Dunmaglass, Captain Shaw of Tordarroch, Bailie
John Mackintosh, Major Allan Duff, Captain Alexander Duff,
and thinks that Mr William Cuthbert was there, but is not positive ; and can recollect no more present, but remembers it was
a full meeting of the Lodge. That he knows a letter was made
out and sent to General Oughton in consequence of the above
resolution ; that, as Secretary to the Lodge, he wrote the letter,
and it was signed by Captain Macgillivray as Master, and Captain
Shaw and Alexander Mackintosh as Wardens ; that the intention
of the letter was to get Mr Warrand removed from the Post-Office,
and that the whole of the members present in the Lodge, excepting two, were unanimous in the application to General Oughton.

AN OFFICE-SEEKER.

Alexander Grant, Sheriff-Clerk of Inverness, deponed— That
from the year 1747 he had known the Pursuer acting in the Post-
Office of Inverness, but in virtue of what commission he cannot
say. Depones, That he heard from the Defender in March 1770
that he had written a letter of complaint to the Postmaster-General
against the Pursuer, but he never heard of the contents of it
till the present Commission to which he was appointed as clerk.
He had heard from Robert Anderson, goldsmith in Inverness,
that several copies of the letter had been made by Robert Rogers,
merchant, at request of Defender. In the Spring or Summer of
1770, witness was walking with Captain Alexander Duff, younger
of Muirtown, by the Shore of Inverness, when, in the course of
conversation about the Pursuer and Defender, Captain Duff, in a
joke, as the deponent imagined, said that Pursuer would be
turned out of office, and that said office would answer very well
for deponent. He remembers, on interrogation, that Captain
Duff gave as his reason for Pursuer being turned out of office

* Of Kingsmills, and thereafter Provost of Inverness.

that it was for malversations, and those complained of by the
Defender. Witness deponed that he had never heard that a bett
or wager had been laid by Defender or any of his friends that
Pursuer would be turned out of office, but remembers to have
heard that Pursuer had said that Captain Duff had wagered
£50 that the Pursuer would be turned out of office by a certain
day. He had also heard that in Spring 1770 that Robert
Anderson, goldsmith, or his wife, had written a letter to the
Marquis of Lorne (now the Duke of Argyle), mentioning that the
Pursuer was to be turned out of office for malversations, and
intreating the Marquis would be pleased to recommend M^r
Anderson for the office. Interrogated, he stated he was a
member of the new Mason Lodge, called the St Andrew's Kilwinning of Inverness since St John's Day 1758. He was not
present at the meeting of the Lodge upon the 5th June 1770.
He had heard of the minute of the Lodge relative to the Pursuer.
He is aware that the resolution was only the deed of the members
that were present that night in the Lodge. Interrogated if he
remembers dining at the house of a neighbouring gentleman by
special invitation in July 1770, replied that he remembers to
have at that time dined in different neighbouring gentlemen's
houses, including that of Mr Baillie of Dochfour and Mr Duff of
Muirtown. He remembers to have been called to Muirtown
about business, and after dinner the Defender and Captain Duff
came in and joined the company; and that after a short time
there was a paper presented and given to Captain Alexander
Shaw of Tordarroch, who was one of the company, which he
read to himself, and said that he liked that paper better than
what he had seen formerly; that the company who were then
present were, Mr Duff, the landlord, Major Alexander Duff of
Inverness; Captain Alexander Duff; the deceased James Duff,
son of the deceased William Duff; the Defender, and Captain
Alex. Shaw. From the conversation that passed at the time, and
what he had heard before the paper, was a complaint against
Pursuer, and intended by the Lodge to be sent to General
Oughton. From his recollection there were some subscriptions
adhibited to it, but who these were he does not know. According to his remembrance he gave his opinion that the paper was
improper, and he refused to sign it. Captain Alexander Duff
found fault with the deponent and said very harsh language to

him on that account, which he thinks improper here to mention, nor choose to do it. Pursuer after left the room where they were sitting, and came to the room where Mrs Duff was. Before the company parted, the paper which he was asked to sign fell by-hand and was amissing; that, as he was leaving Muirtown, the Defender asked him if he had seen the paper, and he replied that he had not seen it since the time he seen it in Captain Shaw's hands. And being asked on whose behalf the said paper was formed or whom to serve, replied that as to knowledge he cannot say, but heard that the paper had been formed with an intention to serve the Defender; but the deponent's own opinion was that it would answer the reverse.

———

[We have sought, in making a selection from the evidence produced in this case, to give only such as best illustrated the Post-Office system in the North 130 years ago in contrast with that which now prevails. The advance is most wonderful;—the number of officials now engaged in the central office in Queen's Gate, Inverness—the various despatches and arrivals of mails—the telegraph and parcels departments, in comparison with the post-master and his wife and the illiterate female letter-carrier who were able to perform all the duties that lay upon them in 1770.

We regret that we are unable to record the finding in the "State of the Process for Defamation and Damages—Robert Warrand, merchant in Inverness, against Hugh Falconer, merchant there." We presume there was a finding, but in the long printed evidence from which we have made the preceding extracts, and which extends to over 500 large quarto pages, none is recorded. There were 55 witnesses examined in Defender's proof, and 39 in Pursuer's proof, besides a number of "exhibits" of letters and documents.

Is it possible, that with the well-known delays in law, the decision may be still at *avizandum* ? /]

JAMES ("JAMIE") PATERSON, POET.

—— o ——

JAMES (" Jamie ") PATERSON, author of the Poem. " Inver
ness Martinmas Market," that follows, was born early in the
present century on the Green of Muirtown, Inverness. as he himself has stated in a song written in praise of the place of his
birth—

> " Dear spot of my birth, tho' the high-swelling ocean
> Should part me, and cause me far from thee to rove,
> While my bosom can beat, I will think with emotion
> On Muirtown, sweet Muirtown, the spot that I love."

His father was John Paterson, a salmon fisher on the Ness, and
known among his neighbours as "Iain-ne Ban 'na Isgair" (Fair
Johnnie the Fisher). James was sent early to school, and while
he made considerable progress in the various branches taught.
he displayed a special talent in arithmetic. This may have led as
he grew up to his turning his attention for a living to that of teach-
ing. His first appointment in this way was to fill up an interval
between the death of Mr Picton— a noted teacher in the Central
School, Queen Street— and the appointment of Mr John Douglas
as Mr Picton's successor. Sometime thereafter he was appointed
to the more permanent post of teacher in the school of Glenconvinth, in the parish of Kiltarlity. While in this secluded district he produced many poems and songs, among others " The
Inverness Martinmas Market." A selection of the fruits of his
rhyming moments he ventured to publish in a very humble *brochure*
of forty pages, which was issued from the press of another local
worthy, John Maclean, better known in his day as " Clach "

James Paterson was an ardent admirer of our national poet Burns,
and in the early spring of 1837, he made what might be looked on
as a quixotic adventure in setting forth on a pedestrian pilgrimage
from the North to visit the " Land of Burns " and other scenes
rendered immortal in the poems and songs of Coila's Bard.
While this journey was not undertaken quite as bare of coin as

that of the penniless journey to Scotland of Taylor the Water Poet, Paterson's purse could not have been over "well lined,' but he had taken the precaution to furnish himself with the names of local bards in places he proposed to visit, while in the towns he knew where to find all the "Clachnacuddin boys," and thus made out his purpose and found friends in almost all the places visited.

Paterson's journey on foot going South was over the Highland road to Perth, thence to Stirling, Bannockburn, Falkirk, and Glasgow ; thence to Ayr and the Banks of Doon. He made a special aside-trip to Greenock to pay a visit to the grave of "Burns's Highland Mary," and to Paisley to visit "Gleniffer Braes, where Tannahill sung his sweetest lays." On the return journey northwards he came by the East coast, visiting Dundee, Aberdeen, etc. Recounting his various adventures on this pilgrimage formed an abundant source of talk among his companions for many a day. Specially did he dwell upon the reception he received from the colony of his townsmen who had taken up their residence in the western capital. The only allusion we have found in his writings referring to this adventure is a poetical epistle addressed from Glasgow to his brother-rhymster "John Macrae, poet [?]. Inverness "—

"My canty friend,—Frae Clutha's stream,
Sae aften sung in poet's theme,
Accept these rhyming lines frae me,
'Tis a' brother bard can gie.
To let you ken what scenes I have seen
In tramps frae Ness to Glasgow Green,
I've roam'd o'er mony a glen and hill
Sin' I trode Druimuachdar bleak and chill."

Paterson must have left Glenconvinth about 1846, as in that year he began to keep a humble venture-school at the Leackhin, near Inverness. It was while here he wrote and published his second venture in poetical literature. "The Royal Visit to Scotland, with other Poems and Songs " (*Inverness*, 1849) The long Poem, which forms the staple of this volume, is a metrical description of her Majesty's Journey to Ardverikie in the autumn of 1847 , the Visit of Prince Albert (Prince-Consort) to Inverness.

About 1850-51 Paterson must have given up the school at the Leackhin, as he returned to Inverness, and took up his residence there with his wife on the Green of Muirtown. For a few years he eked out what was at best a hard struggle with poverty, doing occasional clerking making up the accounts of small traders in the neighbourhood, while in the winter evenings he kept a night-school for young trades-lads employed during the day at labour. To this he added an attempt to give lessons on the violin. One of his pupils informed us he was a poor performer on the instrument, but that he had no small opinion of his own ability. He was invariably ready to play when asked and also to sing. One of his favourite songs, to which he always accompanied himself on the violin, was "Macpherson's Farewell," which our informant heard him frequently perform. When the poet came to the chorus—

> " Sae rantingly, sae wantonly,
> He play'd a spring, and danced it round
> Below the gallows-tree "

—he almost always broke down, affected probably by the bold gipsy's melancholy fate or the charms of the melody—the latter played only very indifferently indeed, as reported to us.

In 1854 he was seized with a fever which was prevalent in the district. Physically he was unfitted to withstand the malignant type which developed, and he fell a victim to it. He died in a humble dwelling in a lane off Queen Street.

INVERNESS MARTINMAS MARKET.

PART I.

WHEN Scotia's hills wi' winter keen
   Hae got their snawy suit on,
And bleak November hirples in
   To gie puir folks their cloutin,
Bare sauls like me feel cauld I ween.
   When wintry storms are spouting,
Come, Muse, we'll seek some couthie ben
   And sing o' Clachnacuddin
      On sic a day.

Auld Ness may as she laves the North
   O' her braw toon be vaunty,
A fairer's nae this side th' Forth,
   Sae brawly busk't and canty ;

Her sons are leal an' fam'd for worth,
Her maids kind hearts ne'er want aye,
Mang them there's south o' fun and mirth,
When Phœbus light is scanty
Or onie day.

At early morn ilk chimla reeks
Wi' lowin' fires fu' gaucie,
When Martinmas sae cauld like keeks
Wi' tents upon our causey.
The red neck'd lads, in velvet breeks, *
Cock up their snouts fu' saucie.
And baton'd knights † as thin as leeks
Parade our streets in raws aye
On sic a day.

Alas! for him who on that day,
Though he left hame fu vogie,
Wha gangs wi' ne'er-do-weels astray
To tipple at the coggie;
Gif he gets fu' and tries to play
The pugilist or rogie,
The batons soon will him o'erlay
Though he were frae Strathbogie,
On sic a day.

Lang lang for thee thou bustlin day
Ilk ploughman chiel was thinkin,
For then ilk buirdly chiel will hae
Coin in his pouches clinkin.
Clad in his finest, best array,
He on his joe is winkin,
How time will gaily pass away
Wi' coortin an wi' drinkin
On sic a day.

---

* The town-officers of those days who did duty as policemen. Their uniform was swallow-tailed coats with red collars. The *velvet breeks* were donned only on Sundays, when they preceded the magistrates to the High Church, and on State occasions. The occupants of the position at the period were Sergeant Alexander Grant ("Supple Sandie"), Sergeant Thos. Tallach, and Sergeant William Chisholm.

† The "batoned knights" were the night constables, old men in their sixties, who did night duty crying the hours. On market days they were called ont for special service. Well do we remember some of these old guardians of the night,—old Donald Macgregor ("*Past eel-e-vaan*," as we boys named him from his crying the hours with a pronunciation peculiar to himself). There was also Macdonald ("*Brogar*"), and others the terror of evildoers.

When Phœbus sheds his scanty light,
   And folk their wames hae stappit,
Our guid toon shows a canty sight,
   Wi' youngsters busk'd and strappit ;
And country folk, frae glen an height,
   In guid braid brechkans happit,
Thrang a' in crowds, sae snug an tight,
   Ere twal-o'clock be chappit
                  On sic a day.

Frae winding Urquhart's flow'ry glen,
   Where Endrick wanders gaily,
Comes canty carlins snod an' clean,
   An' lasses drest in style aye ;
Mair comely lads or strappin men
   Are unco scarce to wyle aye,
And that the Nessian youngsters ken—
   On them a blink they stea' aye
                  On sic a day.

Frae fair Glenconvinth's sunny braes
   In merry bands th'gither,
They trip away as light as fays,
   Frae mang their hills o' beather ;
Her's are the swains wha ken to please,
   An' bloomin' maids to flether.
Wha blithely gang, lac'd in their stays,
   Wi' hearts as light's a feather
                  On sic a day.

Frae ilka airt in crowds they thrang
   On cairts stock'd, heavy laden
Wi' butter kits, baith stout and strang,
   An' fine wove wabs o' plaidin ;
But they, puir sauls, aye think it wrang
   The custom stents * they've laid on
Sic guids as come our streets alang—
   They think that they are played on
                  On sic a day.

Now onward drive ye who can won
   Through sic a thrang and clatter,
The hurry o' the day's begun,
   Ilk ane as brisk's a hatter ;

---

* The petty customs, levied on all goods brought into the town for sale.
Although somewhat modified of late years, their imposition still forms a
bone of contention (1893) on which the fate even of a Councillor's election
depends.

Here's Dan himsel, the chiel for fun,
  How gaily he can flatter
The country chiels, to tak' them in,
  When haflins on the batter
          On sic a day.

His goods are rangit by his side,
  Sic goods as rarely happen
For cheapness, then his jokes beside
  Will gar some een be drappin ;
Gif fun ye want, whate'er betide,
  His match, I'll wad a chappin,
Ye winna find, though ye should try't,
  Twixt Shore Street here and Wappin'
          On onie day.

The chapman billies hae their tents
  Spread out wi' a' things dainty,
Wi' linen cotton, silks, and prents,
  An' preens an' needles plenty ;
" Hillo, hillo, come here wha wants ;
  There's lang sin' I hae kent ye,'
Cheap John cries out, ' Here's sangs an' a'
  An' a' thing to content ye,'
          On sic a day.

Brave jolly tars, on wooden stilts
  Wha aft the lead were heavin'
Wi' " Our Noble Captain cries " an' lilts,
  Our market folk they're deavin',
Fam'd Davidson,* at reel or waltz,
  Though nane can draw a nieve in
Sic grace an' style, at balls or tilts,
  Wi' them's nae worth a shavin
          On sic a day.

Here wale o' bucks, a' frae the west,
  Their tackets are nae sparin',
Guid oak sticks in their nieves they've prest
  For dangers they're na fearin' ;
Ilk ane sae proud gif he's possesst
  O' what can buy a fairin
To gie to her that he likes best
  For nothing else he's carin'
          On sic day.

How vaunty then, in short white breeks,
  Ilk chiel puffs up his noddle,

---

* Donald Davidson. For a notice of this worthy, see *ante*, page 47.

To wair the fee o' twa three weeks
    He doesna care a bodle,
To keep his lass frae dumpish freaks,
    To him she ne'er did bode ill,
An' when the gloamin daylight steeks
    For hame awa they'll toddle
                    On sic a day.

The bagpipe sounds, our causey braid
    Has bauldly marchin' on it
Our country's pride, who foes ne'er dread,
    Nor danger flee, to shun it ;
For these are they who aft were led
    To battlefield and won it—
The lads wha wear the tartan plaid,
    The philabeg, an' bonnet,
                    On ilka day.

The fifes join in the martial strain,
    The rattlin' drum is soundin'
An' mony a bloomin' maid is fain,
    An' patriot heart is boundin'.
Inspired by viewin' sic a scene,
    Sic as our streets abound in,
Their mountain hames o' strath an' glen
    Sic scenes are never found in
                    On onie day.

Haith, Bobbie,† ye should min' your taes
    Tho' fond o' the recruitin',
Altho' ye love the sounds they raise,
    There's danger I am doubtin',
I fear they'll end your loud huzzas
    Tho' mang the bairns ye're spoutin',
Some stots, in shape o' faes,
    May gie your taes a cloutin'
                    On sic a day.

† " Bobbie All." A well-known local simpleton of the day. His real name was James Mackay. He afforded great fun to the boys, who were always teasing him. He was fond of accompanying the recruiting parties in their marches through the town on market and other days, whistling the tune that was played by the band. Bobbie may be indeed said to have been constantly whistling, as, when not engaged with the boys, he was always *shoughling* along the street to his own music. He was very fond of whisky, and many an impish trick he was induced to perform by the promise of a glass. When on his deathbed he had a certain allowance of liquor given him, but Bobbie thought it was too little and demanded more. His mother, poor woman, not to deny him, gave the glass more frequently, but reduced its strength by adding some water. Bobbie happened to see, or suspected, the adulteration, for he was heard to cry out, " Shabby, mother, shabby—cheating poor Bobbie."

Here's Sodger Dan,* Bob's brother chum,
　His trotters ne'er are crampit,
Nane in the fair can march wi' him
　Altho' twal miles he's trampit ;
For jeers he doesna care a flim,
　His spirits ne'er are dampit,
The time o' the loud beating drum
　There's nane like him can stamp it
　　　　　　　Sae weel this day.

Here's Tam,† our ain teetotal swell,
　But he's gien up wench courtin',
And Jock ‡ wi' vigour rings his bell,
　Auld guids for sale reportin' ,
Too lang a tale 'twad be to tell
　O' this day's tricks an sportin',
For wi' her jokes Dame Fun hersel
　To our good toon's resortin'
　　　　　　　In glee this day.

PART II.

Now gloamin her grey curtain spreads,
　The bustle and the hurry
O' this day's done, and canny heads
　Nae langer here will tarry ;
The Black Isle lads, on gude grey steeds,
　Mak' aff for Kessock Ferry,
While inns are sought by drouthy blades
　To tipple and be merry
　　　　　　　On sic a night.

---

* "Sodger Dan." Another well-known character of the day. His name was Donald Macpherson, a native of Cawdor ; he was hence also known as "Dannie from Calder," and in his later years, when he took up his residence almost permanently in Inverness, as "Tiger Dan." This latter cognomen was given him by the town boys from the fierceness with which he resented their calling him names. Little was required to rouse up the latent fire of his wrath the whistling of the tune "Cawdor Fair," or latterly, as the boys saw him approach, the doggrel they sung to the same air—
　　　　　"Tiger Dan is in a lowe,
　　　　　Get the water-engine."
In his younger days he was fond of following the recruiting parties, and also frequented Fort-George.
† "Tam." This was Thomas Fraser, a tailor, known as "Tom-Tit." He was among the earliest converts to total abstinence in Inverness. Tom maintained his principles to the end of his life. He had seen some service as a volunteer in the Spanish Legion. Many were the wonderful stories he told which always had something to do with "When I was in the Spanish Legion, sir, " etc.
　　　　‡ Jock Stephen. See notice, *ante*, page 11.
　　　　　　　　12

By Lucky Gair's* clean chimla lug,
  Where loud the gill stoups clatter,
Where ale gangs round in horn and jug
  As rife as caller water ;
Ilk happy chiel his joe doth hug
  (A' hafflins on the batter),
How happy then he feels and snug
  When near him he has gat her
                On sic a night.

Sweet Celtic lays they loudly chant,
  Bendouran † and *Crochallan*,‡
And notes o' mony a merry rant
  Resound thro' Lucky's dwallin',
Till Clachnacuddin Boys asklent,
  Their throats to moisten call in,
There, sport and mirth to them's nae scant,
  Wi' singin' and wi' bawlin'
                On sic a night.

When hafflin's fou, awa they steer,
  Just like a storm-beat lugger,
Ilk chiel wi' head-piece nae that clear,
  Alang ilk lane they stagger ;
An' thro' our streets wi' boist'rous cheer
  They wi' their sweethearts swagger,
If ane to gang is ablins sweer,
  They are the boys will drag her
                On sic a night.

Waesucks for them wha on that night
  Hae overcharged their stomachs,
'Twere better they in time were tight
  Row'd up within their hammocks,

---

* "Lucky Gair." There were two bowfs in town at this period kept by landladies of the name of Gair. One of these, according to information from an old Invernessian, was in the Black Vennel, now known as Baron Taylor's Lane. The other, and the one most probably alluded to by the poet, was at the top of Wells Street, at its junction with Telford Street. This was, according to an old pupil of Paterson's, one of the houses which he frequented with his boon companions.

† "Beinne Dòrain." A well-known Gaelic poem by Duncan Ban Macintyre.

‡ "Chrodh Chalein." An old Gaelic song, one of those said to be used by the weird women of the fairies to charm the cattle to yield their milk freely. Mrs Grant of Laggan gives a translation of this song in her "Essays on the Superstitions of the Highlanders of Scotland," vol. II. pages 28, 29. See also notice in a paper by Mrs Mary Mackellar, in "The Transactions of the Gaelic Society of Inverness" vol. XVI. page 159, etc.

'Than gaun about in sic a plight
   Wi' lang disordered *gamacks*,
Unfit are they to wield aright
   Their oaken sticks or camacks
             On sic a night.

For our toon lads are *oot an oots*,*
   Their game I winna flatter,
Tho' they wi' greasy, sootie clouts,
   The country chiels bespatter,
And then to fyle their braw new suits,
   To them it doesna matter,
They joy to see folk *up the spouts*,†
   And spoil their wooin' clatter
             On sic a night.

Come, Muse, awa, 'tis time, I think,
   That hame we should be gettin',
For fear our pows may get a clink,
   Ilk callant's bluid is heatin',
And gif the red necks get the wink,
   Frae them there's nae retreatin',
On cauld stanes we will hae to slink,
   Gif 'neath the cock‡ we're put in
             On sic a night.

For unco folk, toon's folk an' a',
   Ne'er dreadin' some folk watch them,
Heez'd up wi' drink, they swear an' blaw,
   That there is nane to match them ;
But our toon guards their heads will claw
   Gif by the lugs they catch them,
To cauldrife quarters in a raw
   Fu' quickly they'll dispatch them
             On sic a night.

Ye hardie sons o' my sweet hame,
   O, for some bard to paint ye,
In strains mair worth a blast o' fame,
   Than those that here I prent ye ;

---

* Shrewd.   † Intoxicated.

‡ "'Neath the Cock " [the cock on the Town Steeple]. This refers to the lock-up cells which were next the Steeple when the Jail was on Bridge Street. We remember it was one of the sights for school-boys to go at nine in the morning to watch "Supple Sandie" release the drunks, etc. We have frequently seen the rush of all sorts and conditions from the "Black Hole."

Au' you, ilk bonny bloomin' dame,
 My wishes here I've sent ye,
May ye, by Nessia's crystal stream
 Be bless'd wi' peace and plenty
  Ilk day and night.

As the poor Muse, forjeskit sair,
 Has had a guid day's wark o't,
She's sung o' drink that drowns dull care,
 But hasna pree'd a spark o't ;
An' fearin' for the midnight air,
 She in my lugs has harkit—
We'll e'en awa, and sing nae mair
 About the Martinmas market
  On sic a night.

———

[The Inverness Martinmas market is now denuded of the picturesque charm which attached to it when the poet wrote—in fact
" all its glories are past." The poem recalls the quaintness of a
condition of things no longer to be found. The charms it had
for the Clachnacuddin boys of the first half of the present century, and the interest with which they looked forward to its advent,
no longer exist.

It was with a feeling akin to that of missing an old friend removed by death from his usual haunts, that we attempted, in
November 1892, the search for some evidence of the old fair.
Gone were the " sweetie " stalls that crowded the south side of the
High Street in the years that are past ; we saw only one table
spread with the syruppy " gundie " or candy that had formed the
main purchases of " Clach " boys. Gone the gingerbread tables,
which were wont to be spread with the birds and animals so
wonderfully and fearfully designed in the peppery stuff. Gone all
the tempting " fairins " of cheap jewellery that used to form the
staple purchases of the " scallags " when treating their lasses.
Gone the old ballad stall of the quiet, placid " Sandie Smith,"
who for years at all the fairs occupied the site on the edge of the
pavement nearly opposite the old Post Office, and who possessed
a stock of " The Ram of Derby " and ballads and songs of
a similar school, with 24-page histories that would be a fortune
now to the old fellow if he were still in the flesh.

On the north side of the High Street no longer were to be found a single stall with the ready-made leather constructions from Fortrose, Rosemarkie, and Campbeltown, where were manufactured the chief displays on the stands devoted to what were called boots and shoes. Once we heard a maiden declare, when it was proposed that a purchase be made for her at the fair of a pair of shoes, " that she was not going to wear any of these ' boxies.' "

Inglis Street had no longer its crowded corner, where a foreigner held a monoply of the disposal of " Fancy Baskets." Across the way were laid out the washing-tubs, pails, etc. of the" timmer trade : " while further down, the " Cheap Jacks " and the sellers of " duffing " watches and purses of half crowns had their stands, and bellowed their loudest to secure victims. The occupation of the latter is gone. The country lads are no longer to be im. posed on, and the purse fakers we hope have taken to more honest callings. It was at this point of the street that itinerant ballad-singers mostly haunted, and the discordant, raucous babel, was loudest as each tried to draw most attention to their wares.

But butter and cheese was the staple of the fair, and from the top of Academy Street, near Baron Taylor's Lane, to Rose Street, we have seen the country carts closely packed together on both sides of the street laden with butter in kegs and jars and kebbocks or cheeses, the produce from their crofts and small farms. The market lasted for three days. As early as Wednesday afternoon might be seen signs of the approaching fair—the arrivals of country carts in town with their loads of produce. On the Exchange or Plainstones in front of the old Town Hall, and crowded round Clachnacuddin stone, were seated old women with rolls of plaiding, bundles of stockings, and homespun thread, while crowds of thrifty housewives discussed the quality and the price. Friday was the chief day of the fair, and on which most business was done and the attendance largest.

The Martinmas market of 1826 was a most disastrous one, and was long spoken of by the older people of the town as " The Wild Martinmas." On the morning of Friday, the 24th November, a heavy snow storm set in, with occasional drifts of sleet, and a violence not previously experienced by the oldest inhabitant. The fall continued for the whole day and the following night. The town was crowded with country people, who, from the severity of the weather, took refuge in the public-houses or any other place

where they could obtain shelter, while many of them started for
their homes in the vicinity of Inverness, which some, alas! never
reached.   Eleven or twelve people perished in the snow within a
few miles of the town, and of these two or three only a short dis-
ance from their own doors.]

POPULAR ENTERTAINERS.

———o———

MR ORD, THE CIRCUS RIDER.

WHO among old Clachnacuddin Boys of "fifty years or more"
but will remember the circus rider Ord, whose wandering
troupe paid an annual or more frequent visit to Inverness?   We
were lately reminded of this popular entertainer by a placard we
saw posted up near a railway station at a seaside resort during the
summer months of this year (1892).   It was the announcement of
another troupe who were then visiting this place and performing
on the Links.   Preceding the programme of the various high-
rope and acrobatic feats to be attempted was the preliminary
introduction, of which this is a verbatim copy :—

"PINDER'S CIRCUS
(Late ORD'S).

"THE name of Ord has been a household word for over sixty
" years.   There are people travelling who use the name of Ord,
" but as there are only three of Mr Ord's family alive, all others
" taking the name of Ord are impostors.   Selina (Mrs Pinder),
" Matilda (now Mrs Shaw), and his only son, Leslie Ord," etc. etc.

The fame of our early entertainer had been assumed by those
who have no claim to it.   But we have no desire to enter on

these disputed claims to the mantle of our boyhood's favourite. Mr Ord's free exhibitions on the Maggot Green alone live in our memory and that of our compeers as affording to us youngsters of those days a fund of delight and pleasure never since enjoyed.

We first witnessed Mr Ord's company perform on the Maggot Green before we had hardly reached our "teens." We have never forgotten the serious advice and warning given to us by a grand-dame on our intimation that we were going to see Mr Ord's performances. This respected personage had a firm belief that Mr Ord and his troupe's performances were aided by the Evil One. The old woman told us the following veritable story in confirmation of her belief in the uncanny nature of the clever feats accomplished.* On one occasion (she said) one of Mr Ord's assistants was performing the feat of balancing large wooden deals 12 feet long—and of which two or three were tied together—first on his hand, then on his chin, and finally on his nose! The old woman with all gravity sought to impress upon our youthful mind that it was all witchcraft—glamour thrown over the eyes of those who witnessed the performance. And this was how it was all found out, she continued : "A woman coming along one day with a burden of grass on her back for her cow, rested for a few minutes on the Maggot Green when the acrobat was peforming this feat, and, attracted by curiosity, watched the performance, but not for long, when she began to cry out that it was not wooden planks that the acrobat was balancing but three straws ; he was only deceiving the people." The woman (said our informant) had discovered the deception attempted to be palmed on the people from the fact that in the bundle of grass she was carrying, there was a four-leaved clover, or shamrock—the popular belief being that this plant has the virtue of showing up any trick or deception to the bearer of it, provided they do not know that they are possessed of the plant at the moment. Had the woman been conscious that she possessed the clover her eyes would have been holden as were those of the large crowd looking on.

With the eagerness of youth we were not to be deterred by the

* We have given the substance of this story of superstition before in a periodical devoted to researches in antiquities and folk-lore.

old woman's tale from witnessing the performance on this occasion, and for many years after we never missed an opportunity of
seeing the gratis exhibitions given by Mr Ord and his company on
the open space where we first saw them performing.

Since that early time we have witnessed many circus performances in cities at home and abroad, but we unhesitatingly say that
as a circus rider we have never seen one who excelled our old
favourite Mr Ord.   His famous performance of riding in eight
character costumes ; his entrance to the ring as a drunken farmer
returning from the fair, his sailor, Sir William Wallace, etc. ; the
quick change of costume on horseback, the dash of his fiery steed
as he galloped round the ring—called forth the loud applause of
the beholders, and is remembered as a unique performance.
Then there was the wonderful sagacious pony, " Cromarty," who
had his own share of popular applause for the wonderful knowledge and training he displayed.   Mr Ord had two daughters who
took their share in the public performance of jumping through
hoops, etc. while on horseback.

Mr Ord's open-air exhibitions usually commenced in summer
about six p.m., and lasted over an hour and a-half, generally
concluding with " Billy Button the Tailor," in which the pony
" Cromarty " took his part in unseating the tailor ; or " Dick
Turpin's famous Ride to York."   Following on that a lottery was
drawn, the sale of tickets—sixpence each—having been going on
by the members of the company during the evening.   From
this source came the profits of the performances.   The tickets
sold contained a few leading prizes, such as a pound-note or a
boll of meal, and were eagerly bought up by the spectators.

On the close of the drawing Mr Ord generally held a dramatic
entertainment in Lowe's Rooms, Church Street, or Lyon's Hall,
Academy Street, at which the stock pieces were Scottish melodramas, such as " Gilderoy, or The Bonnie Boy," " Wandering
Steenie," " Crammond Brig," " Douglas," etc

DELANY, THE CLOWN.

Delany, the clown, was the leading man of the company.   From
our first acquaintance with the circus on the Maggot Green, till we
witnessed the final performance in a large wooden building
which Mr Ord had erected in the autumn of 1849 on the site
where now stand the Markets in Academy Street. Delany was

with Mr Ord the popular favourite. The clown's jokes and his
points and conundrums received hearty laughter and applause,
timeworn as many of them were. Delany's contributions to
the entertainment were not confined to the clowning, for although
a heavy built man, he was the next best performer on horseback,
while his somersaults were eye-openers to the wondering beholder.
As we have said, he was a great favourite with the crowd, and
when they became too pressing on the unfenced ring, his quips
and jokes always got the elders of them to step back, and give
places in front to the small boys, whom he got to seat themselves
on the grass—thus forming a fence in front.

Poor Delany! Some years after, we came across him in an
historical city some hundreds of miles away from the Highland
capital. To all appearance the world was not then prospering
with him. It was in an hostelry in this city which we had
been in the habit of frequenting to enjoy the comfortable reading-
room and the well-supplied stock of newspapers and periodicals
with which it abounded. One afternoon, when the place was
almost deserted, a stranger entered; and on looking up from
the page that was engaging our attention, we recognised in the
new entrant our old entertainer and mirth-provoker—Delany,
of Ord's. Poor Delany! we again say, for he looked the very
picture of being " down-on-his-luck." Dusty and footsore, he had
evidently come a long tramp. The dust added to the shabbi-
ness of the threadbare suit he wore. His feet were poorly shod
with what seemed to be an old pair of canvas slippers that had
trodden the sawdust and formed part of his circus properties;
while a red and white handkerchief contained a further portion of
his belongings. He sat for a time in deep thought, meditating
probably over his journey or his condition. At last he rung
the bell and gave his order to the waiter, whom we were glad to
see return with what in modern parlance would be called a
good square meal. We soon left the room, while he remained
enjoying and replenishing his inward man with the eatables,
ourselves musing over the mutations of human life, and the varying
changes that overtake the worldly conditions of men.

The last visit of Mr Ord to Inverness when we witnessed his
performances was in the winter of 1849. On this occasion, as
we have already stated, he erected a large wooden building as a

13

circus. He had a numerous company, in which Delany sustained
his leading part as usual. The venture was not a successful one.
Although he went to great expense in introducing many new
spectacles and had a large and varied company, the attempt to
galvanise a paying attendance was a failure, and he must have
lost considerably by his venture in seeking to establish a perma
nent circus in Inverness.

RUSSELL, THE WIZARD.

There was another showman who gave an outside stage performance, with whose gratis entertainment we made a still earlier
acquaintance. We could not have been more than eight years of
age when we first witnessed the outside entertainment of Russell,
the wizard, then performing on a piece of vacant ground near the
Capel Inch end of Nelson Street. The place when last we saw
it was covered by several houses. His tent, or ' pavilion," as
he named it, was one of the most primitive order—with a raised
wooden stage in front, the " pavilion " behind was covered over
with what we recollect as pieces of old sails, sacking, and such
like, to cover from vulgar eyes the mysteries of the performances
within. Russell, poor fellow, found it was a difficult job to keep
the Merkinch gamins from getting a sight of the select entertainment, and even at times to penetrate into the interior itself.
Russell, as an advertisement, gave an outside exhibition on the
front stage of slight-of-hand tricks with cards, also sword
swallowing, etc. These were only inducements to the larger bill
of fare supplied in the "pavilion." At this period he conducted
all the business in the " pavilion " without aid, as no other member of a company was to be seen.

The last time we saw him perform was on the vacant space of
ground which was then unfenced, in Davis Square, Green of Muirtown. This open space was at the time a Tom Tiddler's ground,
where sundry sorts of rubbish were deposited, and where, no
doubt, Russell found a free site for his erection On this occasion Russell's pavilion was of a larger size and more strongly
built than the humble one that did duty on Nelson Street. The
company was increased, for he was assisted in his performance at
this tme, by a woman who displayed her accomplishment as a
dancer on the outside stage to her own accompaniment on the
tambourine.

Russell had also another assistant—one Croal, a wandering
pedlar, who was well-known, in Inverness as a dealer in braces
and other small wares, and who occasionally varied it with singing
on the streets when pedling business was dull. He was a
" character." · His songs were largely of the order that prevailed
so long after Waterloo was fought and won—

> " 'Twas on the 16th day of June, my boys, in Flanders where we lay,
> Our buglers did the alarm sound until the break of day ;
> Our British Bulls and Brunswickers, and Hanoverians too,
> Brussels we left that morning for the field of Waterloo."

Croal performed some pantomine business for Russell, got up in
a ridiculous dress as an old woman. The dialogue was amusing,
but frequently bordered on a vulgar obscenity that would in these
latter days bring it within the cognisance of the law.

A fool-hardy performance of Russell's on one occasion has
been recounted to us by a witness of the scene. Russell was
advertising his entertainment through the streets on the west side
of the Ness on horseback, when, on reaching a noted licensed
place in Grant Street, he made a dash into the low and narrow
doorway horse and all, to the astonishment of " Lilias,' the land-
lady, who gave forth some strong expletives in Gaelic at the
strange sight. He barely escaped having his head battered by
coming in contact with the stone lintel ; calling for a glass of
whisky he drank it at the counter, still on his horse's back, and
then by great wriggling managed to make his retreat from the place.

DEVON BROTHERS.

The " Devon Brothers " were contemporaries of Mr Ord.
We have seen Ord's Circus succeeded the following week on the
Maggot Green by the erection that did duty for the Devon
Brothers' performances. This company held forth in a wooden
erection with canvas roof, which had an open stage in front.
There was an outside performance in which the company,
amounting to ten or twelve, took part in a dance, followed by
some clowning, as a prelude to the more serious business in
the inside. This company was ambitious, and performed stage
plays—even attempting some Shaksperian tragedies—but their
chief stock was comedies and melodramas, while wedged in
between were the acrobatic performances of the so-called Devon

Brothers. The most popular piece was "Cramond Brig," and the "Jock Howieson" we never saw better performed, frequently as we have seen it acted since by more pretentious companies. It was in this wooden erection, long before, we had the honour of initiation in a properly constituted Mason Lodge, under the genial Right Worshipful Mastership of Sir Henry Cockburn Mac andrew, that we acquired the Mason's secret," when the dreaded word "Salt beef and mustard" was revealed by poor Mr Dupre, driven to desperation by the nagging of the flaming targe Mrs Dupre.

The Brothers Devon, or at least one of them, must have risen in the acrobatic profession, for some years after we had witnessed him busking in the pavilion on the Maggot Green, we again re- cognised at one of the most popular variety-entertainment halls in the British metropolis one of these brothers, who in buskin and sock strutted the humble stage in the North—only with his name metamorphosed, to please his Cockney patrons, into the foreign one in the programme of Mons. Devonia.

THE GREAT FLOOD IN INVERNESS
IN 1849.

———o———

THE OLD STONE BRIDGE.

THE most disastrous occurrence that has befallen the town of
Inverness within the memory of living individuals was the
great and unprecedented flood of January 1849. The destruction
of the fine old stone bridge of seven arches, which after bravely
standing the floods and stormy tempests of over 160 years,
succumbed to the inundation ; and the laying of a great portion
of the town, especially on the west side of the river, under
water to the extent of several feet, was the cause of great alarm
and distress among the inhabitants. Many of the houses were
deserted, the residents glad to make their escape by boats and
such other means of rescue as could be got at. Happily no
lives were lost, but considerable property was destroyed, and
the whole effect of this calamitous flood was such as to leave an

indelible impression on the minds of those who witnessed the varied scenes involved in the disastrous three days of 25th, 26th, and 27th January 1849.

The weather in the North of Scotland, particularly in Inverness and the surrounding districts, in the month of January was tempestuous to an almost unprecedented degree—long continued heavy rains, accompanied by vivid lightning at night that set the sky along the whole valley of the Ness ablaze with the brilliancy of the frequent flashes ; while the immense quantities of rain fallen brought down the river in an unprecedented seething and angry flood.

On the afternoon of Wednesday (24th) the waters of the Ness had risen to such a height that the roadways at Ness Bank. Douglas Row, Huntly Street, Tanner's Lane, and King Street, were under water, while in many cases the houses had been invaded by the rising flood.   We had occasion on this afternoon to make an attempt to reach the house of a resident in Ness Bank. We found on getting to the foot of the Haugh Brae and on turning round into Ness Bank the waters of the Ness were nearly on a level with the copestone of the railings of the front gardens, After a vain attempt to make progress by walking on the cope stone and clinging to the railings, we had at a little distance to give it up.

About half-past eight the same night, with the boyish feeling of adventure and fearlessness of youth, we crossed the old stone bridge, which had that afternoon been closed by the authorities to heavy traffic, great fears having been entertained as to the ability of the structure to resist the volume of water.   The river at this hour had risen above the piers, and was rushing beneath the arches with the speed of a mighty cataract.   The gateway at the west end of the bridge was closed, and only opened by the policeman stationed there to allow the few solitary foot-passengers to pass who were venturesome or foolhardy enough to make the attempt to cross.   We got safely over, but had not advanced many yards from the gateway of the bridge when we got into deep water, and it was only by using the aid afforded by the walls of the houses as we went along, that we got to dry land, near the point where Greig Street now opens.

Wednesday night was one of great anxiety in the houses on the

west side of river. Popular rumour gave currency to various
stories, as to the safety of the Caledonian Canal and its bursting
the banks. thus letting loose the waters of Loch Ness on the
devoted town became the uppermost topic of conversation during
the wea y hours of watching. Many never went to rest even in
the streets where the flood had not reached. and anxiously
watched the coming of the night-tide, as it was at its full height
at one p.m. On Gilbert Street. a little above the wooden bridge,
the authorities had placed a water–guage so as to ascertain the
progress of the rising of the river, and frequent were the visits
paid by the inhabitants of this district to obtain information as to
the advance of the tide. By many it was anticipated that as the
tide receded so would the river fall, but this expectation was not
realised, for the waters steadily continued to rise. From three
till five o'clock on Thursday morning the most alarming progress
was registered of the increase of the flood in the Ness. The
scene at this hour on the river banks was one never to be forgotten. We stood near the wooden bridge, where we had in full
view the sweep of the mighty stream that rushed down — the
few gas-lamps that abutted on the roadways on the river banks
threw but a weird glimmer over a small portion of the expanse,
and added but additional fear to the terrible scene that lives in
our recollection.

On the upper reach of the river the dreaded fate of the old
stone bridge was realised. At a few minutes before six o'clock on
Thursday morning it fell with a rumbling sound, as described by
the solitary witness. a policeman stationed on Bridge Street, who
saw its fair proportions disappear in the boiling gulf beneath.
Thus fell the venerated landmark that had withstood the spates
and floods of more than a century and a half. It had been a
witness of many scenes connected with Clachnacuddin. In the
fateful year of 1746 it had witnessed a most stirring scene ; for a
brief time it became the rallying-point of some brave Highlanders
who had escaped from the massacre on the bloody field of Culloden, and sought at the western gate of the fallen bridge to beat
back the tiger-like ferocity of the pursuing ruthless Hanoverian
soldiery.

In the Merkinch this Thursday morning, on the fall of the
stone bridge becoming known, the anxious question with the

affrighted inhabitants was how long the "black bridge" was to stand. About eight o'clock a note of alarm was given that one of the Ness Islands suspension bridges was coming down, and we soon saw it being whirled over and over as if it were a log of wood in the rapid current. It was dreaded that if it came in contact with the old wooden bridge, and was stopped by the posts, that the passage would be obstructed, but it fortunately got through without any further damage than the loss of a couple of the posts where it first struck the bridge, and the iron structure got ultimately stranded on the Capel Inch.

We crossed the "black bridge" to the east side of the town about nine o'clock. This bridge was also closed from the previous night to all traffic save the few foot-passengers that ventured to cross. We did the crossing of it at a run, but there was an unmistakeable quiver in the roadway, and it was a marvel how such a frail structure compared with the stone bridge had stood the shock of the rushing waters, but probably the little resistance it offered to the flood was its safety. We found the streets on the east side of the river crowded with people who had been driven from the Green of Muirtown and Merkinch. Many were carrying some of their belongings, and hurrying to the public buildings and institutions that had been opened by the magistrates for their reception.

We were early at Bridge Street to visit the scene of the old bridge's downfall. Policemen were stationed here to keep back the crowd who were pushing to rather dangerous points to gaze on the site. All that remained of the once graceful fabric at the time was the small portion of a parapet and a broken pier. The river here swept up to the very walls of the houses on each side of the street from the corner of Gordon Place to the gable of the picturesque building "Castle Tolmie" that flanked the river front. Looking down the river from this "coign of vantage," the Ness could be seen with its full sweep, and the height the water had reached could be judged when we say that on the west side the water had reached the top of the windows on the first storey.

At Douglas Row the height of the water was nearly as great. There is a view of the river and buildings as seen from this latter point taken by a Mr James Hardie, an architect, who resided here, from the first floor window of No. 17 Douglas Row,

on the morning of the 25th, and which gives a true representation
of the inundation and the appearance of the scene a few hours
after the bridge fell. We produce here a reduced copy of this
drawing—a most interesting and correct memorial of this disas
trous event—by an eye-witness.

VIEW FROM DOUGLAS ROW.

INCIDENTS OF THE FLOOD, Etc.

The authorities were keenly alive to the disastrous appearance
of matters, and took prompt action to aid the people of the flooded
districts. Early on the morning of Thursday the 25th they orga-
nised rescue parties of policemen and citizens to assist in the work
of removing the people from the flooded houses—these removals
became very general—by means of boats and one or two of the
mail coaches the people on the west side of the river were got out
from what appeared to be the most dangerous houses to places of
safety. The poorer of the inhabitants were provided for by the
magistrates who opened the Town Hall, Dr Bell's Institution, the
Poor's House (Dunbar's Hospital), and the Gaelic Church for
their reception, while fire and food were supplied at the town's
expense, and everything done to render their position as comfortable as possible. The removals of the sick and helpless and bed-

14

ridden people, of whom there were several, was attended with some difficulty, but all was accomplished in safety.

In the work of rescuing the people from their houses, the following were prominently active on the west side of the river: John Mackenzie, Ness House ; Colin Lyon-Mackenzie of St Martin's, one of the magistrates ; James Macpherson, solicitor ; Major Macpherson, Drummond ; Andrew Fraser, leather merchant ; George Macbean, shoemaker ; John Macbean, messenger-at arms ; David Anderson, superintendent of police, and his assistant John Macfarlane, and many others. In the Haugh and Ness Bank Dr Nicol and his son D. A. Nicol were active — the latter having taken a coble down the Haugh Road as far as Inglis Court, and removed the people from the houses there.

Amid much that was distressing there were some amusing scenes and ludicrous situations witnessed by the rescuers in their efforts to place the people in safety.

"THE FLOOD A PUNISHMENT OF SIN."

On Duff Street in the early morning, a boat employed in removing the people from their houses came upon an old woman who was wading through the flooded street, carrying on her shoulders a roll of blanketing and some clothing. While making her difficult journey to dry land, under her burden, she was heard loudly exclaiming in Gaelic, " Cha d'thainig so g'un abhar ! Cha d'thainig so g'un abhar !—an thayter mosach ! " (" This did not come without a reason ! This did not come without a reason !—the dirty theatre ! ") The explanation was that at this time a theatrical company, under the management of a Mr Glanville, was performing in Lowe's Rooms, Church Street. The opening of this place for a theatre and the performance of stage plays was strongly and unfavourably commented on by several clergymen of the town the previous Sabbath ; hence old " Ealasaid Bhan's " expressions as to the flood in the Ness being a judgment on the town for its support of the drama.

A FLAG OF DISTRESS.

In the neighbourhood of Duff Street the same boating party came on a curious signal for help. Protruding from the upper window of a low thatched house they observed an old-fashioned tongs holding a piece of burning peat or turf. The tongs was waved about, and the turf threw off sparks. On making for the place, which they reached with some difficulty, they asked the inmate to come out by the garret window, but this he declined to do. All John's wants were, as he declared to the worthy Colin Lyon-Mackenzie, one of the magistrates of the burgh, and who was in command of the boat, that they "would get him a pennyworth of peats and a stale loaf!!" Loaves that were a few days old were then sold at a reduction on the usual price of fresh bread. Old John gave even directions where the goods could be had; but, alas! the huckster's store was flooded, and the dealer had taken flight—but later on a supply was conveyed to the old weaver. The old man was a well-known inhabitant of the Green of Muirtown—"John the weaver"—a local character who had some celebrity in his day in attending on the Rev. Alex. Clark in his catechisings in the district, and who for many years taught a class for the reading of the Scriptures in the Gaelic language in a Sabbath-school held in the neighbourhood. John Fraser was, barring some little eccentricities, a worthy old bachelor. He was in great request among his poorer neighbours when deaths occurred, and at the universal customary "lykewakes" on these sad occasions his services were much sought after for his fervent and unctuous prayers. In his latter years he did no work, but wandered about the town clad with a long camlet cloak in the style of "the men," and depended for his living as the pensioner of respectable citizens who knew him in better days.

MAIDEN MODESTY.

The method pursued in the rescuing of several old maiden ladies in Ness Bank was a subject for laughter and joke for many a day after the flood. In one house there were three ladies, sisters, and when the rescue party found an entrance to their house by the back garden they refused to be carried out on the shoulders of men as had been done by many of their neighbours. "They had never been dependent on men, and they were not going to avail themselves of any such immodest or ridiculous methods." Tom Russell, the blacksmith, who was one of the rescue party, to spare their shrinking coyness, suggested that they should be floated out in a large washing-tub. This plan was adopted, and they had

" a tub of their own at the flood "—but an unfortunate upset of the vessel put an end to this mode of escape and they had at last to submit to be carried out by "those fellows," and got safely landed on dryer territory.

THE TURN OF THE TIDE.

An old ship captain, who resided on Celt Street, was rather disposed to sneer at the alarm of his neighbours at the rising of the waters. On Wednesday night he retired to rest quite at ease in his own mind that with the receding of the tide the Ness would empty itself considerably. Early on the morning of Thursday a friend managed, with great difficulty, to get to the captain's house, and woke him up with " Get up, captain, the flood is coming." The captain replied, " What time is it ? " and receiving for answer " Half past five o'clock," replied, " Get away back to bed, man, the tide is turned." The captain had great difficulty in getting himself and his wife out at an upper window an hour later.

A PHILOSOPHER.

The old building which stood on the north side of Bridge Street at this time, called " Castle Tolmie," was supposed to be in danger of being undermined by the action of the river. " Castle Tolmie," in the 18th century, was the town residence of the Culloden family. It was of early Scotch architecture, with crow-stepped gables, curious narrow windows surrounded with inscriptions and dates, pepperbox corner turrets, and stone turnpike stairs. On Thursday morning all of the roadway in front of the western gable and a wing of the building that faced the river was carried off by the rapid current ; and fears were entertained of the stability of the foundations of the structure not being able to offer much further resistance to the force of the stream.

On the afternoon of Wednesday, when matters first began to look alarming, the tenants in the lower range of the building had taken the precaution to remove their stocks from the small sunk shops to a place of safety. The upper portion of " Castle Tolmie " was occupied as a small hotel, the tenant of which was a John Fraser, known among his familiars as "Jock Beef." The principal portion of John's furniture had been removed, but the landlord himself refused to leave the building, determined, as he said to be buried beneath its ruins rather than take flight.   A few hours after the bridge fell, this philosopher was found sitting at his cheerless fireplace, his only complaint being that " no one had come to ask if he had a mouth on him."   The building withstood the flood, but it had ultimately to make way for the widening of the approaches to the new suspension bridge.

"THE LAST MAN."

The last person to cross the old stone bridge was Matthew Campbell, a sailor—a well-known Royal Academy boy of his day, having carried off the Raigmore gold medal for classics in 1833. He was a son of John Campbell, tailor and musician, who resided in the court now No. 51 Castle Street, Inverness.   Matthew had adopted the sea as a profession, and made long voyages to China, India, etc.   It was on his last visit to his native town that he was able to give his assistance in removing the people from the flooded houses, and on his way homeward in the early morning of Thursday he was the "last man" to cross the bridge.   On his return voyage to India he died there.

THE WITNESS TO THE FALL.

On the recent death of police patrol Donald Macbean, who had been an original member of the new force, it was claimed for him that he was the constable who was on the Bridge Street beat and who saw the bridge fall. We believe that statement to be quite an error.   The policeman who did duty on that night was a well-known member of the force, known as " Red Rory," so called from his carroty poll and red face freckled with pockmarks.   Rory was known to all the youths of the town ; he was the bogey man of the new force, and struck terror into the boys.   The mention of his name soon cleared a corner crowd or scattered a " bike " of marble or top players from the footpaths.

A FALSE PROPHET.

The well known ungallant prophecy ascribed to " Coinneach Odhar " that the bridge would fall when there should be on it three red-haired women and two grey mares, and this would occur when the male sex were so scarce in Inverness that nine

women would be found chasing a cripple tailor ! was falsified in
every detail, as it deserved to be, from such a libel on the fair
character of the women of the Highland capital.

There was another traditionary story connected with the same
Highland seer and the fall of the bridge relative to a gooseberry
bush that grew on the ledge of one of the arches on the southern
side of the bridge. We have often looked down from the roadway above upon this bush. On each returning season it sent out
its foliage and fruit, and the seer's prophecy in this case also came
to nought.

THE BRIDGE DUNGEON.

Between the second and third arch on the east side of the
bridge there was a small dungeon which had been used for crimi-
nals. Maclean, the Inverness Centenarian, gives an account
of it in his "Reminiscences of a Clachnacuddin Nonagenarian,"
and of the most noted prisoners that were there lodged. The
strange prison has been described to us by one who saw it opened
about the year 1845. The bridge was undergoing some repairs
in this year, the roadway had been opened up, and the trap-
door of the dungeon was lifted. Several people went down into
the vault, and our informant was one of those who inspected the
place. He describes the interior stone steps as descending on the
south side of the bridge near to the iron grating in the arch
—the only light into the gloomy cell. When he reached the last
step he found the bottom of the place was bowl-shaped, and at
its widest part not more than twelve feet square. Around three-
fourths of the place a stone seat or settle was constructed, while in
the centre of the place what appeared a small narrow well, as if it
had been an outlet to the Ness.

This place of confinement must have been one of the most
dismal and wretched kind. There have been various stories of
prisoners confined here being eaten by rats, and of others who
had their prison fare supplemented by the passers-by letting
down to them pieces of bread and other food by means of a
string to the grated window in the cell. The same informant
tells us that he had stretched forth his arm to this opening, and
found that he could reach it, so that the story of the extra supply
of food administered was not at all improbable. The place had

ceased to be used as a prison cell for more than seventy years before the bridge fell.

A RELIC OF THE BRIDGE.

On the top of one of the piers of the stone bridge there was an old sun-dial formed out of red sandstone—probably a relic from still older buildings. as much of the material from Cromwell's Fort at the Citadel was used in the construction of the bridge, while many of the stones in this fort had at a still earlier period been, removed from the cathedral at Fortrose and other ecclesiastical buildings. The sun-dial had, on the fall of the bridge, been carried down the stream, and a search was made for it, when the Ness had fallen to a driblet. It was found, and passed into the hands of one of the magistrates of the day, who gave a considerable sum to the finder of this relic. The dial, on the death of this magistrate, passed through many hands, until it appeared as if all trace of it had been lost, but after some years of wandering it was at last discovered, and has found its way into the possession of one of the sons of Clachnacuddin, its most worthy possessor since it became separated from the bridge—Charles Fraser-Mackintosh of Drummond—to whom, on account of his deep interest in Inverness and all that concerns her welfare, may be applied the words of the Psalmist, that he *"takes pleasure in her stones, and favours the very dust thereof."*

ERECTION OF THE STONE BRIDGE.

The bridge was begun in 1681, and was finished in 1684. The cost of the structure was £1,300 sterling, which was raised by voluntary contributions. The following list of private subscribers, and corporate and municipal contributors, is given from a painted board that formerly hung in the Guildry room in the old Town Hall. The bridge, although finished and opened in 1684, there soon arose some difficulties with the builder, or rather his representatives, as to some defects in the structure. The Town Council in consequence, as recorded in their books, took steps to make good their claim against the builder, and took instruments against the representatives of the umquhile Mr James Innes, master-mason." For the maintenance of the bridge a perpetual toll was granted by the Scottish Parliament :—

	Merks		Merks
Al. Dunbar of Balmukite .	1000	Ja. Sutherland, Treasurer of	
Robert Barbor of Milderg .	200	Edinburgh . . .	55
Al. Rose . . .	180	Mr Al. Mackenzie, writer at	
Hugh Robertson . .	200	Ed.	30
Will. Duff . . .	200	Mr Will. Lauder . .	100
Jo. Cuthbert of Easter Drake,		Mr Jo. Lauder . . .	87
Provost . . .	400	Will. M'Bain . .	150
Finl. Fraser, Bailie . .	400	Murd,. Bishop of Orkney .	270
Ro Barbor, do. . .	200	Bishop of Aberdeen . .	518
Jam. Stuart. do. . .	200	Bishop of Murray . .	451
Heu Robertson, do. .	200	The Diocese of Ross .	66
Al. Bishop of Ross . .	180	The Diocese of Orkney .	33
The L. of Cadel . .	500	Hugh English, merchant at	
Sir And. Forester . .	200	Edinb. . . .	100
The L. of Muirtoun .	150	Kinrara . . .	100
The L. of Arkenhead . .	90	Aberdour . . .	133
The L of M'Kinnin .	50	Farr	33
Co. Mackenzie of Cap .	50	M'Intosh . . .	40

The Town and Terri doted as follows :—

	Merks		Merks
Mr Alex. Clark, minister of		Ja. Dunbar . . .	150
Inverness . . .	100	Mr D. Polson . .	100
Mr Gilb. Marshal, do. .	100	Jo. Watson . . .	150
Jo. Hepburn . .	400	Mr Ja. Hepburn . .	100
James Cuthbert . .	336	Mr Al. Fraser . .	100
Da. Foular, late Bailie .	200	Jo. Cuthbert . .	80
Al. Fraser . . .	260	A. Steuart, skip . .	80
Mr Wil. Robertson of Inches	360	Mal. Paterson . .	80
W. Rose of Markinch .	300	And. Mann . . .	80
Will. Duff . . .	150	Al. Neilson . . .	80
Jo. Steuart . . .	300	Mat. Robertson . .	80
Ja. M'Lean . . .	150	And. Shaw . . .	60
Ja. Foular . . .	150	Jo. Cowie . . .	60
Jo. M'Intosh . .	150	Da. Duff . . .	60
R. Neilson . , .	150	Al., M'Bean . . .	60
Ja. M'Intosh . .	150	D, Grant . . .	60
Tho. M'Niven . .	150	Ch. Steuart . . .	60
Wil. Bailie . . .	100	D. Forbes . . .	60
Tho. Hossack . .	100	Al. Dunbar . . .	60
D. M'Lean . . .	100	Ja. Cowie . . .	60
Jo. Lockhart . .	100	Wil. Neilson . . .	60
Ro. Rose . . .	100	Ja. Thomson . . .	60
Ro. Rose, younger .	100	Ja. M'Rae . . .	60
Wil. Thomson . .	100	Da. Fraser . . .	60
Wil. Keloch . . .	100	Jo. Grant . . .	60
Ch. M'Lean . .	100	Wrights and Coopers .	440
Wil, Cumming . .	100	Butchers . . .	104
Ja. Robertson . , .	100	Weavers . . . ,	256
Ja. Robertson, younger .	100	Tailors . . .	285
Geo. M'Bean . .	100	Shoemakers . . .	615
Al. Paterson . .	90	Skinners . . .	390
Da. Cuthbert . .	100	Bakers . . .	104
Da. Smith . . .	40	Masons . . .	105
Wil. Bailie . .	150	Jo. Forbes . . .	158

Subscriptions for Bridge, Town and Terri—(continued)—

	Merks			Merks
Mr Jo. Cuthbert . . .	60	Aberdeen	400
Jo. Barbour ' . .	150	Strivling	107
Wil. Cuthbert . . .	60	Lithgow	100
Jo. Robertson . . .	60	Montrose	190
Da. Bailie	60	Haddington . . .	100
Edinburgh . . .	850	Kirkua	35
Glasgow	609	Musselburgh . . .	80
Perth	200	Dalkeith	65
Dundee . . .	320		

FORMER BRIDGES ON THE NESS.

The earliest notice we have of a bridge on the Ness, is, that in the year 1410, on his march to the Battle of Harlaw, Donald of the Isles burnt the greatest part of the town of Inverness, *and the oak bridge, one of the finest in the kingdom.* On that occasion the following item from an old chronicle of a Clachnacuddin Horatius—

"How valorously he kept the bridge,
In the brave days of old!"—

is worthy of record :—

"One John Cumine, a burgess, son of Cumine of Ernside in Moray, arrayed in his headpiece and armed with a two-handed sword, offered so stout a resistance at the west end of the bridge as would have compelled the assailants, had there been ten such men in the town, to have retired in dismay."

If the "fine oak bridge" was not entirely destroyed by the Islesmen, it may have been the same structure repaired that remained down to 1644 or later.

Richard Franck, a Cromwellian trooper who was stationed in the Citadel here in 1656, describes the bridge then standing in the following uncomplimentary terms : "Yet here is one thing more among our northern novelties very remarkable ; for here you shall meet with a wooden bridge to convey you over the rapid Ness, but certainly the weakest in my opinion that ever straddled over so strong a stream. However, it serves to accommodate the native to those pleasant meadows north and north-west."

On the 28th September 1664 an accident occurred to this bridge, described by the quaint old chronicler, the Rev. James Fraser of Wardlaw (now Kirkhill) : "The great old wooden bridge of Inverness was repairing, and by the inadvertency of a carpenter cutting

15

a beam that lay betwixt two couples to set up a new one, the bridge tending that way, ten of the old couples fell flat in the river, with about 150 persons—men, women, and children—upon it. Four of the townsmen broke legs and thighs ; some sixteen had their legs, arms, and thighs bruised ; all the children safe without a scart. A signal providence and a dreadful sight at ten forenoon."

Following on this accident this bridge must again have undergone a repair, for an early tourist, who visited Inverness in 1677 describes evidently the same erection : " Over the river is a rotten wooden bridge on about ten or twelve pillars. Below this bridge are abundance of nasty women possing [splashing] clothes with their feet, their clothes tucked up to the middle."

THE FLOOD OF 1834.

From a Report furnished to the Town Council by Messrs Mitchell, Maclean, and May, engineers, as to damages done to the river banks by the flood of November 1834, we extract the following :—

" The fall or declivity of the river Ness is very considerable, being at the rate of more than eight feet in a mile till it reaches the sea ; and, when moderately flooded, the velocity of its current has been found to be upwards of five miles an hour. It is also subject, like all mountainous rivers. to frequent variations of level from the effects of floods or continued rains, although to a certain degree usefully regulated in this respect by its connection with the capacious basin of Lochness, which requires a great quantity of water to cause a material rise over its whole surface. A convenient measure of the height to which the river may in such cases attain, was afforded by the extraordinary flood which occurred in the month of November last. On that occasion the river rose to an average height of 7 or 8 feet above its ordinary summer level, overflowing its banks in many places to the depth of several feet, which was a very great inconvenience to the public generally, and was no doubt attended with serious risk and damage to the houses and other private properties that are situated along them."

INVERNESS MARRIAGE ROMANCE.

WE know not if in the following curious Inverness marriage case may be evolved the trite saying of the poet Byron that " Truth is stranger than fiction ; " but, as showing many of the social habits of what may be considered the " upper ten " of Inverness society--their assemblies—card parties dinner parties, and the hard drinking customs and high jinks that pre- vailed among them 160 years ago, the marriage trouble of Sibella Barbour is one of very great interest.

On the 19th December 1732 John Steuart raised an action of declarator of freedom against Sibelia Barbour, while a counter action of adherence was raised by Miss Barbour against him, " before the Masters Andrew Marjoribanks, George Smollet, James Leslie, and Robert Clark, Commissaries of Edinburgh, anent the two several lybelled summonses actions, and causes intended and pursued before the said Commissioners."

Before the case was brought into court there was an attempt to settle it by the offer of a large sum of money if the lady would allow a decreet of declarator of freedom to go in absence at Steuart's instance against her, or pursue a divorce, but all offers of a compromise were indignantly refused by the lady and her friends.

We may state thus early in our narrative that ultimately the Commissaries who heard the case found and declared that John Steuart and Sibella Barbour were husband and wife. We will un- fold the particulars of this marriage case from the MS. record, extending to over 340 pages, now before us.

The gay Lothario is John Steuart (second son of Master Francis Steuart, brother german of the Earl of Moray) who is described by one of the witnesses as " a blooming young man of twenty." The heroine is " Mistress Sibella Barbour, daughter of the deceast John Barbour, late one of the baillies of Inverness, and sister of

Daniel Barbour of Aldourie, merchant in Inverness."* The social
position of the parties was not so very far apart, that a marriage
between them could be looked upon as a *mesalliance*, save that
John Steuart was in the running for the earldom of Moray, to which
his father succeeded in 1735. It may be here however stated
that John Steuart himself died before his father, and never reached
the earldom.

In the year 1730 the young man John Steuart came north to
Inverness on the invitation of John Forbes of Culloden,† as he
said, to visit his friends. At Culloden House, and also at the
town house of the Culloden family—"Castle Tolmie," the old
building which stood near the foot of Bridge Street—he was a
frequent visitor, where were held dinner and wine parties, at
which young Steuart indulged to excess so much as on one occasion at a dinner party at Culloden House, he fell asleep at the
table, and the laird ordered his servants to put him to bed. He
became also a frequenter of the taverns in the town, and engaged
in drinking parties with military officers and citizens who fre-

* John Barbour, bailie of Inverness, acquired the estate of Aldourie.
He had several daughters besides Sibella, who all made advantageous
marriages.

Daniel, the son, and, after his father's death in 1723, of Aldourie, was a
merchant in Inverness. He afterwards, in 1747, joined the army, and
curiously enough, John Stenart, his sister's husband, was lieutenant-
colonel of the same regiment. Had the peace been made up, and had
Sibella joined her faithless one?

We give the following inscription on the tombstone of the Barbours,
father and brother of Sibella, as still existing in the Chapelyard, Inver-.
ness ;—

" UNDERNEATH THIS STONE LYETH | THE BODY OF JOHN BAR- | BOUR
OF ALDOURIE, | MERCHANT AND LATE | BAILLIE OF INVERNESS, | WHO
DEPARTED THIS LIFE | THE 21 DAY OCTOBER | 1723, | AND OF CAPTAIN
DANIEL BARBOUR OF ALDOURIE, HIS ELDEST | SON, WHO DEPARTED
THIS | LIFE THE 24 DAY OF JULY 1758"

† John Forbes of Culloden, the elder brother of the eminent Duncan
Forbes, Lord President of the Court of Session. He sat in Parliament for
Inverness-shire from 1704 to 1727. From his convivial habits he acquired
the name of " Bumper John," and one or two instances of his hospitality
may be gleaned from this case. Captain Burt, who was in Inverness at this
time, and invited as guest to Culloden house, gives the following account of
the hospitality of the laird of Culloden :—

"There lives in our neighbourhood, at a house (or castle) called Culloden,
a gentleman whose hospitality is almost without bounds. It is the custom
of that house, at the first visit or introduction, to take up your freedom by
cracking his nut (as he terms it), that is, a cocoa-shell, which holds a pint,
filled with champagne or such other sort of wine as you shall choose. You
may guess by the introduction at the contents of the volume. Few go
away sober at any time ; and for the greatest part of his guests, in the conclusion, they cannot go at all."

quented these houses of entertainment, where there were prolonged
drinking bouts, with card-playing and more or less gambling, and
it was no uncommon incident as a finish to the night's debauch to
engage in fights.   "One early morning, returning from Culloden,
the party," as a witness states, "got up a quarrel with some
people at a publick wedding at the end of the town of Inverness,
upon which a noise arose, and the mob abused them," and the
young sparks got the worst of it.

These indulgences of Steuart's caused considerable anxiety to his
clansman Bailie Stewart,* at whose house the young man lodged ;
and it was no unfrequent part of the duty he took on himself, to
hunt up the youth at the well-known howffs he frequented. We
will allow the bailie to give his own account of one of these raids
in search of the truant :—

That upon a Saturday he came to the house of John Taylor,
vintner in Inverness, between eleven and twelve at night, to inquire
for young Master Steuart and take him home. That he immediately got access to the company, which consisted of Master Schaw,†
merchant in Inverness, Master Baillie, town clerk of Inverness,
George Mackintosh ‡ a gentleman who resided at Inverness, the
Pursuer (Steuart), and Master Barbour, the Defender's brother.
That they were playing at cards ; that the company drank so hard
that he left them about one o'clock in the morning, the Pursuer
refusing to go along with him. That the Pursuer did not come to
his lodgings till six o'clock in the morning, as the servants informed him. That at this time Steuart frequented the company of
Master Barbour, and turned his back upon him (deponent) and
his other friends, with whom he was in use formerly to keep company, and told his daughter that deponent was officious in ques-
tioning him upon the company he kept, and that if he was another he would slit his nose for his interference. All this time the
Pursuer seldom returned home before three and four in the morning, and always excessively drunk.

* John Stewart, merchant in Inverness, of the family of Kincardine, a
Highland estate now known as Glenmore. The bailie was an ardent
Jacobite, and engaged in the risings of 1715 and 1745. Interesting parti-
culars relative to this gentleman are to be found in Mr Fraser-Mackintosh's
"Letters of Two Centuries," pages 231–233.
† This was John Shaw, a well-known merchant, of the family of Shaw
of Dalnavert, in Badenoch.
‡ George Mackintosh, son of John Mackintosh, advocate, and Mary
Winram. George's grandfather was Collector of Customs at Inverness.

Alexander Baillie,* town clerk of Inverness, called "Clerk Baillie," gives an account of one of the evenings passed at Daniel Barbour's house : That after supper a bowl of punch was brought, and that the gentlemen drank for some time pretty frankly, but at last, about twelve at night (the women having gone off), the deponent challenged Master Barbour's servant for drawing the glass so fast, and threatened him for doing so, they being playing a party at " whisk ;" and thereafter hallenged Master Barbour for ordering or allowing the drink to go so fast round, to which Barbour replied that he wanted more to drink than play. and told deponent that he might drink or not as he pleased, That about four or five in the morning, Master Steuart was very drunk, and deponent overturned the bowl to prevent further drinking, and a short time thereafter Steuart fell asleep and was put to bed in Master Barbour's house.

During this gay and wild time young John Steuart met Mistress Sibella Barbour at her brother's house, and soon fell a victim to the charms of the young lady, although it suited him at a later period to say that he was entrapped into this connection by being " during his stay at Inverness constantly haunted by the Defender's relations." He also pleaded " that from a constant course of gaming and dancing he was brought to drinking to great excess, insomuch that he had scarcely a sober and cool minute all the time he was there from morning to night, and through the night ; and if in this situation inconsiderate expressions tending to a regard for Mistress Barbour might have been thrown out, it was no great wonder. Such incidents but too frequently happen when there is no serious purpose of matrimony." If not an ardent lover in his absence from Inverness on a visit to Morayshire, he addressed the following love-letter to the lady :—

" MY DEAREST SIBBY,—I proposed to myself the happiness of waiting on you on Tuesday, but the people in Moray are so very kind that I cannot get away till Thursday at soonest, though I would much rather dispense with their kindness since it deprives me of the pleasure of your dear company, far more valuable and agreeable than any in Moray or elsewhere, —a least so to me. I would willingly, if I could, write something to divert and make you laugh ; but we have no news here, and since absent from you I want life and spirit for conversation. I believe you heard my friend

* ' Clerk Bailie," a cousin of the laird of Dunean.

John Roy's * resolution of drinking nothing but wine and water, All I can say is, that the water in Moray sends him every night drunk to bed, or perhaps you'll say it is Myrtilla's health that is intoxicating, for he drinks her at least sixty times a-day. And yet I daresay I think more of charming *somebody* than he of her without mentioning her so often. Having this opportunity I could not think of letting it slip without assuring you that no man on earth is, or can be, so much your devoted slave and faithful humble servant as " B."

The wooing of the charming "somebody" must have rapidly advanced, for in the month of November there had been serious talk of a marriage, the lady's brother having been spoken to on the subject.

Mr Daniel Barbour of Aldourie thus gives his version of the interview with his sister's lover: That upon 17th November 1730. he had occasion to be in company with young Steuart at the house of Master Lun, a Quaker, residing then in Inverness. That Master Steuart took him aside and whispered to him to keep himself sober that night as he had something of consequence to communicate to him. That towards eleven of the clock at night the company broke up, when Steuart joined him in the street, and they went together to the bridge. and as they went along he spoke to him of the affection he had for his sister, and the intention he had to marry her and desired his consent and concurrence. In answer to which Mr Barbour thanked him for the honour he did his family, at the same time advised him to give over thoughts of it, because of the consequences, which would ruin both himself and the lady. To which Steuart replied that he very well knew the consequences if such a thing should come to the knowledge of his friends, but that he would keep the affair a secret, and after it was ended he would go out of the country ; and that he would first apply himself to my Lord Isla,† who had given promises to his friends to do for him, and if that failed he would throw himself over upon his brother ; and if that likewise failed he would go to

* John Roy. This is the celebrated Colonel John Roy Stewart, adherent of Prince Charles in the eventful " Forty-five," noted as one one of the best soldiers in the Prince's service ; also not less celebrated as a Gaelic poet. Many of his best songs were written on the events of 1745-46. After Culloden he made his escape to France in the same ship as the Prince, 20th September 1746.
† Archibald Campbell, Earl of Islay, a Lord of Session, brother and successor to the eminent John Duke of Argyll. Lord Islay was a man of rare attainments, and possessed of great power in Scottish affairs. He was hence frequently termed " King of Scotland."

Rome. Deponed—That Steuart next day came to his house and had a further conversation of the same nature, and made an appointment to meet the same afternoon to make a party at "whisk." That accordingly they met at the house of John Taylor, vintner in Inverness, and the company consisted of Master Steuart, Alexander Baillie, town clerk of Inverness, Lieut. Drapper, John Schaw, merchant in Inverness, and George Mackintosh, a gentleman there. It was concocted among them that he should break up the party about seven o'clock in order to concert further about the proposed marriage, and they adjourned from the company and came to his house, and there Steuart renewed his proposals a third time. Daniel Barbour thereon consented to the marriage, but states to Steuart that there would be a difficulty in getting a minister to marry them, to which Steuart replied that it behoved him to procure a minister, and that he would be married if he should go to Edinburgh. Thereupon Daniel Barbour wrote a letter " addressed to nobody," and which letter was delivered to John Anderson, brewer in Inverness, who was to deliver it to any man who would undertake to marry them.

Matters thus far having been arranged, the next step was to proceed to obtain the necessary clergyman to perform the secret marriage,—and here we continue the narrative as given by the witnesses.

THE START FROM INVERNESS.

Daniel Macbaine, stabler in Inverness. deponed—That some time in the winter was a year he was desired by John Mackay, merchant in Inverness, at nine of the clock one night, between Martinmas and the new year to go along with him out of the town about an affair he was to trust him with, which he would rather do in him than in anybody else. As desired he went to the other side of the water of Ness, where he met the Defender (Sibella Barbour) and the Pursuer (Master Steuart), also the said John Mackay and John Anderson, brewer, now deceast. That the deponent lifted up the Defender in his arms, and put her on horseback behind Master Stuart at his desire. That they then went toward the ferry of Beauly—he following them about a quarter of a mile on foot, being ordered by the Defender to walk at the horse's foot to take care of the Defender. He after a time returned because he could not get a horse to ride on. He heard

nothing spoke of marriage that night, but he suspected that was
their design, and next morning he heard it talked that they were
married.

THE BEAULY FERRYMAN CONTINUES THE NARRATIVE.

Simon Fraser, boatman in Beauly, deponed that he knew the
Defender, but knew not the Pursuer.   In the year 1730, and about
the month of November, Mistress Barbour, in company with John
Mackay, merchant in Inverness, and John Anderson, brewer
there, and another gentleman, came to the ferry at Beauly at
about twelve o'clock at night, and raised him out of his bed in
order to ferry them over the water of Beauly, and Pursuer promised him something to conduct the company the length of the
ferry of Brahan, and accordingly he went along with them to that
place.   When they came to Brahan, they asked if Master Æneas
Morison the minister had passed at that ferry, or if they knew
where he was ; who being told he had not passed, some of the
company suggested that he would be surely in the house of Logie
whither they all went. While at the ferry of Brahan, John Mackay
told the deponent that the young folk that were with him liked
one another and that they wanted Master Morison to marry
them, and that he would no longer keep the secret from him.
When they came to the house of Logie, at Mr Mackay's desire
he went to the house to inquire if Master Morison was there, and
was conducted to the room where he was. He found him in bed at
two o'clock in the morning, and having told him that some Inverness people wanted him, he said not to bring them in till he had
put on his clothes.   That deponent at a window observed Master
Morison go into a room, and twice into the laird of Logie's room
to talk with him, but did not know any thing of their conversation.   That when he came out from Master Morison's room to
the company, that gentleman whom he did not know, seemed uneasy about Master Morison staying so long, and the said gentleman, along with the Pursuer, went into Master Morison's room,
and after a short time came again out to the green, where the
company were standing at a distance, but could not (being dark)
perceive whether Mr Morison was among them or not.   That
the company continued together about a quarter of an hour, rather
less than more.   That the deponent was then called upon by
John Anderson to come up to the company, and when he did so

16

he saw John Mackay kissing the young lady and that young gentleman. He then perceived Master Morison going in at the door of
the house. That immediately thereafter he heard the gentleman he
did not know and Mr Mackay propose that they should, for
secrecy, return by different ways to Inverness but finally agreed
to return all one way by the ferry of Beauly, where they left this
witness. The next morning the witness heard that the gentleman
he knew not was Master John Steuart, son to Master Francis
Steuart, and that he and the lady had been married that night.

THE LAIRD OF LOGIE'S EVIDENCE.

John Tuach of Logie,[*] gave evidence that in the month of November 1730, Master Æneas Morison lodged in his house. That
the deponent saw a letter from Mr Barbour brought by John
Anderson, desiring the person to whom it was addressed under
the denomination of " REVEREND SIR," to marry his sister to a
gentleman. That three days after Master Morison came to deponent's house, he heard several horses at the door of the house
about three o'clock of the morning, and afterwards Mr Anderson
got entrance and went into Master Morison's bedroom and stayed
some short time ; that afterwards Master Morison came several
times to the deponent telling him he was desired to marry Mistress
Barbour to an officer of the army, and desired his advice how he
should act in the affair, which he declined to give, and bid him
act in the matter as he would answer to his bishop. A little
while after that, the same morning, he was informed by his wife
that Kenneth Happie, a servant of the deponent's, informed her
that two persons had been married that morning by Master Morison ; and that very day he went to Brahan, and was informed by
the landlord of the change-house there (William Fraser) that
Master Morison had married Mistress Sibella Barbour to my
Lord Murray's representative ; he also told him that any minister
that would marry these two should have six guineas, and at the
same time enjoined secrecy. He also had heard Master Morison
acknowledge that he had received both money and gold for
marrying a couple that morning he was called for out of deponent's house, and complained afterwards that he was cheated—

* John Tuach of Logie. A respectable family of small estate in Ross-
shire. They were noted for their zealous adherence to Episcopacy and the
non-jurant clergy of that denomination.

expecting that he would have received twenty guineas, whereas he only got nine guineas, and seventeen shillings in silver. Discoursing with Master Morison anent the trouble he was to have in coming to Edinburgh to depone, he told Master Morison " that he would save a good deal of trouble to the deponent and others if he would either say yea or nay—considering that he had got money and that he ought to have given penny's worth, meaning that he should have fixed the marriage." To which he replied " that the deponent had pushed the affair too far, and that he would get no trouble." Deponed--That Master Morison never directly owned that he had married Mistress Barbour to Master Steuart.

THE MINISTER'S MAN.

Donald Chisholm, late servant to Master Æneas Morison, could not speak Scots ; therefore the Commissioners nominated Murdoch Mackenzie, son to John Mackenzie of Tolly, to be his interpreter. Donald Chisholm was then sworn in the Irish language, and deponed—That he knew neither Pursuer nor Defender, and was not taught what evidence to give in this process. That he has not received any reward or promise of reward. And being examined if he was threatened by any person forbidding him to come up and give evidence, deponed—That Master Æneas Morison, his old master, told him if he came up to Edinburgh to be a witness in this cause he would be taken and hanged, but that no other person threatened to dissuade him. He then deponed that about the latter end of November 1730, he saw his then master, Æneas Morison, come out of the house of Logie about three in the morning with some company to the easter end of the house, near the garden, and that he saw two persons standing together in the posture that persons usually are when married, and that their hands were joined in one another, and that the man was standing uncovered. That Master Morison spoke to them some time, and that he heard the man make some return, but did not observe the woman make any. He did not observe what passed betwixt them, being ignorant of the Scots language. Depones—That he has seen several marriages celebrated, and that he apprehends that this was a marriage betwixt the man and woman forsaid, and that he did not know any in the company except his master, Simon Fraser, ferryboat-man at Beauly, and John Anderson in Inverness, now deceast. That after what passed the company went off in haste, and at parting, one of the party gave Master Morison some money, but it was not the person he took to be the bridegroom. He heard shortly thereafter that Mistress Sibella Barbour was the woman married ; he also heard the man's name, but does not remember it.

ANOTHER WITNESS TO THE CEREMONY.

Kenneth Happie, gardener at Logie, deponed--That about the beginning of the month of December 1730, Simon Fraser, ferryman at Beauly, came to the house of Logie about three o'clock of the morning, and called for Master Angus Morison, and got access to the room where deponent and Master Morison were lying, and told Master Morison that the parties with whom he had made an appointment were come. Immediately thereafter, John Anderson, an Inverness man, now deceast, came into the same room and told Master Morison the same message and that the people were wearying for him ; upon which Master Morison desired the deponent to walk out of the room. That he did so, and found on going out of the house the company standing on each side of the door, and that after Master Morison came out he went along with the company to the side of the "yeard," where they continued together about half-an-hour—the men standing uncovered—and, as he apprehended, they were celebrating a marriage, but he did nor observe that any one man and Mistress Barbour stood up together, nor did he hear what passed between them. He knew none of the company save John Anderson, Simon Fraser, and Mistress Barbour. That the same morning he heard that Master John Steuart was the person married to Mistress Sibella Barbour.

THE MORNING AFTER THE CEREMONY.

Robert Scheviz of Muirtown * deponed—That he saw the Pursuer (Steuart) come to the house of Muirtown, which leads from the high-road betwixt the town and Clachnaharry, and that he struck up through a fluther (bog) that was on the way. On being further

---

* Robert Scheviz of Muirtown. This gentleman was one of the chief witnesses in the celebrated trial of Simon Lord Lovat for high treason before the House of Peers in December 1746. He gave most damning evidence as to his knowledge of the various plots that his lordship had been engaged in in the interest of the exiled House of Stuart since 1719 ; his aiding in the escape of John Roy Stewart, who broke out of Inverness jail in 1736, and also his sending by the said Roy Stewart a message to the Pretender "assuring him, whom he called King, of his fidelity, and that he was determined to live and die in that cause."

interrogated, deponed—That Daniel Barbour wrote a letter to him, the contents whereof he did not distinctly remember, but that to the best of his memory it was putting the question if the report of Steuart being fuddled when he was last at his house came from his family, since he judged no misrepresentations would come from his house—to which letter he made no answer.

George Scheviz, younger of Muirtown, states that he saw Master Steuart in his father's house of Muirtown, near Inverness, of a morning. That he did not particularly remember the day, but that by hearsay since, it was the 24th November 1730. That he (Steuart) did not appear to be in drink, but rather looked like one who wanted sleep. That he saw him about nine o'clock of the day, and that he had been about one hour in the house before he saw him ; and then, his stockings having been dirty, he had turned them off and put on a pair of Master Cumming's, his brother's stockings. That he did not hear he had come in boots to the house, and he went without being booted. He believed he brought no boots to the house, for he left his own shoes and stockings there. Deponed upon being interrogated — That Steuart slept for an hour in a chair, and thereafter drank some tea. Thereafter deponent and his brother conveyed him to the end of the town of Inverness. That he ¦did not know where he went, but he said he designed going to the house of Culloden. Further deponed—That he heard the day thereafter that the Pursuer (Steuart) was married to Mistress Barbour.

PUBLIC GOSSIP AS TO THE MARRIAGE.

Katherine Duff (Lady Drummuir *), being examined on behalf

* Katherine Duff, wife of Alexander Duff of Drummuir, and mother of Anna, the Lady Mackintosh of Mackintosh of 1715. Lady Mackintosh lived on till after Culloden, and died circa 1750-1, wife of the last Lachlan Mackintosh of Mackintosh, who died 20th October 1731.

Lady Drummuir, with her daughter the Dowager Lady Mackintosh, at her house, which stood on the west side, now No. 45 Church Street, had the honour of entertaining Prince Charles Edward Stuart for some days preceding the Battle of Culloden ; the night of the Battle the Duke of Cumberland occupied the very same apartments. On an allusion by the Duke to his hostess of this fact, Lady Drummuir, with the spirit of her race, answered, " Very well ! your cousin slept in that bed last night, and you can sleep in it to-night."

We may notice that when the old building " Drummuir House," as it was then called, was pulled down to make room for the present structure, portions of the old pannelling were made into two fine arm-chairs. One of these is now in the possession of Mr Fraser-Mackintosh at Lochardill, Inverness.

of Master Steuart, deponed—That she knew both parties. She
heard that Pursuer while in Inverness was drinking and raking.
Further interrogated as to her knowledge of the Pursuer keeping
company with Barbour and his sister, answered—That she as well
as the whole town believed that the Pursuer and Defender were
married some weeks before the time that they are now said to
have been married, for that there was a long courtship, and that
she has seen them frequently walk together on the streets—he -
conveying her home, and has seen her convey him from her
mother's house down to the stair-foot about the hours of nine and
ten at night. She could not positively remember at what season
of the year it was. Further deponed—That she knew no more of
their courtship or marriage. She heard they went out a-horseback
to be married and that he returned by way of Muirtown, and lay
there drunk ; this was the common report of the town, and that
he was drabbed and full of clay and mire, and that he got clean
clothes from Muirtown's son or some other person in that family.

THE OLD LADY'S DAUGHTER CONTINUES.

Mistress Katherine Duff (aged 20, and daughter of the preceding witness), deponed—That she knew the parties, and that it
was about two years ago that the Pursuer came to the north
country. She heard that the Pursuer was keeping company with
Defender and her friends, and was more frequently in the house
of Mistress Barbour the Defender's mother than in any house in
town except Baillie Stewart's, where he lodged, but neither knew
nor heard that he kept company with the Defender at unseasonable hours. She heard of his coming to Muirtown the morning
of the day of his alleged marriage, and that the lady of Muirtown put him into a chair, where he fell fast asleep.

The rumour of the marriage soon spread through the town of
Inverness, and for some time formed the subject of talk for busy
tongues. Young Steuart's friends soon got to know of the rumours,
and he was taken to task by several of them as to the truth of the
story with which the town was ringing. With one or two boon
companions he told the story quite ingenuously—with his older
friends he prevaricated, and denied the marriage.

John Forbes of Culloden, at whose invitation he came to Inverness, was naturally anxious about the matter, and he states the
result of his interview with Steuart as follows :—

He had frequently seen Master Steuart (the Pursuer), Captain Delaune,* and Master Barbour in company. The Pursuer, with several other gentlemen came into his house in town, where he entertained them with some bottles of wine, and in the meantime Captain Delaune came in after the company was set, meaning to have spoke with the Pursuer; whereupon he (the deponent) desired him to sit down that the company might not be disturbed. That after the said Delaune had sat for some short time, he rose two or three times, but still insisted to speak with Master Steuart, which at last he did in a corner, and then he retired In a few minutes thereafter Master Barbour came in, whom he (deponent) made very welcome and desired to sit down, which he did; and after having drunk some glasses of wine he wanted to speak with Master Steuart. The deponent thereupon insisted that there should be no speaking till they had drunk their bottle; but at the same time, Master Barbour being the man that sat next to Master Steuart, it was not possible to prevent them whispering, and after some time Master Barbour retired. Soon after he was gone Master Steuart proposed hard to go away to an appointment he had to drink a bottle of arrack with Clerk Baillie at his house. To which the deponent answered that he must not go, for he must sup with him, but which he absolutely refused; and he saw no more of the Pursuer till Tuesday thereafter that he came out to Culloden to dine, where at table he fell asleep, upon which the deponent ordered his servants to put him on a bed, which they did. When he awoke, which was about supper time, the deponent asked him some questions, particularly where he had been, to which in a confused manner he replied that he could not tell what he had been doing, but that on Monday night he had gone to some place on the other side of the bridge and spent the night there. The Pursuer stayed there at Culloden till Tuesday night, and dined with him on the Wednesday with Ensign Drapper and Quartermaster Steuart, who had come out of town that day; and as they were at dinner, Borlum came in, and chid Master Steuart for having broke his appointment he had made to play at

* Captain Delaune was a brother-in-law of the Defender. Adjoining the Barbour tombstone in the Chapelyard is one erected to the memory of his wife as follows :—
"THIS STONE IS PLACED HERE | IN MEMORY OF MRS LUCY DELAUNE, | RELICT OF | COL. HENRY DELAUNE, | WHO DIED 27TH OCTOBER 1765.

" whisk " with Captain Delaune and Master Barbour, upon which
Pursuer swore and said it was true, but he had forgot; however,
that after dinner he would go and keep his appointment. The
deponent was thereupon very angry to see the Pursuer take such
an idle resolution, and begged of him that he should not go;
however, a short time thereafter he slipt up his hat and left the
room and went to Inverness without deponent's knowledge, and
Borlum followed him. Soon after he was gone, Baillie Robertson
came in and surprised the deponent with the story of a marriage
that had happened the Monday night at Logie between Master
Steuart and Mistress Barbour. The deponent was thereupon so
confounded that he knew not well what he was doing, but immediately sent his servant Thomas Steuart to town to find out the
Pursuer, and not to part with him till he brought him to
Culloden. That accordingly Thomas Steuart went into town and
did not return until the next morning about six o'clock, when he
reported that he had searched all the houses in town where he
suspected he might be found, and had called frequently at Capt.
Delaune's house, but was refused access; but that at last, by
means of a servant of the family, he discovered that Master
Steuart was there, and after calling him to come out and speak
to him, he refused to come out to Culloden that night, but promised to be out next morning, which he accordingly did. As
soon as he came deponent carried him up to his closet and told
him the story he had heard of the marriage, and asked him what
truth was in it. He then in the most solemn manner and with
the most horrid oaths and imprecations, with his hands lifted up
to heaven, said he was as innocent as the child unborn, and not
married to the lady. Thereafter they returned to the hall, where,
as they sat at dinner, Borlum came in and asked Master Steuart
if he did not remember that that was the Assembly night, to
which the Pursuer answered that he did, and was to go to town
after dinner. Whereon deponent took Master Steuart into the
next room and examined him more closely, because he suspected
that notwithstanding what he had said that he had not told him
the truth; and thereupon he (the Pursuer) renewed the same
oaths, denying the marriage and asserting his innocence; upon
which he (deponent) said to him, " John, go into the town this
night to the Assembly; take your leave of the ladies in public,

and as you wish me or yourself well, or expect to find favour with
my Lord Murray and his family, return to me this night; I shall
have horses and servants ready for you that you may go off to-
morrow morning, and if possible be with your father before the
villainous story comes to his ears--and this, with a solemn oath,
he promised to do.   Borlum and Steuart then left and went together to the town, but the Pursuer did not return, nor did he
speak to him ever since.

A BOON COMPANION'S STORY.

Shaw Mackintosh of Borlum * deponed—That about the time
libelled, in the winter of 1730, and three or four days after report
ran in the country of the Pursuer's being married to the Defender,
the deponent went from Inverness to the house of Culloden,
where the Pursuer was, and, as the deponent was informed, had
been sent for by Culloden to know the truth of the report then
going.   That some little time after deponent came to the house,
and after dinner Culloden carried Master Steuart from the company, and they went together by themselves to another apartment
in the house, and after a short stay they returned to the company.
That Culloden said in deponent's hearing, after that Master
Steuart had gone out of the room, that he believed there was no
truth in the report of the marriage, for that Steuart had denied it
to him with imprecations.   Deponed—That Pursuer and deponent
came from Culloden house to Inverness the same evening, being a
Thursday.   That the deponent, being the Pursuer's intimate com-
rade, did take the freedom by the way to talk over the story of
his marriage, and said he should be sorry if such a thing was true,
that he should take such a step without consulting his parents
—which he knew would be disagreeable to them, and that such a
report could not rise out of nothing—and pressed him to tell the
truth of the whole story, and what had passed betwixt him and
Culloden, for he supposed that Culloden had had him upon the
black stone, or words to that purpose ; whereupon Steuart replied
to deponent that he would be ingenuous with him, though he
would not be so to any others save the Defender's near relations
and those who already knew it, and then told deponent that he

* Shaw Mackintosh of Borlum, second son of Brigadier Mackintosh, who
led the Highland army into England in 1715.

17

was married to Sibella Barbour, and would own her as his wife in spite of all the world, and expressed himself on that occasion in strong and affectionate terms towards the Defender—but, in the meantime, it was proper for him to conceal it. The deponent told Pursuer that since Baillie Stewart the Earl's doer, and many others in the country had heard of the story, it was idle for him to keep it up. The Pursuer said he had been recommended by the Earl and Countess of Murray to the Earl of Ilay, when he was last in Scotland, who had promised to do for him, and that he had expected by the Duke of Argyle, the Earl of Ilay, and the Lord Advocate's influence to have a commission in the army, and how soon he obtained it and was settled, he would be in a condition to live without the assistance of his parents, if they continued still to be disobliged, and until then he thought it proper to conceal his marriage ; but then he would own it and live with the Defender all his life. Deponed—That he advised Steuart to return the same evening, and be ingenuous with Culloden as he had been with the deponent, as he could be of greater use to him than any other he could lay stress on in the country in making up the peace with his friends, but Pursuer declined going that night because, as he said, he had an appointment at a dancing in Inverness, where Mistress Barbour was to be present. That, after coming to town, they met together at the dancing, where Mistress Barbour and a good many other ladies were present. That, after coming to that house, the Pursuer told the deponent that he had heard Baillie Stewart was at that occasion to propose to Defender that she should sign a writing disclaiming or owning a marriage betwixt him and her, and thereafter intreated the deponent that he would immediately acquaint the Defender, and tell her from him to sign no writing, as she regarded him or herself, let her say what she would. Deponent accordingly delivered the message to Mistress Barbour, who seemed to be a little surprised, not knowing (as he imagined) he was let into the secret, and said to the deponent, though she had no regard for the Pursuer, yet for her own sake she would sign no writing. Steuart (the Pursuer) told him his reason for employing him in that message was that he did not care to be seen speaking with the Defender in that public place. Deponed—That at that meeting the Pursuer desired of him to press him in public company to sleep with him that night, telling him at the same time it was his design to bed with Defender, as he had not had the opportunity. That, after the Assembly was over, the Pursuer, himself, and others went to a tavern, where he (the deponent) took occasion to acquit himself of his commission, and desired the Pursuer to sleep with him, which he agreed to do—refusing invitations from Baillie Stewart, where he usually lodged, and others who invited him. They left the company, and went together to the tavern where the deponent lodged. They sat up for some little time for Master Drapper, who had told them in the company, before they parted, that he would come to their quarters to drink a bottle of wine with them. That he was uneasy at this proposition, but would not refuse lest it might increase his suspicion. That Master Drapper not coming so soon as they expected, they both stript and went to bed. That Master Drapper and Quartermaster Stewart came after they were a-bed. The deponent and Pursuer had concerted that they should feign themselves asleep that they might go away, but Master Drapper sat down on the bedside and awaked Pursuer, that they drank a bottle of wine together and then they went off. That immediately thereafter, the Pursuer, who had been all the while uneasy, rose up from his bed, and desired deponent to do the same. That they dressed, and he went along with the Pursuer to Daniel Barbour's house, where Pursuer told deponent that Mistress Barbour and some of her friends waited for him—desiring the deponent to keep his lodgings open, that he might have access thereto any time he came—and then he saw Pursuer enter the house by the door, which was cast to but not bolted, and then deponent returned to his own lodgings. Deponed—That Pursuer returned to deponent's lodgings about five o'clock that morning, as he thought, and is very sure it was before daylight. Pursuer told deponent that he had been with Defender, and that he was the happiest man alive. Deponed further—That the same day, being Friday, Burdsyards* came to Inverness, as he thought, upon the alarm of the marriage, and kept pretty close company

* Robert Urquhart of Burdsyards, Forres—now incorporated in the estate of Sanquhar. Mr Urquhart was a witness in this case, but his evidence only amounts to a statement of Steuart's denial of his marriage; and on Burdsyards urging him to disclaim it, Steuart replied that " there was no need of a disclamation, for the thing never was in being."

with the Pursuer, who told the deponent that Burdsyards had questioned him pretty hard upon his marriage, which he had denied; but told the deponent that he had so much perplexed him he would own it : but he advised Pursuer, because of his own project to conceal it, that if he was to own it after so long a denial, his best way was to throw himself at the Earl of Murray and his parents' feet, and own it to them, and probably his lady mother's clemency would be of use to him.   At a subsequent meeting the same day or next with Pursuer, he told him that he had still denied the marriage to Burdsyards, who carried Steuart out of town with him on Saturday or Sunday.   While they remained in town he heard Burdsyards had slept with him, and, so far as deponent knows, the Pursuer never again returned to Inverness, nor has he seen him since.

ANOTHER BOON COMPANION.

George Mackintosh, son of John Mackintosh, advocate, deponed—That he knew both parties. That towards the end of 1730 he had frequently seen the Pursuer in company with Daniel Barbour and others ; that he himself was with them, and that their ordinary exercise was talking, dancing, playing at cards, and drinking.   Sometimes they parted at good hours and at other times at unseasonable hours.   He saw the Pursuer once drunk in Master Barbour's house in company with Masters Drayson, Barbour, Alexander Baillie, and himself. That Master Barbour pressed the Pursuer to drink, and heard Master Barbour afterwards say that his design of bringing the Pusuer to his house was to make him drunk.   Deponed—There were further in company Mistress Barbour, junior (the Defender), Mistress Mackintosh, spouse to Collector Mackintosh, and Mistress Baillie, spouse to Alexander Baillie, town clerk ; and that the women went off a long time before the rest of the company. Deponed—That he heard the Pursuer express himself very kindly of the Defender.   He knew nothing of the Defender's character but what is highly virtuous ; and in reply to question if he heard anything to the prejudice of her character, replied that he was not obliged to answer that question, because he thought them idle and without any foundation.

A LADY FRIEND OF MISTRESS BARBOUR.

Anne Baillie, daughter of William Baillie, Commissary of Inverness, and wife of Duncan Grant, junior, merchant in Inverness, deponed—That she knew the parties ; that she had been sometimes in company with the Pursuer while he was in Inverness. That one night, in company with the Pursuer and Defender in Mistress Barbour's mother's house till one or two in the morning playing at cards. That deponent thought Master Steuart was perfectly sober and behaved exceedingly mannerly, and talked very affectionately to the Defender, and that on that night she thought he talked more affectionately than she had heard him do at any other time ; that he hung about her neck, and called her many times his " dear Sibby "—he said grace before and after supper, and served the company at table—and from his familiarity, and Pursuer's seeming fondness and regard for the Defender, she apprehended that they might have been married. This happened about the first eight days of November 1730.

DEFENDER JOCULAR IN HIS CUPS.

In the month of October preceding (Mrs Grant continues), as she and Mistress Deborah Dunbar were of a night going down the Kirk Street, the Defender came from the house of John Taylor, vintner—having spied them passing by—without hat, sword, or cane (and she supposed, from that circumstance, was somewhat in liquor)—and walked along with them to the said Mistress Dunbar's lodgings, and in that lodging, in a jocular manner in the presence of the said Mistress Dunbar, proposed marriage to her (the deponent), and said he had ten guineas, and fifty shillings in silver, which he had gained at cards, and that he would give the ten guineas to Master Jameson * the non-juring minister at Inverness, or any other minister that would marry them. To which she replied, that the fifty shillings would not last him long if he parted with the ten guineas. She further said to him he would do well to take care to whom he made such offers, lest some time or other he might be held to his offer ; and further deponed, that when she had occasion afterwards frequently of

* The Rev. Robert Jameson was settled as Episcopal clergyman in Inverness about 1710, and continued his ministry there till 1734. He left his library by deed of mortification to the Episcopal congregation in Inverness, and among the managing committee named in the deed are several of the witnesses in this Barbour case. Some years ago the library was disposed of for a trifling sum by the managers of the congregation of St John's, Inverness.

seeing him, and sober, he never renewed that proposal, and she
never afterwards saw him drunk. She saw him frequently in Defender's company, and she always heard him talk affectionately
and respectfully of Mistress Barbour.

ANOTHER WITNESS'S STATEMENT AS TO THE MARRIAGE.

John Stewart,* Quartermaster in the Grey Dragoons, deponed
—That in November 1730 it was currently reported in and about
the town of Inverness that the Pursuer and Defender were married, but that the first time he put the question to Steuart, and
for several times thereafter, for three days, he denied it ; but
shortly afterwards he begged Pursuer to tell him what was in
the affair that made so much noise. and he answered him in
these words, to the best of his remembrance : " Dear Johnnie, I
am afraid there is too much in it. What shall I do ?" or " How
shall I behave ? " or words to that purpose. Some time thereafter Steuart acknowledged that he and Mistress Barbour went to
Master Morison (a deposed minister, as he was told) and desired
him to perform the ceremony of marriage betwixt them or words
to that purpose, which he refused to do ; upon which the Pursuer had said that he and Defender would marry themselves, and
desired Master Morison would give them a blessing. That
Master Morison said, " The blessing of God and mine go with
you ; " upon which John Mackay, then present, said it was
enough. Deponent further said—That upon the report running
through Inverness, he went to Mistress Barbour's house, and
asked her if it was fact ; and upon her denial, deponent desired of her to write a letter to him signifying the same, which he
would send south to prevent Pursuer's friends being alarmed upon
such a report. To which she replied that the deponent was to
give credit to her word, and if he did not she did not think herself obliged to write upon the subject ;—that the witness replied
he was satisfied with what she said. That Mistress Barbour then

---

* Quartermaster Stewart. This was John Roy Stewart, see *ante* page
119. He held an appointment in this cavalry Regiment, in which he served
with considerable distinction. On application for transference to the command of a company in the Royal Highlanders then vacant, his claims were
overlooked. He thereupon deserted from his own Regiment, went over to
France, fought against the British in Flanders, and in 1745 joined the
standard of Prince Charles Stuart.

said if the Pursuer (Steuart) would desire it of her to write a letter that she would do it. That a little time after he met with Master Steuart, to whom he communicated the conversation that had passed between Defender and him, and told Pursuer it would be prudent in him to ask such a letter from the lady in order to satisfy his friends, to which he condescended ; and ac-cordingly they went to the Defender's house together, when deponent again broached the subject. Whereupon Master Steuart said it was an idle story and was not worth his notice, and it was idle in any lady to ask such a thing of him, and he refused it- This conversation happened before Pursuer had said to him, " There is too much in it," as above set down. Further deponed —That on a Sunday towards the end of November 1730, he, along with Ensign Drapper of Handyside's Regiment, went along with Pursuer to Mistress Barbour's ; that, that very day Steuart was to leave Inverness, as he accordingly did ; that the conversation turned upon the report of the marriage, and he heard the Pursuer say to the Defender, " Dear Sibby ! conceal it from all the world till you hear from me from the south." That deponent was enjoined by Burdsyards and some others in the company they had left, when they went to Defender's house not to let Steuart stay with her, but to haste back ; and Chamberlain Russell came after them to the room to hasten them away. That at parting, the deponent saw the Pursuer and Defender embrace one another affectionately, and shed tears each of them, at the seeing of which he was also affected. Deponed further-- That some time after, in Edinburgh, when the Pursuer was asking deponent's advice if or if not he should write to the Defender, he (the deponent) gave it as his opinion that he ought not to write to her. That he doubted not but at that time the Pursuer might have expressed himself affectionately towards the Defender, and acknowledged that he had heard him upon several occasions both before and after the time they were said to be married express himself affectionately towards the Defender. Deponed—That when he parted with Pursuer, who was going on board ship for Holland, he said to deponent to take care of his character in general, as he could, for him ; and if he could see the Defender (whom he called " Sibby "), to make an apology for not writing to her, and to tell her that he (the deponent) had dissuaded him from it. Deponent thereon told the Pursuer that he was straitened on seeing the Defender for fear of disobliging the family of Murray Deponed—That some short time before the marriage was said to be celebrated he had seen several letters that had passed between Pursuer and Defender, and the letter produced in process, of 7th of June last, beginning "My dearest Sibby," he took it to be very like the handwriting of Pursuer.

EVIDENCE OF BROTHER-IN-LAW OF DEFENDER.

Henry Delaune, captain in Colonel Harrison's Regiment, depones—That upon the 23rd November 1730, the Pursuer came to his house about seven o'clock at night, and told him that he and the Defender resolved to go that night and be married, and asked witness to along with him ; to which he replied that Pursuer would do better to let it alone that night because of the badness of the weather, and that if he would delay it he would go along with him to-morrow morning to any part of Scotland. The Pursuer supped with deponent on Wednesday thereafter, being the 25th of November, when he told witness that he was married to Defender, and that the minister that married them was like all other priests, for that he had billed him out of a crown in regard that he had refused a bank-note—not liking to take paper—and was obliged to give him five guineas. Deponed—That on Thursday night (26th), he was sent for to Master Barbour's house between eleven and twelve o'clock, being desired by Master Barbour to be present at the young folk's bedding.* That deponent was actually in the house when Pursuer came there about two o'clock of the Friday morning. There were present Master Barbour and his lady, Master Mackay, Pursuer and Defender, and deponent. After drinking a glass of wine in the outer-room, the Defender retired to her bed-chamber along with Mistress Barbour (sen.) ; and he (the deponent), along with the foresaid company, went soon thereafter into the said room with

* This custom, which at one time was very common among all ranks in the Highlands, has now happily fallen largely into disuse. We have been present on several of these occasions, where considerable rough fun prevailed—the flinging of the bride's stockings among the gathering being a leading item of the business ; while the bridegroom rewarded the friendliness of the company by distributing among them flowing bumpers from a bottle provided for the purpose.

the Pursuer, when he undressed himself and went to bed to the Defender ; and deponent saw the Pursuer and Defender sit up in bed, while he and the company drank a glass of wine or two to the health of the young folk. The deponent remained in Master Barbour's house till between six and seven in the morning, when he went along with Pursuer to Borlum's quarters ; and the Pursuer told the witness by the way there that he was the happiest man in the world.

STEUART'S FLIGHT FROM THE NORTH.

Young Steuart was soon, on report of his marriage scandal spreading, hurried off from the north by the friends of his family. On Sunday, 29th November 1730, he set out from Inverness, accompanied by James Russell, Connage, chamberlain in Petty to the Earl of Murray. Mr Russell " saw him over Spey " on his way to Edinburgh. No sooner had he arrived there than he found it convenient to deny the marriage that had taken place in the north to his relatives, and having through their influence obtained an appointment in the army, he soon sailed for Holland to join his Regiment.

Early in 1731, at the instance of himself or his family, the action of " Declarator of Freedom " was begun for the purpose of annulling the marriage ; while Miss Barbour commenced her action for " Declarator and Adherence," affirming the marriage to be true and valid. Before the actions were raised, as we have already stated in the early part of this narrative, there were diplomatic attempts made by the Pursuer's friends to come to some compromise with the Defender. An agent was sent to the north with a commission to take evidence in the affair, Commissary Stewart being employed for that purpose.

DIPLOMACY.

John Baillie, Writer to the Signet,* deponed—That he was with Commissary Stewart in the Town-House of Inverness at a solemnity kept there on the occasion of the King's birthday ; and after they had drunk some glasses to public healths, Commissary

---

* John Baillie, W.S., was the 3rd of Leys, Inverness. He was the father of Dr G. Baillie, who was succeeded in Leys by his son Colonel John Baillie, who represented the Inverness Burghs in the first Reform Parliament, 1832–33.

Stewart took him aside, and told him he wanted to see the Defender, and thought witness a proper person to introduce him, since he was to cause summon the lady before the Commissaries of Edinburgh, and did not care to do it abruptly without giving previous notice ; but as the affair in question of the marriage was like to make a great noise, and would cost a great deal of money, which his, the Commissary's friends, would expend to know whether it were a good marriage, he thought it more prudent in Mistress Barbour and her friends to disclaim it than to stand trial ;—and if it was so agreed to, he doubted not the lady would get a bonnie thing, or a sum of money, which she would be sure of, though he had not the money himself to give her, or a direct commission for it. To which the deponent replied that he would go along with the Commissary to see the lady, but would not mention anything else to her or her friends without some authority, since he believed they would not accept of money. The Commissary allowed him to mention the above, which he did, to Daniel Barbour—not as the deponent had received the proposals from any other person, but as proceeding from himself as a friend—but Master Barbour assured the witness he would not propose any such thing to his sister, for he knew she would accept of no money whatsomever, not the greatest sum that could be mentioned.

" MEPHISTOPHELES."

The Rev. Æneas or Angus Morison, the non-juring minister of Contin, is the Mephistopheles of Sibby Barbour's romance. Morison, although an Episcopalian, managed by some means to retain the church of Contin after the Revolution. He was summoned before the Presbytery for some part he is said to have taken in the rising of 1715 and other illegal proceedings, and, refusing to appear before the reverend court, he was deposed, and the church of Contin was declared vacant. He continued, however, preaching in meeting-houses, and celebrated marriages and baptisms in the parishes of Contin, Fodderty, and Urray, until, in 1716, he was brought before the Circuit Court at Inverness, and sentenced—a sentence that never was enforced. Mr Morison died at Castle-Leod, Strathpeffer, about 1739.

His conduct in the case of Mistress Barbour reflects very unfavourably on his character as a clergyman. He prevaricated to

a great extent, as will appear from admissions in writings under
his own hand, and from the evidence that follows, given by witnesses of considerable standing and undoubted honour—many
of them friends and patrons of the parson, and of the same religious persuasion.

MORISON'S STORY AS TOLD TO JOHN BAILLIE.

John Baillie, W.S., gave further evidence, and deponed—That
he was in company with Master Æneas Morison both at Master
Mackenzie of Dachmaluag's house, at the Ferry of Kessock, and
at Baillie Alves's * house in Inverness, as he thought in October
1731. The first two meetings were accidental, and the third he
was called to by Daniel Barbour to meet with Master Morison
by Commissary Stewart's appointment. At Dachmaluag's house
he took occasion to talk with Morison on the subject of the marriage, who told him a long story that he had been written to by
Daniel Barbour or some other person to come and marry his
sister to an English officer, and had refused to do so; but that
afterwards he was written to again, but the deponent did not re
member whether he agreed to come again or not,—only he
thought Morison told him that he had acquainted his bishop of
what he had done in the affair, which would exonerate him in his
conscience,—and then the conversation ceased. Some days
thereafter he met Morison accidentally at Kessock, and he
showed deponent a letter or two he had from Commissary Stewart
upon the affair, and desiring him to come to Inverness to meet
him, and told witness he was going there. Next day he met
Morison at Baillie Alves's house in presence of several gentlemen
on both sides, where Master Morison was interrogated by both
parties, as to the question of the marriage. He answered that a
young, lusty, blooming gentleman whom he did not know, but
called himself an English officer, with whose countenance Morison
was frighted, came to his bedside at Logie, desiring the minister
to marry him with a young lady who was at the door, but Morison
refused at first; but the gentleman pressed him so hard, being

* Baillie Alves. A merchant in Inverness, and proprietor of Shiplands,
His son, Dr John Aives, was principal practitioner in Inverness for some
years : one of his daughters married, 1796, George Inglis of Kingsmills;
another daughter married William Arbuthnott, Lord Provost of Edinburgh, and who was created a baronet.

flusht with passion, that he agreed to come out to them, and that accordingly he did come.   That the said young lady and gentleman came before him in the fields at the end of John Tuach's house and joined hands together, and (as he believed) took the matrimonial engagement together, but that he (the minister) was so frighted that he could neither remember nor repeat the marriage solemnities as he usually did in such cases, but that they themselves, having sought his blessing or benediction, he said to them "God bless you! and go your ways."   The minister being then asked if he did declare them married persons, he replied that (to the best of witness's recollection) he did not doubt but he did so if they asked him, and would give a declaration to that purpose for every day in the year, for he knew what such a marriage as this would be described or thought by the canon law, whatever the laws of the country might make of it, and that he declared his sentiments of it to his own bishop, which were (to the best of the deponent's memory) that it would be a subsisting marriage by canon law.   In reply to a further question put to Master Morison, If he knew Master Steuart the Pursuer, he answered, That he knew none of the family of Murray further than he read of them in history, and that he did not know Master Steuart the Pursuer had a commission in the army or served any other station at the time, but thought he had heard him on some occasion express his inclination of going into the army.

A FRIENDLY WITNESS TO PURSUER.

John Stewart, W.S.,* Commissary of Inverness, deponed—That he knew both Pursuer and Defender. He wrote a letter to Master Æneas Morison desiring to be informed by him of the truth whether he had married the parties in this case, to which he returned an answer; but whether the answer was addressed to him or jointly to another, he could not be positive till he searched his papers.   Deponed further—That he never made any proposal to Daniel Barbour or the Defender of giving her a sum of money in allowing a decreet of Declarator of Freedom to go against her, nor had he any authority to do so; only he remembered that in a conversation with Master Baillie he said that if Master Baillie, as

* John Stewart, W.S., acted as agent for the Earl of Murray and other northern proprietors.

of himself, being a wellwisher of the lady, could bring about an overtour from the other party as to the trial of the marriage and preventing the charge thereof, he (the deponent) would use his endeavours to procure her a compliment. Further deponed— That he believed he did desire Master Mackenzie the minister, to write Master Morison to the same purpose that he (the deponent) had wrote him ; and he thought Master Mackenzie did so, and had a return from Master Morison which he showed to the deponent. Further interrogated, he deponed—That the Pursuer never did acknowledge to him his marriage either by word or writ.

A CLERICAL WITNESS.

Master John Williamson,* minister of the Gospel at Kilcowie, deponed—That he knew the Lady Defender, but not the Pursuer. That some short time before Christmas last he was in company with Master Æneas Morison in the house of Kilcowie, where he took occasion to expostulate with him upon a report which deponent had heard that Master Morison had celebrated a marriage betwixt the forenamed parties ; and the deponent having said to him that if he had celebrated such a clandestine marriage, it would be a grievance to him and a reproach upon the clergy, Master Morison replied that it would be a marriage in Moses' time, or in the time of the Council of Nice, whatever might be made of it by the laws of Scotland. Deponed further—That Master Morison's wife meeting the witness one day at Contin market, she accused him for not going to visit her husband—his brother—in his present distress, on account that Captain Monro of Culcairn had orders to apprehend him with a party, on account of having celebrated marriage between Pursuer and Defender ; to which he made an apology of having business, although he had great inclination to visit him. Interrogated by Mr Stewart, Procurator, Whether or not he (the deponent) or any other person,

---

* The Rev. John Williamson. This non-juring clergyman seems to have acted as chaplain to the family of Kilcoy, and also ministered to the Episcopalians in the parish of Kilearnan. In 1726 a process was raised against him by the Presbyterian party, but it came to nothing. He appears to have drifted in 1737 to Gairloch, on the west coast of Ross, and ultimately to the Island of Lewis, greatly exercising the Presbyterian brethren in the various places by his being "active in preventing and drawing aside the people from attending their ordinances."

to his knowledge, offered a reward in money, victuall, or other
ways to Master Morison or his wife, at that or any other time, on
condition that he would grant a certificate of the said marriage,
or that he would grant the same without any consideration whatever ?—Replied in the negative, and that he never spoke to
Morison or his wife on the subject, nor did any other person to
his knowledge.

ANOTHER WITNESS ON MORISON'S STORY.

John Stewart,[*] merchant and late Baillie of Inverness, deponed
amongst other items of his evidence—That he never had any
letter from Master Morison directed to himself concerning the
celebration of the marriage libelled, but remembers to have had a
letter from the said Morison to Commissary Stewart, which he
(deponent) read, and, as he thought, it contained a denial of the
marriage. Further deponed—That he knew nothing of threats
or promises to induce him to deny the celebration of the marriage
upon the part of the Pursuer, but that he has heard the said
Morison and his wife say that such threats and promises were
made to them upon the part of the Defender to make him give a
certificate of the said marriage, and that he has heard the same
frequently—and that it could be proved, he thought. The witness
did exert himself as a friend and servant of the Earl of Murray's
in expiscating the truth of that story, though he was not desired
to do the same by any person ; but the Pursuer being lodged in
his house, he thought himself obliged to take some care of him.
Deponed—That in Baillie Alves's house in Inverness, Master
Barbour asked Master Morison if he had married the Pursuer to
an English officer of the name of Steuart, and that he answered,
that the first time he was spoke or wrote to upon the subject by
Master Barbour that it was to an officer of a name different to
that of Steuart ; but when deponent spoke to Morison at the
house of Kilcowie, he (Morison) mentioned one Steuart, a gentleman. or officer in the army, a Borderer. Morison also owned
that Defender and a gentleman came to Logie's house, that the
gentleman was muffled up in a greatcoat ; by his speech he
knew him to be a Scotsman, and therefore he refused to marry
them lest he should be trepanned. Upon which the lady and
gentleman made a fashion of marrying themselves, and that he

* John Stewart. See *ante* page 117.

then desired them to go, and God be with them. Whereupon the lady said, " Is this all we are to get ? " and Mr Mackay, who was present, said, " Sibby, it is enough ! " ·

For the part of John Steuart the Pursuer, objection was taken to the next witness—Donald Mackenzie of Kilcowie—for that it was offered to be proved that he had given partial counsel and assist- ance in the cause by collecting information from persons called as witnesses, and others, in order to the founding and carrying on this cause to serve the Defender ;—that he had tampered with several of the witnesses, more particularly with the pretended celebrator of the alleged marriage and his wife, to give declarations as if the said Morison had celebrated a marriage betwixt the said parties, and made him sign some declaration thereanent. The objec- tion was considered by the Commissaries, and they allowed Kil cowie's evidence to be received.

KILCOY'S EVIDENCE.

Donald Mackenzie of Kilcowie * deponed—That he never gave any assistance to Defender in getting information from persons called as witnesses in this cause, and in reply to interro- gation, If he obtained any declaration from the pretended cele- brator of the alleged marriage and his wife in favour of Mistress Barbour ? deponed—That he had received by the hands of Master Morison's wife a missive letter, unsubscribed, but which he knew to be holograph of Master Morison, addressed to the lairds of Highfield and Ord, which he now produced, and is dated 21st December 1730. He received the letter the day thereafter. That he was very much importuned by Morison's wife to meet with her husband, and at last was prevailed upon by her tears to yield to her request. That she told the deponent the reasons of the meeting she apprehended to be, that he might hear from her husband's mouth, and acquaint the late Lord Seaforth of the story of Master Steuart's marriage as far as Master Morison was concerned,—and as to which she referred the deponent to the contents of the letter then delivered to him. That on the next day he met with Morison at Kinettas, a small town near the house. Morison asked deponent if he had seen Lord Seaforth, and if his

* Donald Mackenzie, 5th of Kilcoy.

Lordship had shown him a letter which he (Morison) had written
him, desiring him to send deponent, or Highfield, or Ord to discourse with him concerning Master Steuart's marriage—adding
that any other person sent by his Lordship would not be accept-
able, nor could he talk so freely with them on that subject. To
which deponent answered that Lord Seaforth had shown him the
letter.   Master Morison asked further of deponent if Master
Forbes of Culloden was importuning the late Seaforth to know if
there was any marriage betwixt Pursuer and Defender. The deponent told him he did. Whereupon Master Morison told the
witness that the late Lord Seaforth had communed with him on
the subject and seemed displeased with his answers, charging
him with disingenuity (he sometimes seeming to acknowledge
and deny the same facts). Deponed further—That Master
Morison wrote with his own hand, and of his own dictating, a
declaration concerning said marriage, and signed the same, and to
the doing of which deponent gave him no assistance or direction :
and the said declaration Morison gave to witness, desiring him to
give it to the late Lord Seaforth—which deponent accordingly
did. On interrogation anent Master Morison's condition in that
conversation and while he wrote said declaration, replied—That
to his observation he was in his ordinary state of health and
and reason, so as he had known him for years. Deponed further
—That he asked Master Morison what he meant by keeping himself so obscured in that little hut? he answered, that, being informed that Monro of Kincardine, commander of one of the
lesser Independent Companies, had a warrant to apprehend his
person, and for preventing his arrestment he chose to keep himself obscure and retired. Further, witness deponed—That at the
celebration of the marriage Morison received from the bridegroom,
or some other for him, three guineas and seventeen shillings, and
that getting the money in the dark, he fancied it was twenty
guineas. This was truth, as he should answer to God.

The following is the missive letter referred to in Kilcoy's
evidence :—

"HONOURED SIR,—I am unjustly treated in Master Steuart's story. It
is true that when I was at Kilcowie last year a certain person called me to
Andrew Tulloch's, and showed a letter from Daniel Barbour intreating
marriage to his sister. The letter went back with a refusal ; and seeing

Daniel again at your house, I called him and asked his meaning. He told me it was an officer, and that there was reason for privacy.

"I parted him with a refusal after midnight, and at Tuach's house. I declare it was not by appointment. Some of them were at my bedside or I knew. The gentleman came in single. I asked him what he was. He said he was an English-born officer in the army, and asked marriage service of me with Mistress Barbour. 1 asked him, why so obscurely? He told me he feared displeasure of some superior officers, and intended to keep it secret for a year, till he would make his case good with these; that they intended to go soon till Killchuan and leave her for a time, but if he had not his business now he feared a disappointment. I declare I declined him : by this time she was entering the door, and I resisted. Before that motion ceased we were at the head of the house, and they put themselves in the situation usual with parties expecting church service. I told them expresssly that they might marry if they pleased, but that they needed not expect the ceremony of me. It is true their zeal pitied me, so as leaving them I said, 'God Almighty bless you !' All the while I knew not that he was such a man as he is called now. They may be married, or not married, but I refused my part, viz. the ceremony. Now that which I call the ceremony—first, a proper prayer concluding with the Lord's Prayer; a sermon on the real notion and incumbent duties of marriage; and to end with the proper benediction, viz. 'The grace of our Lord,' etc.—I absolutely refused. There was present with them but one man, and if he be honest he will agree to what I say. They tell me there were gazers, but I am sure not within distance of hearing, or perfect seeing, else I would have seen them for it was half-moon. It must have been they that spread the story, but falsely as to my part. It is true I saw them join hands and interchanging the matrimonial vow. If that be really a marriage before God in case they come together, I leave that decision to divines. I fancy Isaac had no more. But how can I be called in question when I denied my part. I had two reasons to write this to Kilcowie, Highfield, and Ord by your care—first, because so many false stories spread ; secondly, altho' I be persuaded that Seaforth has good will to do me assistance as best he can, yet there are that to divert him (I meet St Paul's lot), who reckoning his   , took false friends for the worst of them. Except Kilcowie, Highfield, and Ord, and another besides Seaforth for my chief friends, I find them not. I wish therefore that it please Kilcowie if he can bring Highfield and Ord to come to Brahan to-morrow, and apply him therefore, by his last letter, that he is anxious, not willing to displease me, and willing to please his friend Culloden, which both may be done. If more of you come by Seaforth's desire, and if he send any other I will not trust any but one of you three. What I said is truth. If there will be any more for satisfying the question, I will not trust to write but will trust it to Seaforth by one of you, which may cease the trouble. And you will see by Seaforth's letter that he will be pleased with one or all of you to see him.—Your very obedient humble servant, ——— ———, 21 Decr.—Scruple not that I do not subscribe on this point till I be out of terror."

Addressed thus : "To the Lairds of Kilcowie, Highfield, and Ord."

19

EARL OF SEAFORTH'S EVIDENCE.

William Earl of Seaforth * deponed—That he knew both Pursuer and Defender. Sometime in December 1730 he got from
Master Mackenzie of Kilcowie, at his house at Brahan, a declaration signed by Æneas Morison concerning a marriage betwixt
Master Steuart and Mistress Sibella Barbour—which declaration
is produced. He also received letters from Morison ; has seen
him write, and knows the declaration exhibited to be holograph
of Morison. Deponed further—That it was commonly reported
and believed in that country that the Pursuer and Defender were
married, and the deponent himself believed it from the common
report. Being shown a missive letter exhibited and addressed to
the Lairds of Kilcowie, Highfield, and Ord, deponed—That he
believed all the said letter to be holograph of Master Morison.
Deponed—That Mistress Barbour has the character in the
country and amongst all his acquaintances of a virtuous young
lady, without any blemish.

*Declaration mentioned in Seaforth's evidence, the tenor as
follows :—*

"I, Master Æneas Morison, Minister of the Gospel in
" the Diocese of Ross, declares that ——— Steuart, is
" married with Mistress Sibella Barbour, and that I declared
" them so of — December current 1730. As witness these
" at Kinettas, 22 December 1730, by me subscribed,

"ÆNEAS MORISON."

FURTHER EVIDENCE OF JOHN STEWART, W.S.

John Stewart, W.S., being again sworn and examined anent
letters and papers in relation to the marriage libelled, said—That
after diligent search he had no writing in his possession which
could be probative of the marriage unless it be the following,
exhibited by him, viz., a missive letter from Master Æneas
Morison to deponent, dated the 5th of January 1731 ; a letter by
said Morison directed to Master James Mackenzie, minister of
the Gospel, enclosed with the other, and a list of money affairs—
of gold to Master Morison for private marriages—also a letter to

---

* William, 5th Earl of Seaforth, who took part in the rising of 1715, and
was known among his clan as " Black William " (" *Uilleam Dubh* ").

deponent from Morison dated 26th February 1731, with a paper therein enclosed without date or subscription, beginning with the words "You must not lett any man see this snippat;" also another letter by said Morison to deponent, whereof two pages are on one paper and one page on a separate paper, but neither of them signed. Of which missive first mentioned the tenor is as follows :—

"DEAR SIR,—I received your friendly letter. I am sorry that you doubted that I would answer, for it seems you have not so bright an opinion of me as I have of you, otherways you would not doubt my answer, tho' it were for life, for I might trust life to you with the greatest confidence. You have a real and particular account of all the particulars you mentioned in your letter in the Information herewith sent, wherein you see if that was a marriage I am free on my part. I was terrified by many that the Earl of Murray intended vengeance against me. If I had really given my part in that pretended marriage and knew that man to be such a relation to him, the Earl of Murray might be provoked. And now since your friendly letter gave me opportunity to show the truth and that I am free, I am persuaded the Earl of Murray has greater reason to be pleased with me than offended for my caution, and say it without flattery that my caution was not for his sake, but for my own credit. In the meantime I say that if I knew that man to be so nearly interoped in the Earl's family I would be more cautious, perhaps call for friends to repell them. But I would not be at that pains with a pityful officer for whom a refusal was enough. I think I see some treachery in the case, that Daniel Barbour should offer to impose the Earl of Murray's apparent heir under the name of an English Ralph, or a pityful officer, but let the Traitor answer for that. I promised in the Information to tell you in this letter the cause of my fear, viz., that in the preceding month a gentleman to whom I refused twice private marriage did watch me till he got me at a distance and alone, and keeped his sword to my breast swearing that he would have my life or service. By good providence I escaped with my life, and seeing such as Master Steuart soon thereafter who had such high blood in his face and in the rage of filthy love, and the world knows men in the height of brutish passion cares not what they do, it was not wonder though I might be teared and amazed, but the gentleman indeed threatened violence, which I reckon myself happy to escape with the refusal of the ceremony. Pray acquaint me if you are satisfied with my conduct in this misfortunate occurrence, who am your very humble servant, "(Signed) ÆNEAS MORISON.

Lyle, Jany. 5th, 1731."

The tenor of the Information enclosed in the preceding missive is as follows :—

" Ane Information with respect to Commissary Stewart's Letter dated at Edinburgh, 26th December 1730, concerning the marriage, or alleged marriage of Mistress Barbour with the man now called Sir Francis Steuart's son, etc.—

" The Commissary's letter requires, first, a real Information of the fact and as well of the circumstances, concurrence, and if there was a marriage line : which is as follows, viz.—The minister declares that upon a Sunday about the end of November last (and after sermon) a certain Inverness man applied very zealously, having an indifferent sort of a letter from Daniel Barbour, earnestly entreating the minister to go to Inverness to give marriage to his sister with an officer in the army, and that at his coming to Inverness he would get all the conditions of a lawful marriage clear before him, only that the marriage should be private, and that the minister should go *incognito.* The minister refused. The next day, the minister happening at Kilcowie, the same person called him out and showed him a more particular and pointed letter from Daniel Barbour : the minister refused as formerly, but instantly upon his return to Kilcowie Castle found Daniel Barbour there, who renewed the matter to him with great earnestness ; and upon the minister's refusal Daniel intreated him to keep secret, to whom he (the minister) told that if he would do them no good he would do them no ill —and so they parted. That night (and after midnight) they surprised his quarters with much beating at the door, and had a candle, and one of the party at the minister's bedside before he knew ; and after silence the minister asked the man what he meant ? He told that Mistress Barbour and a certain gentleman would speak. The minister put on his clothes and went to the landlord's bedside to consult if there was a way of making his escape out of the house, and told the whole story to the landlord, but could have no solution nor escape, because the gentleman possessed the door without ; but upon his return to his own chamber the gentleman came in. The minister asked him what he was ? He answered that he was an Englishman born about the Borders, and gave himself a strange name and that he was an officer in the army, and that he would have matrimonial service with Daniel Barbour's sister. The minister —studying what pleasant answers to give him to evade the apparent difficulties—told him that Mistress Barbour had partial consent, and 'spear'd' whether he had such clearances from his superior officers as was practical in such case ? He said No, because that he feared the displeasure or envy of some of his fellow-officers, that he would not discover his intention to them, and that they were going shortly to Kilchuan, and that if he would not get his business settled ere then he feared a disappointment. The minister made the want of his clearance of that sort the argument of his refusal then. The gentleman, after some more discourse, went out, perhaps to consult further ; but the minister seeing the maid instantly press in he resisted her at the very threshold, and before that motion ceased they were all thrown out—the minister, the maid, and the gentleman—and immediately a fourth person starts in to them, and then they renewed their application with uplifted hands begging the minister to give them ceremony, but he declined, and told them they might marry as they pleased and said, ' God's blessing be with you ! ' They stood as amazed, till by good-luck the man that started in said ' that they might be going—that there was enough,' and so the minister parted ; and you may be sure he was glad of their humour, for he had ground enough to fear violence.

" The Commissary requires the witnesses.—The minister has not these to give, for there was not such a thing as a bottle drunk, or witnesses ; for if the man who started in (if he was the man that was told to the minister thereafter), is no habile witness for the proximity of relation. There was a Highlandman hard by, by chance. God knows where he is now ; but the minister knows well that he was a stranger to the English language, and they all spoke English :—so that he cannot say in any practical sense that there were any witnesses.

" The Commissary's letter speaks of a marriage line, and subscribed with two witnesses.—The minister knows nothing of it, but this he knows, that if there was such a writ the witnesses were great knaves, for the man that started in ought not to subscribe by reason of proximity ; and the Highlandman could not subcribe, and be sure he never saw the party before or after :—so there must be a falsehood in this information.

" The Commissary says that the gentleman and the woman deny the marriage.—And when the minister did not give the ceremony who is obliged to move the question ? If they married themselves let them answer for it before God and their own conscience, but what is that to others ? "

Likewise the tenor of the missive letter directed to Master James Mackenzie :—

" REV. DEAR BROTHER,—If it were not my being in deep sickness, that therein I gave myself over twice for death, I had wrote to you before now concerning the unjust and calumnious story that goes—that I should give give church marriage to the Earl of Murray's heir with Sibella Barbour. I declare I knew not whether

Sir Francis Steuart had either son or daughter till some days after Barbour had stormed my quarters in a public inn, and then she had one English Ralph by the hand. I'm wearied with the question by many, whether they are really married. I ordinarily answer with a distinction that they had no church marriage off me ; for you know there was marriage from the beginning of the world, and I find feasts at marriage too—such as Jacob's marriage with Leah, Asuerus with Esther, and the marriage in Cana of Galilee—but all the while no mentioning of sacerdotal office, but Isaac's marriage (viz., to choose and enjoy), which to this day I think is the original and essential way of marriage. Nor do I find that church office was enjoined to it till Constantine the Great's time, or thereafter when the church mixed with the civil state, and then it was thought expedient that a churchman should be still at marriage to give instruction for duty to the parties and to give his benediction. Now dear brother, as you have seen the Informaton, notwithstanding that I was violently attacked, I neither prayed, preached, or gave the benediction ; and tho' he were the king's heir I could withhold nothing from him but my own part,—so that fault or no fault I am innocent. Those minsters that study secrecy in this service are not spoke of or come to peril because they please, but it's my resistance that brought me to this peril of death before now and occasioned this noise, because that I did not please that busy maid. But the gentleman is juster to me, as Commissary Stewart writes to me from Edinburgh that he denies any church service from me. I intreat you acquaint my brethren at Edinburgh in this case, for a calumny is no just balance for a churchman's reputation. I intreat that you write to me with the first post, who am, dear brother, your humble servant, " (Signed) ÆNEAS MORISON·

"Lyle, Janr. 11th, 1731."

" P.S.—I sent the Information of the fact herewith and the Lists of my refusals to show that I was neither active nor covetous in such cases, by which I think I deserve rather the thanks of the church than their displeasure by reason of my resignation and caution."

Directed thus : " To the Reverend Master James Mackenzie, Minister of the Gospel at Edinburgh."

Further, the tenor of the list mentioned in Commissary Stewart's deposition :—

" A List of moneys, more offers of gold to Master Morison for private marriages, and refused—

Primo. From Novar for his brother Andrew, Fifteen Guineas and a half chalder of Bear—refused, and Nineteen Guineas.

Item. From Skipper Mackenzie in Cromarty, by William Fraser in Ferntoun—refused, Ten Guineas.

Item. From Lady Stirrack, by the Chief of the Gunns in Sutherland—refused, Ten Guineas.

Item. From Munro of Teanaird, by Chirurgeon Munro—refused, Ten Guineas.

Item. From Culrain's sister, two intreating letters from Inchcoulter and his sons—refused, Ten Guineas.

Item. From A. Long, Chamberlain in shire of Lorn, by the foresaid William Fraser—refused, Ten Guineas.

Item. From ane Edgar, an officer in the army—refused, Ten Guineas."

The haill amounts to seventy-nine guineas. They are but the principal offers; I do not doubt of the smaller.

In like manner the tenor of the other missive mentioned in the said Master Stewart's deposition, directed to himself as follows :—

" SIR,—I had an account from your cousin, showing me that the young gentleman approves my account to you in every point excepting one point, viz., that he did not promise marriage before me to that busie maid. The truth is, that I was in such amazement in that short stance (for I left them very soon) that I cannot say upon certain memory whether he gave promise or not, but that I heard a promise called and offered among them ; and though I might have mentioned his promise in my Information to you, it's what I cannot warrant upon perfect memory. But there is one point that you will need care for, viz. ; I do not doubt but that the Presbyterians have ' portuous ' rolled * out to me for that alledged marriage. It's the interest of your friends to take me out of the portuous roll when it comes to Edinr., which is very easily done if you get justice when the man denies the marriage. For in the sense of our Canons—and I think your Canons and Scots law agree tolerably well in the matter of marriage—for in that sense *vir est semper pars potior*, especially if no coherence follow upon the congress ; and if the woman assert against the man in such case, the Canon interprets her to be but proditory of her own shame, and declines her, as the Canon provides—*assorere suam turpitudinam fides non adhibenda.* So that

* Portuous or Porteus Roll. A list of persons indicted to appear before the Justiciary, given by the Justice-Clerk, so that those indicted present themselves personally.

your friends have just ground to plead me out of the portuous roll.—I am, sir, your humble servant,

"(Signed)   ÆNEAS MORISON.

"Lyle, Feby. 26th, 1731.

"P.S.--If you see my brother and good friend Master James Mackenzie, tell him that I intend, God willing, to write to him soon, for really writing is a burden to me since I took my great sickness."

Directed "To Commissary John Stewart, Writer to the Signet at Edinburgh."

Follows the tenor of the paper that was inclosed in the said missive, and mentioned in the said deposition :—

"You must not lett any man see this snippat but a person that may be of use to you in the following overtures, and conceal my name, but as if ye had these 'notify' from some other hand. Some friend came to me under the fairest pretence about Christmas last, and I in high raging and rowing fevers—took advantage by that disturbance, and had a writ of me, which by after accounts displeases me, It lays in Seaforth's hands. I had no conference with Seaforth since, for I am yet very weak ; but you will cause some fit person to write to Culloden (who has great power with Seaforth) or both, if Seaforth has any writ that speaks of that alledged marriage that he should conceal it. *Secundo*, That ye find some fit person to write to Bishop Dunbar * that he should not meddle farther in the matter or that marriage ; and if he give commission for trial of it that he should recall it— for he sent a commission to Jameson to convene me. Now I am not able to attend such a meeting without danger of life, because of my sickness ; and if they convene without me, all is in danger, first, because Master Jameson is wonderfully violent for the Barbours ; secondly, for fear of false witnesses, which they prepare—for in truth there was none within sight of that short stance but John Mackay. Now if your friends take no care of me or themselves, now, I declare, I'll turn my back on you all. *Vale*."

Also, the tenor of the letter upon two separate papers, mentioned in the said John Stewart his deposition, is as follows :—

"SIR,--From further discoursing had you not discouraged me when we parted, I might have prevented the trouble of this letter, or had I seen the double of that nonsensical paper the Baillie

---

* Bishop Dunbar. The Rev. William Dunbar, M.A., parson of Cruden, Aberdeenshire. Appointed to Cruden 1691. Elected Bishop of Moray and Ross, and consecrated 1727, and held this see till he was elected Bishop of Aberdeen 1733.

had from Seaforth ; for really I knew not so punctually what stuff was in it, my memory being so confounded when it was taken from me in the rage of sharp fevers, wherein I sometimes raved, till last month a certain friend, who read it so oft with Seaforth, told me the man's name or designation was blank, and the date not consistent with that mischance. Now whether I be a good or an ill man, I'll answer my God for it, and I hope to die in his peace. But my acquaintance will not believe if I were in solid sense then that I would sign such a nonsensical paper as a marriage line to a blank person and of uncertain date. God forgive the man that took me at such disadvantage. When I came to solid memory after that great sickness, I wrote to Seaforth to suppress that paper till I would see it, and wrote to you that the Earl of Murray should write to Seaforth to give it up in his favour ; and I wish the Earl write now and without delay : for tho' the nonsense of it may not prevail before a judge, yet it may occasion dispute, and far better have it out of the way. They fleg me with the tenor of a charge to Edinburgh. I am sure your friends have greater sense than to wish so ; for whatever freedom I used with you in your particular information as the opinion of the Church, it is what you might not wish to hear before a judge,—not that we dissemble ; if that man proceed sinfully let the sin be at his door, we are no debtors further than we are asked. But I think no Scots law obliges any to declare his private opinion before a judge, yet the dispute of advocates is a little rash and may make the event uncertain. Nor must you ask your bishop, for tho' he got a headfull of calumnious interpretations before he saw me, when he saw at meeting that I was deceived and that I could not behave more cautiously, we resolved, in our mind, viz., not to be officious, and leave every one concerned to his own consciousness, and I presume that the bishop will do nothing in it without me ———. If the Barbours charge me, I may allow them to prove that fact, which I fancy they cannot ; but when they might, I may hound them after a Borderer,—for I really know not whether (and your partisanpage is thus) Sir Francis Steuart had son or daughter, or if the Earl of Murray had such a brother. Let her find her Borderer if she wants him. But far better that with God's help you prevent any such charge, for neither party may gain by my compearance. However, I am brought to extreme poverty and misery by it. A band of my best friends and maintainers, being so interoped in the Barbours, abstracted themselves, and abused my greatest friend in the world and others, that I am not this day sure of bare bread. But little needed I want of gold if I yielded to a certificate that is not consistent with truth.

"I fancy I need not sign, for you was four times acquainted with the hand.— 11th Jan. 1732.

" Let no man know that I correspond with you, and if you

20

write, as I fancy you will, how things go thereby, your friends
can admonish him that none know it, or then we will all be mis-
interpreted. I bid you again that the Earl of Murray write to
give that senseless paper to him or me. I am in the physician's
hands this while ago."

Directed "To Commissary John Stewart, Writer to the Signet,
Edinburgh."

Having now followed the tortuous explanations and reiterations
of the Jesuitical non-juring parson of Contin, we will bring this long
marriage case to a termination. There were several other witnesses who appeared, but as there was little or no additional matter
of fact in their statements that has not been already adduced, we
omit further repetition of evidence. Throughout we have adhered
closely to the manuscript volume of the case. The subject of
this marriage occupied the attention of the Commissary Court for
nearly twelve months : at last, on the 11th December 1732, the
Commissaries " Found and declared the said John Steuart and
Sibella Barbour husband and wife, assoilzied Mistress Barbour
from Master Steuart's process of Declarator of Immunity, and
decerned him to adhere to the said Sibella Barbour, her fellow-
ship and company, and to treat and entertain her at bed, board,
and all other conjugal duties as becomes a lawful married husband
to do and perform to his lawful married wife, and that during the
whole time of their conjunct lifetime."

LOCAL CHARACTER.

JOHN MACRAE, "THE POET."

IT has been said that the success and fame of Robert Burns, the Scottish Poet, led to the publication of a host of volumes of indifferent verse, which it would have been better for the writers and the world had they never seen the light so far as either have been advantaged. Almost every town, village, and hamlet in Scotland has produced one or more of these local bards. Men who would have been successes in life in the sphere of labour in which they started have been induced on the pressure of indiscreet friends who flattered them as possessing poetical genius, and also the vanity of seeing themselves in print, rushed into publishing, and have thereby become quite unfitted for the soberer affairs of business.

Inverness has furnished several examples of these hapless versi-fiers—Andrew Fraser ("Goggan"), gardener and poet ; "Jamie" Paterson, teacher, and writer of verses ; "Davie" Macdonald, baker, and author of a volume of poems published in 1838, among which are some in Gaelic ; and John Macrae, waiter. the subject of this notice.

For more than forty years Macrae was a well known figure on the streets of Inverness, as he paraded the High Street daily whatever might be the state of the weather. The High Street was almost invariably his favourite haunt, with occasional turns on Inglis Street, not omitting his solitary daily forenoon walk to the " Wine Shop," where he always got his morning bitters in the days of Provost Fergusson, and which is said to have been continued by the various succeeding proprietors, till poor Macrae was laid aside and unable to tread his daily beat.

Our first meeting with Macrae must have been somewhere about 1844. We had known his figure a year or two earlier. Some companions had pointed him out to us as " Macrae the poet," a *rara avis* to us boys in those days as one who wrote poetry and " had made a book." Crossing the New Bridge— as it was called fifty years ago, to distinguish it from the Old or Stone Bridge—one winter night, our juvenile courage was screwed to its testing-point by seeing a tall individual declaiming with loud voice and extended arm, some verses—

" I stood on the bridge "———

but within two hours of " midnight," and as the man continued to speak his lines, we drew near and found it was Macrae—invoking probably the assistance of the Muse. We braced our courage when we knew our man, and, boy-like, spoke out—

" *You are John Macrae the poet !*"

—when he immediately replied, with pleasant voice and pointed finger at us—

" *Yes, boy, thou speak'st truth—I know it !*"

The acquaintance thus begun was continued, and many a verse of " crambo" was interchanged in various bouts in after years when we met. All his rhymes in these little combats, when the rhyming vocabulary got exhausted, used to end with—

" By hill and brae—your humble servant, John Macrae."

In our early acquaintance Macrae appeared a handsome well-built man with good clear-cut face, well dressed, and scrupulously neat in his attire, while his well-polished tall hat always shone most brilliantly.

John Macrae was, we believe, a native of Moniack. Inverness-shire. He must have been born some year in the last decade of the eighteenth century, for we find him in Inverness publishing his first volume of " Original Poems and Songs " in 1816.* At this time Macrae was a waiter in Geddes's Royal Hotel, and afterwards in the old Commercial Hotel, Castle Wynd. He has been described to us by a townsman who knew him in those days as " one of the smartest waiters in town." He had also as a young man filled situations as valet in various families in the neighbourhood of Inverness—Inglis of Kingsmills, Mackintosh of Balnespick, The Chisholm, etc.

The volume issued in 1816 extends to 193 pages, and is dedicated " To The Most Noble the Marquis of Huntly." Macrae received considerable support for this work, as there is a list of subscribers (chiefly gentlemen in the town and neighbourhood), extending to sixteen pages, who took upwards of 500 copies. at 6s per copy. In his preface he sets forth that he was induced at the particular request of friends and acquaintances " to publish the productions of his " untutored muse, with all its imperfections on its head, and he humbly hopes it may meet with the approbation of the public." To those who disapprove of his propensity for rhyming his answer is " *Better employ the leisure hour to a recreation of this nature than to run in the face of vice or embrace folly in the dark.*" The italics in this extract are Macrae's own, and we leave them here without comment.

In 1828 Macrae again tempted Fame and published a small brochure entitled " The Muse Revived, or a Selection of Poems and Songs (never before published), together with a Specimen of the forthcoming ' Martinmas Market.' " It is from this small col-

---

* Macrae must have been born in 1791, if his tombstone in the Chapel-yard Burying-ground. Inverness, is correct :—" JOHN MACRAE, POET, DIED 15TH NOVEMBER 1864, AGED 73 YEARS." ETC. ETC.

In 1832 another little publication of Macrae's appeared, entitled, " Duncancroy, or The Northern Racecourse ; with Original
Poems and Songs." There is a sad falling off in all the pieces in
this latter gathering of 48 pages, and it is the last published collection we believe, that Macrae issued. All his future pieces appeared
as printed leaflets on any theme that he wrote upon, and copies
were offered to such as cared to buy them. These latter lucubrations are some of them the veriest doggrel, written on occasions
of marriages, births, and deaths in families in Inverness and its
environs. He appears to have established himself as the " Poet-
Laureate " of every occasion of domestic joy and sorrow in the
Highland capital : A birth, marriage, or death, was an opportunity for producing an Ode or an Elegy. The starting of a
new business establishment afforded him a favourable chance of
which he largely availed himself. Acrostics on the names of individuals, was a favourite mode that his verse assumed. On subjects
occupying public attention John was always ready with a rhyming production suitable for the occasion. He evidently knew the
weak side in human nature, for in these lines he is always an
adept in praise or flattery, indeed somewhat nauseous in com-
pliments to the subjects of his pieces. His rhymes in these " fly
sheets " we have seen are almost always of the very lankiest and
most limpid character, while his metres are often incorrect and
false.

John's method of composition was eccentric. At the time,
when full of the subject of his intended effusion, he might be
seen at the corner of the street of his favourite promenade,
or by the margin of the Ness, or on the old stone bridge—declaiming his lines, " his eye in a fiery frenzy rolling," labour-
ing at his production, and giving forth passages, unconscious of
passers-by. The repeating of lines or couplets was a common
practice with John. On one of his daily turns an informant
told us of a scene in which two dogs and the poet took part.
The dogs began quarrelling, and Macrae, as he contemplated
the growling curs, gave forth the following lines of crambo :—

> " You are Kennedy Macnab's dog,
>   I know you by your ways ;
> But I am Donal' Jron's dog,
>   And I'll give you sixty days "

The explanation of the story is, that one of the dogs belonged to Kennedy Macnab, the bellicose editor of the once notorious "Inverness Reformer," a print for particulars of which we refer to the "Bibliography of Inverness Newspapers" that follows in this volume. The other animal was the property of one of the town bailies, who was known as "Donal' Iron" from his calling as an ironmonger ; the severity of whose sentences while for the short time he occupied the magisterial bench secured himself some unenviable celebrity—even a notice from the Government of the day in the case of one of the members of the military re-cruiting party stationed in town. A soldier, one night at an untimely hour, was found in the kitchen of a house making love to the servant-girl ; her employer, who permitted no followers, sent for the police, who next morning brought the son of Mars before the bailie. The sentence, as usual of sixty days' imprisonment, was inflicted, and it was very soon brought under the notice of the authorities at the War Office by the officer in charge of the party at Inverness, with the result that the magistrate was deprived of the power to treat all and sundry offences with the same indiscriminate punishment. Macrae's allusion to the characteristics of each owner is well hit off in his rhyme on the two dogs.

Our portrait of John Macrae is taken from a photograph, and is a good likeness of the old man a year or so before his death. He appeared then but as a wreck of his former self.

In his latter years Macrae was largely dependent on the support of old friends, and the many Invernessians, or "Clachnacuddin boys," as he called them, who, on their return to their native town from the Southern cities and abroad, kindly remembered the old poet.

The stanzas that follow on the Rifle Volunteers we give a place to in our pages, not for any merit they possess, but partly as a commemoration of the patriotic movement which the poet celebrates in his halting verse—and further, as probably the last of the "fly-sheet" productions that were issued by Macrae. To citizens of Inverness of the present day it is scarcely neces-sary to say that the gentlemen mentioned in the second verse were—Colin Lyon-Mackenzie of St Martin's, Provost of Inver-ness, captain ; Donald A. Nicol of the Tweed Mill at Holm, first

21

lieutenant; and Sir Henry Cockburn Macandrew, second lieutenant. The latter gentleman attained to the rank of honorary
colonel of the Battalion at the time of his retiral.

As already said, we give in its entirety the " Tailor of Beauly "
as the best specimen of Macrae's rhyming talent at his best
period.

The Inverness Volunteer Rifle Corps.

Tune—" A Highland Lad my Love was born."

I'VE heard it lately whispered here
   A loyal band would soon appear,
Combined as one, and now 'tis clear
     We've Clachnacuddin Riflemen.

We've seen our Lyon at their head.
And Nicol true, with martial tread;
Macandrew too, an ensign made,
     To lead our gallant Riflemen.

Shoulder to shoulder onward go,
Through summer's heat and winter's snow,
And let each stern invader know
     You're some of Scotia's Riflemen.

With patriotic feelings crowned,
May you united all be found,
Sincere in heart, and always sound,
     Our Invernessian Riflemen.

Should danger threaten, staunch convene,
And as true sons of Mars be seen,
To guard our Isle, Consort, and Queen,
     As heroes born, and Riflemen.

That ages yet unborn may boast,
And sound it round from coast to coast
Each in himself was known a host
     In days of Nessia's Riflemen.

With martial spirit then shine forth,
And lauded be from south to north;
For independence, sterling worth,
     Long still be known our Riflemen.

Throughout the empire round and round,
Now volunteer, new corps are found,
Whom long be spared to keep their ground,
    As loyal British Riflemen.

Propitious years long may you share,
Remote from foe and enemy's snare,
As pure you breathe mountain air,
    Onr native true-born Riflemen.

A phalanx firm be seen to stand
As guardians of your Fatherland,
Repelling each invading band,
    As brave and sterling Riflemen.

October 17, 1859.

——*o*——

THE TAILOR OF BEAULY.

A Tale of Tradition.

———

" Let such teach others who themselves excel.
And censure freely who have written well ;
Whoever thinks a faultless pieee to see,
Thinks what ne'er was, nor is, nor e'er can be."—POPE.

———

AROUND the fire in friendly chat,
    The farmer and his neighbours sat :
Long they conversed of what had been
About the kirk at midnight seen ;
Each awful tale awoke their fears,
Till ev'ry spark a fire appears ;
And granny's old asthmatic hoast,
Bore all the terrors of a ghost.
" If there be ghosts, what can they do,"
A neighbour says, " to me or you?
We honest folks have nought to fear."

    A knock was heard. " Oh ! L——d be here ! "
Around the ring in hurry flew,
And closer to the fire they drew ;
With open mouths, and lengthen'd ears,
They wish'd to hide, but shew'd their fears ;
With trembling lip the landlord said—
" The cow to chew her cud is laid ;
Or gussy to the beam has broke."
They wish'd to laugh. A second knock

Dissolv'd the charm ; their fears increas'd,
And still more close and close they press'd.
A third still louder than before—
They knew the third was at the door.
" Wife, you are nearest, go and see
If any neighbour calls for me."
She ask'd the rest if it was fair
That she should go, and Thomas there?
They all agreed, 'twas more beseeming
The men should go, than send the women.

The tailor, who had been abroad,
And knew each alehouse on the road,
Had brought for Tommy a new suit,
And thought they kept him long without,
Quick drew the latch, and in he flew :
A piercing scream escap'd the crew.
In haste they fly to hiding holes,
To pray in secret for their souls ;
In hurry they impede each other,
And knock and crack their heads together :
Just as the brood upon the roost,
When the sly fox disturbs their rest,
Some dash themselves against the wall,
Some aptly in his clutches fall.

" Faith " says the tailor, " one would think,
So much you tremble and you shrink,
That Beauly's ghost had broken loose,
And taken lodgings in your house."

" Is this you, Will ? we got a fright,"
The landlord says, "for all last night
The kirk was filled with such like things
As those with which the country rings :
Now awfu' gleams flash thro' the kirk,
And now 'tis clear, and now 'tis mirk ;
Now moaning sad will fill the pile,
Then laughter's heard for mony a mile."

"Tales, tales," quo' Will, " I'm none of those
Who think that ghosts leave their repose.
Now, Thomas, say what will you stake,
But I a pair of hose will make
At midnight, in the kirk alone,
Tho' that the ghost should roar and groan."

" I'll give you, Will, a boll of bear,
And four half-crowns in honest gear ;—

But if you fail, I nought shall pay
For all the clothes you've brought to-day."

"A bargain be't—this night—I've thread ;
And ev'rything, in short, I need."

The night was dark, and wind and rain
Beat round the house, but beat in vain—
No rain could pierce the thatch above,
No blast of wind a stone could move.
Quick pant the neighbours' hearts with fear,
As midnight hour approacheth near.

With solemn face, they grave, exclaim,
What a great sin it was and shame,
That man, to whom a state is given,
To angels next, that dwell in heaven,
Should place his soul within the pow'r
Of wicked sprite at midnight hour :
And awful 'twas, they said, indeed,
That he should go and meet the dead.
They all protested 'gainst the act,
And wish'd the tailor to retract ;
Told thousand tales how fiends had drawn
Men to their snare, and how, ere dawn,
Their mangled limbs alone could tell
The horrid fate which them befel !

The tailor had a heart of steel,
And had no fear, nor fear could feel.
The hour was come of dead midnight ;
He gaily called aloud for light :
With well-oiled lamp, and heart so stout,
He ask'd the neighbours round about,
If they would go the road awhile,
And bring him to the old kirk-stile :
Some bid him pray, and take good heed,
While some as gravely bid him speed ;
But *all* the awful task refuse,
To stir a step beyond the house.

His fav'rite Kate, whose jet-black eye
Gave love the watchword and reply,
With secret step the circle leaves,
.While anger in her bosom heaves,
To see a crowd so frail of soul,
As fear the road, whilst Will, the whole
Of that long night, alone must spend,
And hold discourse with horrid fiend.

With tartan cloth and pocket sheers,
The tailor and his lamp appears ;
With outstretch'd neck and gaping glow'r,
They push and press around the door .
But none would dare the road to try—
The hour was late, the kirk was nigh.

Will met, at length, his faithful Kate,
And ask'd her where she went so late ?
She answer'd—" She had ta'en a whim
To go and spend the night with him."—

" It is agreed, and 'tis but right
That I alone should spend the night ;
I know the fondness of your heart—
But THIS, my dear, before we part."

What more then pass'd, I cannot tell ;
But this, all Beauly knows full well,
Ere six months' end there was a flaw,
And ere the tenth she took the straw :
While some weep tears, some sport and fun ;
The stranger squeak'd—it was a SON.

But to my tale.   He leaves the maid
With cautious step, but not afraid ;
He strives to shun each rough grave-stone,
Nor cares to stumble o'er a bone :
He op'd the door with manly pride—
He had no partner by his side ;
He hurl'd it back with sudden fling,
And, with the sound, the rafters ring.
His feeble lamp sent scarce a smile
Across the benches of the aisle :
With steady step he reach'd a table,
That had been cover'd o'er with sable—
Tho' some say not, 'tis my opinion
It had been us'd for the communion.

When he had cut the cloth with care,
Whistling, the while, some merry air,
A groan throughout the kirk was heard ;
But not a pin our hero car'd.
And as the groaning louder grew,
The lamp before him burning blue :
At length a scull, with hollow voice,
That had no tongue to cause the noise,
While, on the opposite pew it sat,
Without or beard, or wig, or hat—

"See, mortal, see who is thy guest!"
The tailor rais'd his hand in haste,
And, planted straight before his eyes,
The speaking bone the tailor spies—
" My head is bare, and I am old ;
O ! tailor, I am poor and cold."

"I have no time, nor words to waste ;
I hear and see—but am in haste."

His arms and shoulders next appear,
And to the tailor, thus, severe—
" My shoulders are both thin and bare ;
Tailor, my shoulders claim thy care :
For countless years no cov'ring warm
Did e'er defend my wither'd arm."

"I cannot listen to thy woe,
So do not frown upon me so ;
For faith, and truth, the hose I'll make,
Or else I lose the goods at stake."

A lengthen'd body, slimly built,
With various signs of daggers' guilt,
Arose upon our hero's sight,
And thus address'd the wond'ring wight :
" Hast thou no pity—canst thou see
A form so weak and frail as me,
Without a plaid, thus strive in vain
To shield me from the wind and rain ?
Now thro' my ribs, with whirring song,
The mountain winds their blasts prolong."

"My honest friend, be not offended,
For now your case can scarce be mended ;
And if it could, what's that to me ?
Pray, go your way, and let me be."

And now it stands upon its feet—
A skeleton in parts complete.
"Oh ! mortal, see me, lean and tall ;
Hast thou no sympathy at all .
Tho' weak and wretched, yet I see
No tear of pity start for me ?
Hast thou no remnants left of cloth,
By cheating, cabbaging, or both,
To shield my ancient feeble form
From summer's sun or winter's storm ?"

Our hero, who was near an end,
And wish'd a parting with this fiend,
With hasty hand drew ev'ry stitch
And wish'd himself beyond his clutch.

"Sir," says the tailor, "I'm not rich ;
And if I were, of clothes and such
Like useless things, what need have you ?
My pity for your person grew."

With piercing shriek, thus laugh'd the fiend—
"I spoke you thus to gain my end ;

I have no pow'r till this I'm grown—
I took a temper not my own ;
So now thy life is but my due."

His task being done, the tailor flew—
And, being seated next the door,
Skimm'd lightly o'er the flagged floor ;
And as the kirk the wight forsakes,
A pouncing aim the phantom takes ;
In haste to seize his prey, now gone,
His fleshless fingers cleft the stone ;
And even to this day, we see
The mark of thumb and fingers * three.

The tailor won the bet, I trow,
And nobly too, you must allow :
He got the bear, and all the rest
As promis'd, and herein express'd.
Then as you pass by Beauly Kirk,
In morning clear, or ev'ning mirk,
Be you prudent man, or railer,
Call to mind the *Beauly Tailor*.

* It is a positive fact, that the mark of three fingers and a thumb are
perfectly visible on the stone at the present day ; and the story alluded to
is extant among the country people.

PUBLICATION OF THE CULLODEN PAPERS.

———

THE letters that follow came into our possession some time ago. We think them of sufficient permanent interest to occupy some pages in our "Miscellanea Invernessiana." Everything in connection with the publishing of a work possessing the historical value of "The Culloden Papers" is worthy of preservation and of the attention of the student of history and antiquarian lore. The families of Forbes of Culloden and the Duffs of Muirtown have been so long and honourably connected with the town of Inverness that this of itself is an additional reason for including in this work these byways of our local history.

The editor—Hugh Robert Duff of Muirtown—was a gentleman possessed of considerable literary judgment, and with a strong inclination to literary pursuits. His merit as editor of "The Culloden Papers" has been attested by Sir Walter Scott in his article reviewing the work in "*The Quarterly Review*," May 1816. Mr Duff also edited "Genealogy of the Family of Forbes." Inverness, 1819, which became rather scarce and difficult to procure. This work has since been reprinted, Inverness, 1883.

The originals of the correspondence have recently passed into the possession of Francis Darwin, Esq., who married Miss Duff, heiress of Muirtown and grand-daughter of the editor of "The Culloden Papers."

———

No. I.

Addressed to Messrs Cadell & Davies, booksellers, Strand, London.

Muirtown, Inverness, *22nd July*, 1812.

GENTLEMEN,—By course of post I should be glad to know whether perhaps it might not be more eligible to publish the book the subject of a correspondence in quarto instead of octavo ; secondly, whether you mean, in the clear divisible profit

22

being £750 or £800, as one to be divided, or is it the share of *each party*—the *publisher* and *proprietor* of the papers—as if it is *not*, it is a much smaller sum than has been offered in Edinburgh; and thirdly, whether after inspecting the papers you would not be disposed to give a certain sum at once for all property in them. I beg leave by *direct course* to have a precise answer.—With esteem, I am, gentlemen, your humble servt.,   H. R. DUFF.

My last letter might be called an acknowledgment of a handsome offer rather than an acceptance, which I do not consider it to be, there being other articles besides price in an agreement of the sort.

No. II.

Messrs Cadell & Davies's reply.

London, *July* 30, 1812.

SIR,—It is very far from our wish to consider your letter of the 3rd instant as binding you to a positive acceptance of the terms proposed, if you have since found cause for thinking that more advantageous terms have been offered by any other persons. We are still, however, of opinion, that, on further consideration, you will find our proposal to be as fair, and upon the whole as advantageous to you, as can possibly be made, particularly when it is recollected that, though we have not seen a single line of the papers in question, we have undertaken, not only to print an edition, which will cost us at least £800, but also to pay to you, on the day of publication—before a single copy is sold—one half of the divisible profits, which we have estimated may probably amount to from £375 to £400, besides furnishing you with copies for yourself and friends free of expense, and securing you a further advantage contingent on our finding encouragement to print a second edition.

These terms, we beg leave to assure you, we should never have offered had we looked at the transaction in a mercantile point of view merely. If on turning the matter further in your mind you wish us to inspect the papers and then to make an offer for the whole property, and form an opinion whether the publication should take place in quarto or octavo, we will do so with the utmost pleasure, and with all practicable dispatch, whenever you favour us with an opportunity.—We are, Sir,   C. & D.

P.S.—The edition might certainly, by the retail price being fixed higher than £2 8s in boards be made to produce greater profits; but we are not very fond of having our publications called dear.

No. III.*

Addressed to Messrs Cadell & Davies.

8th Sept. 1812.

GENTLEMEN,—When I delivered over the Culloden papers yesterday, I told the gentleman sent by you that though the papers before 1704 were not arranged yet that they were most valuable ; among them is the minute † (Aug. 1650), of the transactions at the *West Kirk*, his participation in which is one of the principal articles against the Marquis of Argyll in his indictment. Some of the others, from the signatures. must be equally curious —though ftom the old hand hard to read.

In presenting the Culloden papers in the state I have done you may observe that it would have been as easy for me to have curtailed them into a state fit for publication, without selection ; but then I might have hurt the mass of the work by striking out papers which may be found worth preserving, and the labour is not much enhanced by the trouble of rejecting the few which may be found fit for rejection. Besides, I think that the choice has been already nearly sufficiently rigid, and that but very few letters will be found which either do not gain value from general bearing upon points of early history, from throwing the President's life and habits into a clear light. or from elucidating the history of the Rebellion of 1745 beyond the necessity or possibility of any future effectual narrative.

The points upon which the letters and essays are supposed to bear, and upon which their value must be established, are those above stated, and the period extends from (say) 1625 to 1748— an extent of time full of political change and eventual settlement of the highest importance, indeed comprehending the English history from the first shaking of the throne under the Stuart race untill their final overthrow in all their hopes of regaining the sovereignty of Great Britain. The arrangement for the publication being chronological cannot be difficult, and the selection being easy, you cannot be sorry to have your own judgment somewhat employed in a work become your own property.

A work of this kind derives from various sources its interest. Some comes from the events narrated, and some from the narrators when the events have little or no moment,—and we are glad

* This letter was written from London by Mr Duff, who left Muirtown on 14th August per packet, arriving in London on the 24th, and on same date notes in his diary the disposal of the Culloden papers to Messrs Cadell & Davies. This information has been kindly communicated by Colonel Warrand of Ryefield, grandson of Mr Duff.

† No. 8 of the series of documents printed in "The Culloden Papers," see page 6 of that work.

to trace an acknowledged great man into his retirement and private habits when we are perhaps tired of the scenes which have constitued the basis of his fame.

From the printed volumes it is presumed that some curious papers may be selected, particularly some regarding Simon Fraser (afterward the unfortunate Lord Lovat). I shall esteem the favour of being freely consulted upon any difficulty, as from my situation in the north I may easily get information not readily to be got here.—Wishing long success to the work, I am, gentlemen, your most obt. servt.,   H. R. DUFF.

No. IV.

Addressed to Messrs Cadell & Davies, booksellers, Strand, London.

Muirtown, 25th Jany. 18!3.

GENTLEMEN,—I beg to inform you that I shall send off the Introduction to the Culloden Papers, by the boat * which leaves Inverness to-morow, so that the sixth day after you ought to receive the parcel. The 42 and 43 pages are left blank, as I shall require a few days to finish them, when I shall forward them by post. The pages opposite are left reserved for notes and omissions, and I hope that you will make some allowance for the inaccuracy of the writing, as, in fact, I am only slowly recovering from a rheumatic fever, and the manuscript was found (?) " FORMED " in bed since 3rd Jany. ; but I have no fear that the manner of conducting the Life and the Notes will be found sufficiently accurate and interesting. It will require, on account of the way (somewhat confused) that the paper is drawn up, that a person careful and who can make out an indistinct hand, and who understands punctuation and Latin, should have the superintendence of the Introduction both at the press and before it goes to it. I shall esteem extremely a letter by course regarding both the receipt of the *parcel* and everything else which may inform as to the publication, its form, etc.—I am, meantime, your most obt. servt.,   H. R. DUFF.

I have again to state that it will require a clever clear-headed person to manage the arrangement of both notes and text.

* At this date trading smacks sailed at stated times from Inverness to London.

No. V.

Addressed to Messrs Cadell & Davies, booksellers, Strand, London.

Muirtown, *11th March* 1813.

GENTLEMEN,—I have been for sometime anxious to hear from you, because I am certain that my having (now my health is somewhat restored), time and opportunity of examining *my* Life and Notes would be of service to the work. As I have some additions to make to the notes and text, as well as several corrections a perusal of a fair copy of the Life, if such has been made would be of use to me ; or a copy from the press provided the types could be kept in for alterations, till I had 2 or 3 days to examine what would be done with propriety, and to compose and arrange the requisite writing.

I hope you will take this communication as proceeding (as it does) from my goodwill towards the work, and I may add that I judge the whole will not be the worse of a free correspondence with me during the preparations for publishing.—I am, gentle·men, your most obedt. servt., H. R. DUFF.

It is almost impossible for me to state all the advantages which may result from my knowing further the state of the work, and having the *above* advantage. I hope I may express a hope that the Life is not ill executed, as I think it is not amiss, and I may add that the materials were very scanty. H. R. D.

No. VI.

Addressed to Messrs Cadell & Davies, booksellers, Strand, London.

Muirtown, 13*th July* 1813.

GENTLEMEN,—Mr Forbes of Culloden being here to dinner yesterday, informed me of having sent you a letter a few days before, and likewise of his great anxiety regarding his papers and his perfect amazement at your conduct regarding them ; he resolved to procure the delivery of them without loss of time. It might, perhaps, be disagreeable to relate the various reports and even private assertions of influence to suppress the papers and the Life. I had myself never had any suspicion except in two quarters, bnt Culloden has mentioned a third, and with various pretty curious circumstances. It will therefore save much trouble that you at once (without the least delay) either state the papers are ready for re-delivery, or else for publication in some reasonable time.—I have the honour to be your most obedt. servt.,   H. R. DUFF.

No. VII.

Messrs Cadell & Davies's reply.

London, *July* 23, 1813.

SIR,--You may safely assure Mr Forbes that all his apprehensions respecting the Culloden papers are perfectly groundless. The unexpected difficulties which (as we already informed you), we found in getting the *MSS.* put into anything like a proper arrangement prevented our getting the volume printed in time for publication during the present season, and therefore it necessarily stands over for the winter—for to publish it later than July would be quite destructive.

We believe that nothing can prevent to setting the printer to work early in September, and in that case it may be published in December, which is quite as early as would be advisable to us to bring forward the work as soon as we prudently can.—We are sir, your very obedt. servants,   C. & D. (Cadell & Davies).

No. VIII.

Addressed to Messrs Cadell & Davies, Strand, London.

14 Suffolk Street, Charing Cross,
20th Nov. 1813.

GENTLEMEN,—Not being favoured with an answer to my last, and being in town, in great measure for the purpose of receiving Mr Forbes's papers as delivered in Sept. 1812, I shall be glad to be informed when such delivery may be agreeable or convenient to you.

I judge from several circumstances that a sale of the right of publication can easily be effected in town. and as I should be very unwilling to do or say anything which might compromise your names, I would be glad to know if such a measure would be agreeable to your wishes--at the same time at this writing taking no right upon myself to enter into any transaction of the kind. I only ask in order to be enabled to make proper inquiries. which could not be done without more or less giving publicity to our intercourse.

I expect the favour of an answer,—being, gentlemen, your most obt. servt.,   H. R. DUFF.

No. IX.

Addressed to Messrs Cadell & Davies, Strand, London.

14 Suffolk Street, *20th November* 1813.

GENTLEMEN,—I think it proper, since hearing Mr Davies express his desire of my meeting him in company with Mr Jones regarding the Culloden publication to state my sentiments regarding such meeting.

(1st), If it is to promote the publication in any way, I have no objection to it ; but, (2nd), If it is for the purpose of persuading me out of the value of the papers, or of the propriety of publication, I must say it can only be a nullity, for I am not an —— to —— anything from the terms settled. I am not capable of being argued or worded out of an opinion duly founded on facts, unless the facts are nullified, even if all the *literati* in Europe were to place themselves against me in opinion. Mr Jones is un-unknown to me in every regard. The meeting might end in altercation (a very unpleasant thing), or my silence might be taken for admission of what I did not mean to assent to. Everything of this kind is best managed in wriiting—*litera scripta manit*—but to consent to interviews of this sort would only perplex parties as to what they have said, or think they have not said—a thing most cautiously to be avoided, because it is indeed an indirect way of loosening Positive and Evident Engagements.

I have little doubt the papers if still as I delivered them, will find a purchaser ; but I must decline any correspondence except in writing for the above reasons and others I could state.—I am, yours, etc., H. R. DUFF.

If you please I shall beat about for a publisher or purchaser.

No. X.

Addressed to Mr Mutlow, at Messrs Cadell & Davies's, Strand, London.

14 Suffolk Street, Charing Cross, *23rd Nov.* 1813.

SIR,—I have received your letter, and I may hope repeat my belief that the papers are still a saleable article. At the same time if they are really and *bona fide* to be published, and that soon by Messrs Cadell & Davies, I beg to suggest how extremely convenient, and to the advantage of the work it would be, that I should have the inspection of the sheets, etc., before they are finally printed off. Even the correction of proper names would be an object of itself, and you may observe that the Life is far from being finished as I could wish either in respect of extent or accuracy. This being the case, and my stay in town not being for more than 10 or 14 days, I beg to know when the work is ready to go to the press. Mr Davies mentioned that it was much looked for in Edinburgh, and feared disappointment, but I trust no reasonable hopes can be disappointed.—Your most obt. servt.,   H. R. DUFF.

An answer is requested as soon as possible from Mr Mutlow, who has ever been extremely civil.

No. XI.

Addressed to Mr Mutlow, at Messrs Cadell & Davies, Strand, London.

14 Suffolk Street, Charing Cross,
9th Dec. 1813.

SIR,—I have just received the *copy* of part of my Introduction, which is extremely erroneous in point of accuracy of orthography and punctuation.

I am glad the Introduction is to be seriously set about, as I shall get my part finished before leaving town ; and I do believe it will be most essential to my credit in a work which will at least be imputed to me (if my name is not to it), to be upon the spot when the press is going. I observe a manuscript notice upon the printed page, " that it is to be set in new English " ! ! * I do not fear this *squib*, though it may be the forerunner of the more heavy thunder of the *Review*. I am, indeed, a Scot, and one born in the far distant North ; but my life has been passed in milder climes and with men who have never been remarkable for bad English or undue Scotch bias. Still, when Mr Jones or any other person can catch me at a Scotticism, an omission, an erroneous sentiment, or in short any other impropriety, their censure at *once* expressed I shall esteem— for just criticism in due time is the best boon a person publishing could receive. Besides, of what I have written much could be changed, abridged, enlarged, and mended upon the fair perusal in print by myself, and much of the notes perhaps with propriety be transferred into the text.

As my presence is required at home, and my other cause of

---

* An amusing mistake on the part of Mr Duff—" to be set in new English " being only a direction on the printed proof as to the special type in which the printer was to " set " the Introduction. We would not, however, miss such mistakes as caused the production of such a spirited defence of Northern English from the laird of Muirtown.

being in town (my appeal) near over, I hope you will not allow any delay not necessary. —I am, your most obed servt.,

H. R. DUFF.

What is sent to me as printed is what I conceived when I wrote it as the flattest part of my Narrative, for the subject was only just broached and did not admit of either grandeur or solemnity or sentiment, as if one was beginning the history of an Empire.

I beg I may be sincerely treated with.

No. XII.

Addressed to Mr Mutlow, at Cadell & Davies's, Strand, London.

14 Suffolk Street, 29th Dec. 1813.

SIR,—I beg to send the 20 pages, which I think are now correct. I beg they may be carefully printed off and the *notes inserted.* Mr Jones has written on the margin that part of the manuscript sent did not come back. There is some mistake in this, as none of it is here but what came to-day, and will be sent herewith. The hamper has some time past been in "The Fame," which comes to Down's Wharf, Wapping.

I cannot help (tho' humbly) recommending the adoption of such a title-page * as I wrote in March last about, as the

---

* The following is the title-page referred to from MS. copy in Mr Duff's handwriting in our possession. It varies from that published :—

CULLODEN PAPERS.

CORRESPONDENCE,

CHIEFLY RELATING TO

THE REBELLIONS
IN
THE YEARS 1715 AND 1745 ;

INCLUDING MANY LETTERS FROM THE UNFORTUNATE LORD LOVAT.

TRANSCRIBED FROM THE ORIGINALS IN THE
POSSESSION OF
.. .. .. D U F F, E S Q. O F M U I R T O W N.

TO WHICH ARE PREFIXED,

MEMOIRS
OF
THE RIGHT HON. DUNCAN FORBES OF CULLODEN,
MANY YEARS
LORD PRESIDENT OF THE COURT OF SESSION
IN
SCOTLAND.

23

expense would not be much, and the effect and application very
correct.   I beg to have a corrected copy to send Culloden of
what is sent this day, and one for myself.   The sheets I now
send need not be sent back, nor will the *Introduction* be handed
about in any way which can affect the sale of the work when out.
—I am, sir, with compts. of the season, yours, etc.,

H. R. DUFF.

No. XIII.

Copy Letter from S. Jones to H. R. Duff, Esq , Suffolk Street.*

2 Red Lion Passage, Fleet Street,
Feb. 5th, 1814.

Sir,—I shall by Tuesday next have got through the contents of
the hamper, and shall then immediately go to press with the
Correspondence.

The sheets, as they are printed off I should suppose, might be
sent to you under Mr Strahan's franks ; and such an explanatory
Preface as you allude to would be a very useful addition to the
work.

The Dedication will be the last thing wanted by the printer.

I should before this time have written to you to report my
progress with the hamper but that my attention is always indis-
pensably occupied for several of the *latter days of the month* by
my connection with some periodical publications.—I am, sir, with
respect, your obedt. humble servant,

S. JONES.

No. XIV.

Addressed to Thos. Cadell, Esq., Cadell & Davies, Strand,
London.

Muirtown, *17th March* 1817.

Sir,—I am induced, as a last request (unwilling to the
extreme to resort, as I have been long advised, to legal steps), to
address you, reverting to my late communications to Mr Sn. Jones,
Mr Mutlow, and Cadell & Davies.

The restoration of the Culloden papers is (by deeds now here)
most strenuously agreed on in Sept. 1812, to be made spring
1813.   4½ years have elapsed, and still illusory and vain answers
are given.   This, I am sorry to say shall be the end of my
amicable application, and I, as such, now send you this,—being
truly your obt. servt.,

H. R. DUFF.

* This letter has been kindly sent to us by Colonel Warrand.

No. XV.

Copy of letter sent to H. R. Duff, Esq., Muirtown, Inverness, in answer to the foregoing.

London, *March 25th.* 1817.

SIR,— I received your letter of the 17th, and much regret that Mr S Jones had not sooner enabled Mr Davies and myself to comply with your wishes respecting the restoration of the Culloden papers, which we have been prevented effecting by his not having been able to spare sufficient time amongst his other numerous literary avocations to put them sooner into some degree of proper order. Some weeks have, however, now elapsed since the papers have been sent to us by Mr S. Jones, and we have deferred taking further steps respecting them as we expected that the gentleman by whom we have frequently been applied to upon the subject, and who did not communicate his name and address would have taken charge of them ; but he having called two or three days ago, declined doing so, at the same time saying he would write to you respecting the papers. We must await your instructions.— I am, sir, your obedt servt.,   THOS CADELL.

No. XVI.

Addressed to Messrs Macqueen & Mackintosh, W.S., Edinburgh.

Muirtown, *2nd Feby.* 1819.

GENTLEMEN.— I have not the least expectation that any result will be found different from what I have stated as to the documents you wish, as I was careful in my perusal with views directed to the subject.

I send the order you wish, and,— I am your very obedt. humble servt.,   H. R. DUFF.

No. XVII.

Addressed to Messrs Cadell & Davies, Strand, London.

Muirtown *2nd Feby.* 1819.

GENTLEMEN,— As Mr Forbes of Culloden has (as I understand from his agents) use for the papers, which have been in your hands six years for publication, and as they are to be employ'd in some proceedings for his advantage, I beg these documents may be delivered to the order of his agents, Messrs Macqueen & Mackintosh, W.S., of Edinburgh. As they have made the request when they were delivered over to me by Culloden, they were gifted to do with as I chose, and were not meant to be returned. I have, however, neither kept nor alienated any of them.— I am your obt. servt.,   H. R. DUFF.

No. XVIII.

Addressed to Messrs Cadell & Davies, Strand, London.

Muirtown, *2nd Feby.* 1819.

GENTLEMEN,—Mr Forbes of Culloden's agents have some project with the Treasury which makes them wish for the letters in your hands. They were gifted to me spontaneously, and were indeed saved by my happening to be at Culloden from being used as loading-paper by the gamekeeper, as my first acquaintance with them was from a parcel lying on the table for that purpose. The letters on the other side can be of no use to the agents in this pursuit ; and though I made the note I gave to them a general one, yet I beg by this letter (which will come to hand first) to reserve them, and beg they may be delivered in a parcel to my address to Mr Stoddart, 2 Cleveland Row, St James's, London. —I am your most obedt. humble servt.,   H. R. DUFF.

Mr Stoddart is my halfpay agent, and for any kindness you are pleased to show in complying with my request, I shall be much obliged.

BOY FIGHTS.

——o——

THE "BIG GREEN" *versus* THE MERKINCH.

THE reader of Lockhart's "Life of Sir Walter Scott" will be
familiar with his account of the illustrious author of
"Waverley," in his High School days, partaking in the boy fights
or "bickers" in which the youths of the school fought with the
Edinburgh street *gamins*, and in which the redoubtable "Green-
breeks" sustained so prominent a part. In Inverness in our younger
days similar fights were indulged in between the boys of one quarter
of the town and another. The Petty Street boys were in a chronic
state of warfare with those of Rose Street, alternating with an occasional brisk brush with the boys of the Royal Academy. Tomnahurich Street and King Street had quarrels with the "Big Green"
—Muirtown Street—and the various streets and closes that diverge
from it towards the river. But the most desperate fights were
those carried on between the "Big Green" youths and the boys
of the Merkinch. These outbreaks appeared in the season as
regular as marbles in dirty spring weather, or as football in these
latter days with the approach of winter.

It is with the fights between the Green and the Merkinch that
our reminiscences have chiefly to do, as for three or four years
we took part as a combatant among the ranks of the latter. Indeed our position at that time was not a very enviable one, as,
while resident among those whose side we aided, we had daily to
attend the Central School that lay in the heart of the district of
the "Big Green." We must say, looking back on those days, that
the boys of the "Green" were not a very magnanimous lot ; for a
party of six or seven used to watch at the corner of Wells Street
or sometimes Celt Street for the arrival of the one or two Merk
inch youths who attended the Central School. We could hardly

pass without a charge from the enemy, in which a few good
knocks were exchanged on both sides.   On the occasion of one
of those unfair attacks, the odds were very unequal, and if it were
not for the unexpected arrival on the scene of good John
Douglas, head master of the Central School,* one or two of his
pupils would have fared badly at the hands of the " Big Green "
assailants.

There was a tradition among the boys that, some years preceding the date of which we write, in one of the encounters a life
had been lost—one of the boys belonging to the Green having received a blow from a stone on the head from which he
never recovered.   Another story was that the Merkinch youths
had seized in a fight on one of their opponents and had pushed
him into the " Abbey "—a sheet of water that then lay in the
hollow between Abbey Street and Telford Road, but has since been
filled up and partly built on - and that on his finding his way out
he returned home only to take to his bed, never recovering from
the severity of the attack made on him.   Our own personal
experience was that these fights were not always bloodless to
those engaged in them on either side, and were most dangerous
to innocent people who happened to be in the neighbourhood of
the battlefield, to say nothing of considerable destruction to
property.

One personal experience which caused us some alarm we give
as we ourselves were the offender.   On the occasion we refer to
there was a battle of stone-throwing—although many of those engaged were provided with sticks for use at close quarters.   When
the skirmishing began, many of the assailants on both sides were
provided with slings, which threw stones a long distance and with
great velocity.   Those who used the slings were in the habit, in-

* Worthy John Douglas, who died only a year ago at a ripe age, was
a painstaking teacher, although his scholarship was not extensive.   What
he did undertake, he, however, did well and thoroughly, and we will
ever venerate his memory.   Many promising youths were under his
tuition in the later "thirties" and in the early "forties."   Were we
to name those of our compeers at this time the list would be an extensive
one of successful business men at home and abroad, and others who
attained celebrity in literature   Notably among the best pupils at the
time to which we refer were, Malcolm M'Lennan, author of " Peasant
Life in the North," "Benoni Blake," etc. ; his two brothers—John F.
M'Lennan, author of " Primitive Marriage," and Donald M'Lennan,
barrister, who edited two editions of his brother's writings.

stead of throwing the stones direct, to fire them against the dyke that lined Telford Road, and which from thence ricocheted with considerable force among the combatants. The writer of these notes drove a stone in the manner described, and which struck first the wall, and rebounded among the opponents on the other side, striking a youth on the arm. On receiving the blow he retired from the field, and the fear fell on us that it must have been a dangerous blow that would have induced him to leave his post. Years after he recounted to us the pain he then suffered and for many long weeks, but we are glad to say no permanent harm was done him ; and after fifty years he is still alive and well, a prosperous London citizen, and ready to fight his battles over again when we meet.

We could not have been more than ten or eleven years of age when we took part in our first fight on Telford Road. A message had sped like the fiery cross in the days of clan raids that a fight was on, and we were wanted to help to drive back the enemy from the sacred soil of the Merkinch. There was soon a crowd gathered, and Joe Wishart, who led the Merkinch division, soon drove back the foe to their own ground—the Abbey gate marking the division between the opposing parties. It was on this occasion that one of the youths in this moment of triumph gave forth in rhyme, or rather the parodying of a verse of an old Scottish song, which follows, to one of his companions, what after became the rallying song of the Merkinch boys, and to which they marched as long as the writer continued to take part in these fights :—

> " March ! march ! to the Abbey gates,
> The foe is now before us ;
> We have fought them bravely,
> They no longer triumph o'er us."

The most of the Telford Road fights took place in the early summer, but when the long autumn nights set in the *venue* was changed to Gilbert Street, and Huntly Place, and Huntly Street. These were the more dangerous encounters, as the flying stones in the darkness could not be seen nor avoided— broken heads were more frequent, and damage to property greater. To add to the inspiriting of the combatants, the " Big Green ". got up a fife and drum band, and the Merkinch youths

24

followed suit. This development of musical talent had not the usual effect of " soothing the savage breast," for the contending forces now marched more eagerly to the scene of conflict. This state of matters continued for two winters, until the early spring of 1849, when, in the famous potato riots of that year, they came into conflict with the authorities. The bands of both the Merkinch and " Big Green " had been requisitioned by the rioters, but the magistrates made short work of the bands. When peace was restored they seized on the instruments of both parties, and that was the end of the fife and drum bands, and so far as our connection went with these fights, the last in which we bore any part.

It may be asked where were the police when such scenes were enacted as we have been describing. In those days there were only the three burgh officers—Sergeants Grant, Chisholm, and Tallach—who attended to matters in the burgh during the day, and we can only remember seeing them once on the occasion of these numerous fights. The three officials appeared one day suddenly in rear of the Merkinch band, when immediately there was a cry of " Police! " The enemy in front saw the position of affairs, opened their ranks, and received the flying Merkinch boys. The joined forces were now arrayed against the representatives of law and order. These officers were soon scrambling over the dyke and flying across the ploughed field where the Militia Barracks now stands—nor did they again show face on Telford Road that day. On the retreat of the officers of the peace, a parley was held among the conjoined force of the " Big Green " and the Merkinch, when a truce was agreed on, and each party marched away to their respective quarters to " fight another day."

Ex-Provost Alexander Ross, LL.D., President of
the Inverness Scientific Society and Field
Club, and a frequent contributor to the
Society's " Transaction " volumes.

BIBLIOGRAPHY OF INVERNESS NEWSPAPERS
AND PERIODICALS.

The following notes regarding Inverness Newspapers and
Periodicals, written by Mr. Noble, appeared in the columns of
"Scottish Notes and Queries" during the year 1888 :—

1807. " The Inverness Journal and Northern Advertiser," 4
pages, double crown folio, price sixpence, a weekly newspaper, was the first printed in Inverness. The first
number was issued in August of this year, by John Young,
Printer and Bookseller. Mr. Young was publisher of
several works in Gaelic and English. A fair specimen of
his capabilities as a printer, and reflecting credit on his
press, is the edition of " Poems, chiefly in the Scottish
Language," by Dr. Robert Couper of Keith, 2 vols., post 8vo,
Inverness, 1804. Dr. Couper is author of another work,
well known to Aberdeen collectors, " The Tourifications of
Malachi Meldrum," issued from the Aberdeen press. Mr.
Young also published a very handsome edition of " Ossian's
Poems," Macpherson's translation. Mr. Young is said to
have conducted the " Journal " himself for a little time, but
early in its career the editorial chair was taken by David
Carey, a native of Arbroath, who discharged the duties for
nearly five years. Carey was an author of considerable
versatility and ability—a poet, novelist, and successful
pamphleteer. While in Inverness he published a volume of
poems, printed by Mr. Young, "Craig Phadric: Visions of
Sensibility, with Legendary Tales and Occasional Pieces,"
8vo. Inverness, 1810. This volume is now chiefly valuable
for the notes to the piece Craig Phadric, containing as they
do much information on the early history of Inverness. In
connection with the " Journal " it may be mentioned that
a younger son of Mr. Young's, Murdo Young, was long
editor, and latterly proprietor, of the London " Sun " and
"True Sun" newspapers. The "Journal," about 1814,
changed hands, for the numbers of that year bear the
imprint that it was " published for himself and the other

proprietors by James Beaton." In a few years thereafter
the imprint bore as published for the proprietors by James
Fraser. It was understood at that time the proprietor was
really the late Lachlan Mackintosh of Raigmore, who continued the "Journal" till his death in 1845. Raigmore
had under him as sub-editors at various periods in succession, James Beaton, David (?) Stalker, and Donald
Macdonald. Mr. Stalker was sub-editor at the time of a
celebrated assault case, arising out of an article which had
appeared in the "Journal," reflecting on several townsmen.
The late Sheriff George Cameron of Dingwall, at that time
a writer in Inverness, was put on his trial for horse-
whipping the proprietor, Raigmore. Henry Cockburn
(afterwards Lord Cockburn) appeared for the defence, and
in his address to the jury played on the name of the sub-
editor, Stalker—"that he was put forward as a stalking
horse," as the writer of the offensive article. Another story
connected with the same trial I have heard told by the
foreman of the jury (a deceased county gentleman) that,
without leaving the jury-box, he had turned round, and
consulted with his fellow-jurymen for a minute, when suddenly, before some jurymen had quite made up their minds,
he announced that the jury by a majority found the defender
not guilty. On Raigmore's death in 1845 the "Journal"
was stopped for a time, but was resumed in 1846 by Donald
Macdonald, but continued to be published for about two
years only, when it finally ceased at his death.

1817. "The Inverness Courier, and General Advertiser for the
Counties of Inverness, Ross, Moray, Nairn, Cromarty,
Sutherland and Caithness," was commenced on 4th
December, 1817, and continued to be issued as a weekly
newspaper from that date till August, 1880. It was then
published three times a week till the end of 1885, and
since the latter date it has been published twice a week.
It still flourishes. The first editor was Mr. John Johnstone, husband of Mrs. Johnstone who conducted "The
Edinburgh Tales," and authoress of "Clan Albyn," a novel,
and other works. Mrs. Johnstone contributed to the
columns of the "Courier" while it was under her husband's

management.	Before the appointment of the late Dr. Robert Carruthers as editor, the late Mr. James Suter superintended the original matter that appeared in the " Courier," and in its columns first appeared (1822) " The Memorabilia of Inverness," recently reprinted in a small volume (1887) from its pages, by D. Macdonald, Inverness. In 1828 Dr. Carruthers became editor, and afterwards sole proprietor. He continued to edit it till his death in 1878. He was succeeded by his son, the late Walter Carruthers, who died in 1885, and he again was succeeded by its present editor, Mr. James Barron.	The London Letter of the " Courier " was for many years a feature of some note for its excellence. The first writer of this weekly budget of London Gossip in Politics, Literature, etc., was Mr. Roderick Reach, sometime a solicitor in Inverness, and who in his later years took up his residence in London, when he began contributing his weekly letter. On his death it was continued by his son, Angus Bethune Reach, one of the writers to " Punch," and a prolific contributor to the comic and lighter literature of his time.	The late Shirley Brooks, editor of "Punch," contributed the London letter for a year or two during the illness and till the death of Mr. Angus B. Reach.

1836. " The Inverness Herald." A Weekly Newspaper. Commenced on the 15th December, 1836, and " Printed for the Proprietors by Duncan Davidson." Strongly Conservative, and ultra Protestant in Church and State. At its first start it was edited solely by the late Rev. Alexander Clark, at the time Minister of the Second Charge, Inverness. Mr. Clark was a steady contributor to the columns of the "Herald" during its ten years' life, but he passed over the editorship very soon to the Rev. Simon Fraser, a probationer of the Church of Scotland, who was in time succeeded by the Rev. Donald Munro, also a probationer of the Kirk, who resigned the conducting of the " Herald " on his receiving the charge of a Presbyterian congregation at Alnwick, Northumberland. The last editor was Mr. Charles Bond, who conducted the paper till it was discontinued in July, 1846. Mr. Bond came to Inverness from Hastings, in

Sussex. He had published a small volume of Poems, in that
town, circa, 183(?), entitled, " Coronalis, a Poem designed
as a Memorial of the Coronation of Her Most Gracious
Majesty, Queen Victoria."   While acting editor of the
" Herald," at Inverness, he edited " The Reminiscences of
a Clachnacuddin Nonagenarian."   Inverness, 1842.   The
" Nonagenarian " became afterwards well known as " The
Inverness Centenarian.   Bond's little work, " The Reminiscences," became in course of a few years rather a scarce
book, and when copies appeared in local sales, sold at a
good price. It was republished last year (1887).

1839-40. " The Clachnacuddin Record."   A Weekly crown folio
sheet of 4 pages of local news, and literature. I write of
this periodical from recollection only. It had a brief existence—about 20 months, probably—1839-40. In 1851,
turning over the old periodical stock of a local bookseller,
I came on two different numbers. My recollection of its
date of publication is confirmed by a townsman who in his
early days had been employed in the " Herald " office, and
who at that time, on nights of publication, gave a hand,
both at case and press, to the printer and proprietor of the
" Record." John Maclean, the printer, was well known to the
older generation of Invernessians. He had a small jobbing
office in a court off High Street, now built over by the
Caledonian Banking Coy.'s offices. He was familiarly
known as " Clach," derived either from his newspaper, or
more probably as an Inverness boy, from the ancient stone
which forms the palladium of the Burgh—" Clachnacuddin,"
or the " Stone of the Tubs." Curiously enough, he is not
the last connected with the Inverness press who has borne
this designation, as at this very time (1888) the redoubtable
editor of another local newspaper is known by the popular
cognomen, " Clach." After the cessation of the " Clachnacuddin Record," Maclean gave up his jobbing office, and
passed a few years of Bohemian life about Inverness, living
on some little means he possessed. During these purpose-
less years of his life he made his old fellow-" comp." his
banker, as he could not always trust himself with the
possession of his means, and in applying for any sum he

needed, he always passed this characteristic cheque—" To
the Agent of the Caledonian (Canal) Bank, Pay to the
Editor of the ' Clachnacuddin Record' the sum of——.
(Signed) John Maclean, Editor." The latter years of his
life John Maclean spent as a compositor on the "night shift"
of a Glasgow newspaper. He died rather suddenly, a few
years ago, in the Western City. Alas! poor Clach! thou
wert deserving of a worthier end. The last we saw of his
open, jovial, Highland face was among the gathering of a
few Inverness boys in the city where he died.

1845-46. "Inverness and Northern Agriculturist." A Monthly
Journal. Published at the " Courier " office, Inverness, by
Robert Carruthers. A demy 4to sheet. About 18
numbers were issued. Entirely devoted to articles on
Agriculture, Sheep Farming, and kindred subjects. Among
its chief contributors were the late James Baillie Fraser of
Reelig, the celebrated Persian traveller, and the late
Kenneth Murray of Geanies. The latter, on the discon-
tinuance of the "Agriculturist," continued his monthly
article on Agriculture, etc., in the columns of the "Inverness
Courier " till his death.

1849. " The Inverness Advertiser, Ross-shire Chronicle, and
General Gazette for the Counties of Elgin, Nairn, Cromarty,
Sutherland, Caithness, and the Isles." Price 4½d., stamped.
A weekly newspaper of 8 pages double crown folio. The
first number was issued on 19th June, 1849, bearing imprint
—" Printed every Tuesday Morning, by Gavin Tait, and
published by him for the Proprietor, James M'Cosh." Mr.
M'Cosh came to Inverness from Dundee, where he had conducted the " Northern Warder." He was well known on
the Evangelical side of the Non-intrusion controversy.
" The Wheat and the Chaff," a pamphlet which he published
at the Disruption, exposing the flaming profession as Non-
intrusionists of many of those who remained in the Church
of Scotland, is well known to collectors. The success of the
" Advertiser " was great, but Mr. M'Cosh lived only for a
few months after its start. On his death it was carried on
by his representatives, the editorship being undertaken

temporarily by Mr. Thomas Mulock, father of the late Mrs. Craik, authoress of "John Halifax, Gentleman," and numerous other works. Mr. Mulock had brought himself into notice in the North by a series of letters and articles which appeared in the "Advertiser" on Highland evictions. These articles were afterwards reprinted (1850) under the title "The Western Highlands and Islands of Scotland Socially Considered with reference to Proprietors and People." Those fond of pursuing researches into the by-ways of literature will find an interesting notice of Thomas Mulock, as founder of a new religious sect, in "Tait's Edinburgh Magazine" (circa 1844),—his rough treatment by a mob of students at Oxford, and his attempts to propagate his peculiar views in the Pottery districts. I think the paper was written by William Howitt. In 1850 the "Advertiser" was purchased from the relatives of Mr. M'Cosh by the late George France of Silverwells, Inverness, the number of 8th October of that year being the first with his name as proprietor. He had successively as editors Mr. Dundas Scott, a translator of several works from the French ; Mr. Robert Gossip, now connected with the newspaper press in Glasgow ; and latterly Mr. J. B. Gillies, now a printer and a Town Councillor of Edinburgh. In November, 1855, the plant and copyright of the "Advertiser" was bought by the late Ebenezer Forsyth, who before coming to Inverness had connection with several newspapers in Edinburgh. For upwards of a year after this purchase the "Advertiser" was edited by Mr. Donald Maclennan, now a Barrister in London, when Mr. Forsyth took the reins of office, and retained the same till his death, in May, 1873. He was succeeded by his son, W. Banks Forsyth, who conducted the paper till it was discontinued in December, 1885, when the copyright was purchased by the proprietors of the "Inverness Courier." The "Advertiser," it may be noted, was issued from its commencement on 19th June, 1849, till 3rd February, 1860, as a weekly paper. From this last date till 16th September, 1882, as a tri-weekly (Tuesday, Friday, and Saturday). The Saturday issue was numbered independently, and in this day's publication, it may be mentioned, first appeared the valuable "Antiquarian Notes" of Mr. Fraser-Mackintosh,

M.P., which ultimately developed into a large volume with this title, printed in 1865. Another volume, reprinted from serial articles which appeared in this day's publication, was the "Notes on Shakespeare," by the editor, Mr. Forsyth. The "Advertiser" from 22nd September, 1882, till it stopped, on 25th Dec., 1885, was resumed as a weekly.

1853. "Caraid nan Gaidheal: or the Highland Friend for the Highlands and Islands of Scotland." A Monthly Magazine of 16 demy 8vo pages, with printed cover, price 6d. No. I. was published in July, 1853, by Gavin Tait, printer, 76 Church St. (the same office as that at which the "Advertiser" was printed), and sold by K. Douglas. W. Smith, C. Keith, and D. Fraser, Inverness. The proprietor and editor of this short-lived periodical was James Ross, a working journeyman shoemaker with an employer in Castle Street, Inverness. He furnishes one more example of many contributors to literature of the sons of St. Crispin, and the "pursuit of knowledge under difficulties." Mr. Ross afterwards became manager of the Reformatory, Inverness. The contents of "The Highland Friend," No. I., are about three-fourths printed in the Gaelic language: the articles are of a moral and religious character. One of the articles in English by the Editor—"Familiar Words across the Counter "—is really lessons to a beginner in Gaelic. The instructions, if not useful to the learner, are, at least, both novel and amusing to the reader. Mr. Ross thus curiously set forth his aims in starting "Caraid nan Gaidheal" in his address "To our Readers" on cover. While he admits that various publications in Gaelic have been published in the south of Scotland, but the whole of them had only a short reign, he claims for his periodical—"This is the first of its kind ever attempted in the Highlands. Inverness," he continues, "is a little spoken of as a favourable place for new speculations, but we will not say much in case our own reign may be far shorter than any of the above. By what wonderful means do we think to succeed? Is it by our superior talents, etc.? No. Is it by trying to work wonders in the midst of a crooked and perverse generation? No. Is it by attempting to knock down all opposition, as

a butcher unmercifully does an ox? No ; for, strange to say,
there is no opposition ; but if we dig deep till we find the
' gold,' we shall, undoubtedly, share the same fate with the
California Miller" (sic ? Miner). So much for the editor's
style ! " The Highland Friend " was fated to live a much
shorter life than even its southern predecessors. No. 1 was
published ; No. 2 never saw the light of publication.

1855-59.   " Inverness Times and North of Scotland General
Advertiser." A weekly newspaper of 4 pages, double crown
folio, printed and published by Charles Merrilees & Son,
2 Church Street, and latterly at 45 High Street. At its first
start three pages of the paper were printed in London.
The front page, printed in Inverness, contained advertisements, local news, with prose and poetical contributions.
About eighteen months after its commencement two pages
were printed in Inverness. Its editing for a time was hap-
hazard—chiefly by Mr. Merrilees, junior, while in 1857-59
the chief contributors were two or three young men, members of a local Debating Society, who at the time were
strongly infected with "cacoethes scribendi." These
aspirants got up the local leaders, tales, poems, and even a
novel that ran for some months. The latter was contributed
by the chief of the trio. It was done with considerable
power, and while appearing it was with some amusement
to those who were in the " know " that the hero in course of
moving incidents by " flood and field " was landed in the
great Metropolis, " near where the shadow of St. Paul's
throws itself across the way "—a city in which the author
had then never been. Years after, one of these young men,
on his first visit to the great city, made his way purposely
to St. Paul's in search of the spot where Mac's hero was so
suddenly transplanted. As might be expected from young
men fresh from the inspiration of Plutarch, and the
oratorical displays at the Inverness Literary and Debating
Society, the leaders were strongly flavoured with a dash of
Radicalism. Twice or thrice a week meetings were held,
where articles, correspondence, etc., were considered and
decided on. These meetings still live green in the
memories of two at least of the contributors, who, though

separated by nearly twenty years' wanderings in two hemi-
spheres, some three years ago had, on the banks of the Ness,
an opportunity of renewing with much glee a talk over the
lucubrations at these symposiums and their connection with
" The Times " in earlier years. In the summer of 1859 the
publishers got into difficulties financially, and the " Time (s)
was no more ! "

1856-58. " The Inverness Reformer." A weekly newspaper of
4 pages, double demy folio, price 2d. Like its contemporary " The Times," as already mentioned, the " Reformer "
was only partially printed in Inverness—the front page only
—three pages coming from London. The imprint, however, bore as " printed for the proprietor, by John Reid, 9
Church Street, Inverness." The ostensible Editor of the
" Reformer " was the late Kennedy M'Nab. In the
original prospectus, now before me, the principles on which
the " Reformer " was started are set forth as " thoroughly
independent of all local influence. It will take the Liberal
or rather Ultra-Liberal side in politics. It will advocate
extension of the suffrage, vote by ballot, shortening the
duration of Parliament, etc. ; the union of the Free and
United Presbyterian Churches, as the sure and effectual
means of overthrowing the Establishment, as an Establishment, and with it all religious endowments." Abstract
reports of the Town Council were only to be given, "unless
any comedies or farces are enacted in the Town Hall, when
full reports will be given and the Actors mercilessly ridi-
culed and satirised." It was not long before the " Reformer " and its editor were in a sea of troubles, legal and
financial, and the publication was frequently interrupted
and delayed, until finally the editor was laid up by the heels,
the result of an action, and the paper was stopped, at least
for a time (1857). The "Reformer" was probably unique
in Scottish journalism—its violent personal attacks on prominent public men—its satirical notes on the peculiarities
and angularities of quiet and inoffensive citizens, who were
easily recognised through the thin veil of anonymity thrown
over them—even the very family circle was invaded—and to
many the " Reformer " became intolerable and looked on

as a nuisance to be put down. I have heard an irascible
citizen at this period, who was asked if he had read it, express himself—" Read it, Sir!—No, Sir! I would not touch
it with the tongs!" He, however, was hardly an unpre-
judiced witness—he figured in the columns of that morning's issue of the " Reformer." As above stated, the attacks
on public men laid the editor open to several actions, and
in course of the processes, the sheets of the " Reformer,"
received from London, were several times arrested at the
Railway Station. As showing the sonorous Junian hand
of the editor's writing, I may quote from a handbill issued
by him on one of these occasions. It is dated 24th November, 1856, with M'Nab's name as Editor of " Reformer " at
bottom. The bill is headed—" The Lawyers of Inverness.
—Notice to the Public."—The arrestment is denounced as
a regular combined attempt on the part of a number of
members of the bar to crush " The Reformer." " The
Editor has a little story to tell his legal friends :—Once
upon a time an indignant Irish orator in the Parliament at
College Green, was venting his wrath against some one,
when a cry got up to take down his words. His answer
was ' Stop a little and I'll give you something worth taking
down ' and then went on ten times worse than before.
Now, we tell the lawyers, stop a little and we'll give you
something worth stopping the ' Reformer ' for. Let them
look out for the next number. We pledge ourselves to
shiver their reputation to atoms by telling the Truth."
Even the threat of " giving wood engravings of not a few
of them, in proper attitudes," did not save the persecuted
" Reformer " at this time. After several months' suspension it, however, reappeared. To give a favourite quotation
of the Editor's—" It springs again like a phœnix from its
ashes," and he promises " it will be regularly continued.
Legal oppression will not put it down." It had now become
more a magazine, a weekly periodical of 16 pages, 8vo,
entitled " Macnab's Inverness Reformer and Review," No. 1
appearing on Friday, 5th March, 1858, price 2d, and
" printed for the Proprietors by Kennedy Macnab, Ramsay
& Co., 13 Petty Street, Inverness." The sheet was really
printed in Edinburgh. It was but short-lived. Whether

from the failure of the sinews of war, or that the soothing effect of the discipline the editor had undergone had helped to tone down the acerbity of his pen, the paper ceased to sell up to the paying point, and at the third number of the new issue it came to an end—wood engravings nevertheless. The last number is dated 19th March, 1858. It contains a woodcut portrait of Alex. Campbell of Monzie, then a candidate for the representation of the Inverness Burghs in Parliament. Another cut in this number is intended for a portrait of an unpopular factor in a Northern Isle. The Inverness bar escaped being portrayed in the "proper attitudes."

1857-58. "Merrilees' Pictorial Monthly Magazine of Instruction and General Entertainment." Demy 8vo, with printed cover, price 2d. The early numbers extend to 20 pages, but ultimately enlarged to 24 pages. Of these at first only 4 pages, and on extension 8 pages, were printed by the publishers, Charles Merrilees & Son, at the "Times" office, 45 High Street. Sixteen pages, with woodcuts throughout all the numbers, was a sheet issued by Cassell of London. The original papers printed in this periodical contained contributions by C. H. Morine, late professor of music, Inverness, Mr. Findlay, Reelig, etc., but the majority of articles were contributed by the same trio as in the "Times" Newspaper, published by this firm. A series of articles on events in the Early History of Inverness, short tales and poems, were their chief contributions to its pages. The periodical was only short-lived, about 9 or 10 numbers. The last, now before me, is dated March, 1858. A curious circumstance in connection with the printing office, and as showing how sometimes most valuable historical documents disappear, may be here mentioned. This place, a year or two preceding, had formed part of the Chambers of the Town Clerk for the time being. At his death a quantity of papers connected with Burgh were stored in an underground cellar. When the premises were relet, they had been overlooked or forgotten on the removal of the other effects. One day a visitor to the printing office, looking at a small hand-press which a boy was working at, discovered that the tympan of vellum or parchment, had some old writing on it, and asking the party in charge as to it, was told with a chuckle that "they did not require to purchase tympans now," as the P. D. of the establishment had discovered a find, and was making use of papers in the cellar for lighting his fires, etc. The visitor warned them of the seriousness of what they were doing, as well as the Vandalism they were guilty of.

1857-58. "The Institutional Gazette." A Monthly Sheet of 8 pages, foolscap 4to, price 1d.   Printed at the "Courier Office," Bank Lane, by Robert Carruthers. This small sheet, consisting of short essays, papers on education, poetical pieces, etc., was got up by the senior pupils and a few of the pupil-teachers of the Free Church Institution—an educational seminary started by the Free Church party a few years after the Disruption—and ultimately merged in what is now called the High School, Inverness.   The Institution had at this time as rector Thomas Morrison, now Principal of the Free Church Training College, Glasgow. Many of the pupils attending the Institution at Inverness had imparted to them much of the energy and literary taste of their rector, and in the "Gazette" found a small field for exercising their acquirements and youthful exuberance. Some of the contributors to this small brochure were very successful, and came well to the front in their varied careers in after life.   It was an open secret at the time of the appearance of this publication that the chief contributors and conductors of the "Gazette" were the present Dean of Faculty and Queen's Counsel, Wm. Mackintosh of Kyllachy, and "Alec" Fraser (so familiarly known to his old school fellows), now a Lieutenant-Colonel of the Royal Engineers, stationed in India, and eldest son of Captain E. B. Fraser of Redburn, Inverness. The "Gazette" extended to about 8 numbers.

1861-63. "The Highland Sentinel—with Gaelic motto following the general title—"Tir nam Beann nan Gleann 's nan Gaisgeach—The Land of the Bens, the Glens, and the Heroes —the well-known motto surrounding the bank note of the

GAELIC SOCIETY OF INVERNESS.

——

Some contributors to the " Transaction "
volumes :

Sir Henry Macandrew.

Charles Fraser-Mackintosh of Drummond.

Kenneth Macdonald, Town Clerk.

William Mackay, First Secretary of the Society.

——

View of the Castle from the River.

Caledonian Bank. A weekly newspaper of 8 pages, demy folio, price, unstamped, 2d. It was started in July, 1861, by Robert Maclean, a jobbing printer in the Athenæum Buildings, 3 High Street, Inverness. It was only partly printed here, 6 pages coming from publishers in London, as did its predecessors, the " Reformer " and the " Times." Indeed, the material from which the pages were printed locally, came from the office of the latter, Maclean having purchased the chief part of the types, etc., at the dispersion of the "Times" plant; and in the year after it began, the "Sentinel" occupied the same office, at 45 High Street. In the end of 1861 Maclean was joined in partnership by a relative, and the firm became Maclean & Paterson. On the removal of the office a change was made on the " Sentinel." It then appeared as a four page, double crown size, all printed locally, and the price was reduced to a penny. The "Sentinel" had no responsible editor—the local paragraphs, and the usual scissors and paste was done for a time by Maclean, with the occasional aid of any outsider who could be obtained for an original article. Mr. Angus Macdonald, the first Bard of the Gaelic Society of Inverness—a Gaelic poet and scholar of some note, worked for a time on the " Sentinel." I can also discover in looking over some of the numbers in its latter days, the hand of Kennedy Macnab, the whilom editor of the deceased " Reformer," but robbed of much of the seasoning that gave his paragraphs a zest in his own publication. The " Sentinel " was not a financial success, and after an existence of two years it stopped.

1872-88. " Transactions of the Gaelic Society of Inverness." Vol. 1.—year 1871-72.—" Clann nan Gaidheal ri Guaillean a Cheile." 8vo, Inverness: printed for the Society by William Mackay, 14 High Street, 1872. Thirteen volumes of the Society's Transactions have been issued up to date (1888). These vols. were printed at offices in Aberdeen and Inverness, and bear various imprints. They vary in quantity of matter, the tendency of later volumes being to double the quantity of the pages of Vol. I. The contents contain full reports of the annual meetings, also of the papers read before the Society. These papers are valuable, and bear on the furtherance of the objects for which the Gaelic Society was founded, viz., the use of the Gaelic ; the cultivation of the language, poetry and music of the Scottish Highlands ; the rescuing from oblivion of Celtic poetry, traditions, legends, etc. There is a Publication Committee to aid in getting up the Transactions, but the burden has pretty well lain on the shoulders of the Secretary for the time being. William Mackay, Solicitor, Inverness, and editor of Captain Simon Fraser's " Collection of Airs and Melodies of the Highlands and Isles, " as Secretary, had charge of the first volume. In vols. 3 and 4, published in one volume, appeared as intro- duction, a " History of the Origin and Aims of the Gaelic Society." This double volume was edited by Alexander Mackenzie, now editor of the " Scottish Highlander," and William Mackenzie, then Secretary, and now First Clerk to the Crofters Commission. This latter gentleman continued as Secretary to the Gaelic Society from 1875 to 1886, and edited the various volumes of the Transactions published in this interval,—viz., volumes 5 to 12 inclusive, as well as vol. 2. Vol. 13, the last issued, is edited jointly by the present Secretary, Mr. D. Mackintosh, and Mr. Alex. Mac- bain, M.A., Raining's School, Inverness.

1873-82. "The Highlander." A weekly newspaper of 16 pages, crown folio, price 2d. Printed for the Highlander Newspaper and Printing and Publishing Company, Limited, by Alex. Macbean, at the office, 42 Church Street, and pub- lished at the office, Exchange, Inverness. The name of Alex. Macbean, as printer, it may be noted, only appeared on Number 1, issued on the 16th May, 1873. He was really only the manager of the printing department of the Coy. The "Highlander" was started by the Limited Com- pany as already noted with Mr. John Murdoch, a retired supervisor of Inland Revenue, as editor, a post which he continued to fill during the existence of the newspaper. Mr. Murdoch was well known in the North as holding advanced views on the Land Question, which he had promulgated by lectures and newspaper contributions. The chief objects of the promoters of the paper were, to quote their original

GAELIC SOCIETY OF INVERNESS.

Some contributors to the "Transaction"
volumes :

Sheriff Blair.

Duncan Mackintosh, Secretary.

John MacDonald.

William Mackay, Printer of Vol. i., 1872,
and printer of the "Agricultural
Register."

View of Inverness, after Turner, R.A., and
reproductions of the Burgh Arms.

"THE HIGHLANDER."

———

Editors:

John Murdoch.

Lachlan Macbean.

John Whyte.

———

View of Castle Wynd, Commercial Hotel,
and Old Town Hall.

prospectus, "To foster enterprise and public opinion in the Highlands and Islands of Scotland; to advocate, independently of party considerations, those political, social, and economic measures which appear best calculated to advance the well-being of the people at large; and to provide Highlanders at home and abroad with a record and review of events in which due prominence should be given to Highland affairs." A prominent feature of the "Highlander," and one which excited interest among the Highland people, was that a large portion of its pages was devoted to articles of an interesting character in the Gaelic language, as well as a profusion of Notes and Queries on the lines of "Scottish Notes and Queries," bearing upon Celtic and Highland matters. There also appeared, from time to time, Gaelic songs and poems, the former with music in the Sol-fa Notation. This department was one of peculiar interest, and makes the file of the "Highlander" a repertory for future compilers of song and lore. Early in its career the "Highlander" experienced some of the vicissitudes attendant on newspaper criticism. An action was raised against it for libel, and damages were awarded in the case, which proved a staggering blow to its prosperity. Friends, however, came forward, and the "Highlander" was enabled to tide over its difficulties for a time, but the Limited Company found it necessary ultimately to wind up its affairs, and in November, 1878, the whole concern passed into the hands of Mr. Murdoch. The number of the "Highlander" for 23rd November bears the imprint as printed for John Murdoch, at the office, 87 Church Street, and was continued by him till the end of January, 1882, when it ceased to be issued. The original size of issue underwent various changes throughout its chequered career. Starting as a 16 page crown folio, it changed, on 30th May, 1874, to an 8 page double crown folio, giving it more of the form of the ordinary newspaper. In 1877 it was again changed and enlarged, and later, underwent one or two more alterations of form and size, till in the end of May, 1881, it was converted into a Magazine of 40 pages, demy 8vo, with cover, and published monthly. The contents of the monthly "Highlander" were

25

now more of the literary Magazine but still bearing entirely
on Celtic subjects. It was numbered anew—Vol. I., New
Series—Nos. 1 to 6. This was the last part issued, and is
dated December-January, 1881-82. It may be mentioned
as of some interest, that the only known complete set of
the "Highlander" is in the Library of the Gaelic Society,
Inverness.

1874. "The Auctioneer:" price Not one Half-Penny. A post
4to of 4 pages, printed at the "Highlander" office, Inverness, for A. & W. Mackenzie, Auctioneers. Only three
numbers were issued, October and November, the last number issued being No. 3, dated 16th November, 1874. It
was intended as a bi-monthly publication, the object contemplated being a furtherance of the business of the firm,
advertising their sales by auction, and articles for sale by
private bargain. It, however, contained, throughout all
its issue, critical articles upon local Municipal matters, the
Elections to Town Council, Burgh Accounts, etc. This was
the first news publication of the now Editor of "The Scottish Highlander," and late Editor of the "Celtic Magazine."

1875-88. "The Celtic Magazine: a Monthly Periodical,
devoted to the Literature, History, Antiquities, Folk-Lore,
Traditions, and the Social and material interests of the
Celt at Home and Abroad." Conducted by Alexander Mackenzie, and the Rev. Alexander Macgregor. Inverness: A.
& W. Mackenzie, 2 Hamilton Place. Beginning as a 32
page demy 8vo, price 6d., it has been enlarged from time
to time to 40, and latterly to 48 pages, besides the printed
cover and advertising sheet. The purpose for which the
Magazine was started is very fully set forth in the general
title. In the original prospectus, as also on the title page
of Vol. I. of the magazine, it is stated as conducted by Alex.
Mackenzie and the Rev. Alex. Macgregor, M.A., Inverness ;
but I understand that the rev. gentleman had nothing whatever to do with the editing, although he contributed several
papers to the earlier volumes, in his own name, as also
under the nom de plume "Sgiathanach." In the "Celtic
Magazine" appeared Mr Macgregor's "Life of Flora Mac-

"THE CELTIC MAGAZINE."

———

Editors:

Alexander Mackenzie.

Alexander Macbain, M.A., LL.D.

Rev. Alexander Macgregor, M.A.

———

View of the High Church from the River Ness.

donald, and her Adventures with Prince Charles"—the first authentic narrative of this famous Highland heroine that has appeared. On the author's death it was reprinted from the pages of the "Celtic Magazine," with memoir of Mr. Macgregor in a cr. 8vo volume (1882). The sole editing of the Celtic was done by Mr. Mackenzie, the proprietor, to the close of Vol. xi., when the editorship was taken over by Mr. Alex. Macbain, M.A., a well known member of the Gaelic Society of Inverness, and a contributor of most valuable papers on Celtic Philology to the Society's Transactions. The "Celtic Magazine," it may be stated, is the most successful effort made in Highland periodical literature. At no previous time has any Magazine connected with the Highlands, on the furtherance of Highland interests, continued to exist for half the period this one has done, and it still pursues its prosperous career. The following bibliographical facts may be given as of interest in connection with this publication:—In its pages first appeared the several works on H'ghland Family History, etc., as follows—they having been reprinted with some additions, viz., "The Prophecies of the Brahan Seer (1877), several editions of which have been issued; "History of the Clan Mackenzie" (1879); "History of the Clan Macdonald" (1881); "History of the Clan Matheson" (1882); "History of the Clan Cameron" (1884.) In the current volume (13), now issuing, the "History of the Clan Macleod" is appearing, and on completion will appear as a large volume similar to the others.

1878 (?) "Fraser's Illustrated Monthly Magazine." 8 pages, royal 8vo, price 1d. Published by Donald Fraser, 15 Union Street, Inverness. About this date a periodical with this title was issued. Not more than three numbers were published. It excited no interest, and as a periodical under its Inverness title, it may be reckoned among the "lost books." I have failed to find a single number among those who usually set aside local efforts of this class, and my application to the publisher has been as fruitless. In fact, Mr. F., when applied to first, had no recollection of ever having issued such a journal. After giving him sundry pieces of information in regard to it, stored in my own memory, he at length recollected something of it. The most palpable fact, however, in his mind regarding it was, to use his own words, "The affair did not pay." How much infliction the world would be spared if only that which "paid" was alone printed. The life of newspapers and periodicals would then, as in the doctrine held by some in reference to the natural world, be that of the survival of the fittest. Only one page of "Fraser's Magazine" was printed locally, the other seven pages in this case, as in the other local ventures of a like character, being supplied by Messrs. Cassell of London.

1879.   "Two Stories": "Schoolmaster's Abroad," and "In the the Way of Business" (Chap. i., ii., iii.) No.1—September, 1879.   London and Edinburgh.   Aberdeen: W. & W. Lindsay.   Inverness: W. Mackay.   112 pages post 16mo, price 6d.   This small serial was issued from a private press in Beech-Tree House, Drummond,—a suburb of Inverness. The Rev. Mr. Parminter, Incumbent of St. John's Episcopal Church, Inverness, had a press, from which he issued several small educational books, based on a scheme which has been largely adopted by school book publishers since, that is of issuing Classics, arithmetical works, etc., in small sections or portions suitable to the progress or standards of pupils. The "Two Stories" were intended as a serial, if successful. The authorship of the stories, the printing, etc., were all done by Mr. P., following the noted example of Samuel Richardson, the author of "Clarissa Harlowe," who set his own type and composed his novel at the same time. I do not know if any more of the "Two Stories" were issued, as shortly after No. 1 was presented to me by the Author, he removed from the North. The rev. gentleman had been, previous to his incumbency at Inverness, in South Africa, and had contributed to the press there. If I mistake not, several articles of his appeared in the "Cape Monthly Magazine," then under the Editorship of Professor Roderick Noble, an old Clachnacuddin boy, and a Gold Medallist of the Royal Academy, Inverness. While noting the issue of the above, it may also be here mentioned, that about this date, or a year or two earlier, there was another

"NORTHERN CHRONICLE."

———

Portraits of Charles Innes, late Chairman of the
" Northern Chronicle" Company, and of
James Livingstone, late Manager.

———

View of the " Northern Chronicle" Publishing
Office.

privately printed periodical issued in the neighbourhood
of Inverness. At Gollanfield House, near Fort George
Station, occupied then by Hector Mackenzie, Esq., his
daughter, Miss Isobel Mackenzie, issued for some time a
monthly magazine, the editing, printing and publishing of
which was done in this mansion house. I expect to be able
to supply the exact title, date, and extent of issue, in my
concluding article of this bibliography. It may be here, however, said of the editress, Miss Mackenzie, who died young,
that she possessed considerable hereditary claims as a
writer, as niece of the world-wide boys' author, R. M.
Ballantyne, and grand-daughter of James Ballantyne, the
friend and publisher of Sir Walter Scott.

1880-81. "The Invernessian: " An Independent Journal, published on the last Saturday of every month, conducted by
Alexr. Mackenzie, F.S.A. Scot., price one penny. A foolscap
folio of 8 pages, printed by James Black, Elgin, for the
proprietors, and published by A. & W. Mackenzie, "Celtic
Magazine" Office, 2 Ness Bank, Inverness. This journal
was not so much a newspaper as a critical comment on
passing events in the Burgh of Inverness and the adjoining
county, on the lines of the Society Journals. In the
"Random Notes," and the "Local Notes," the editor, as
a "Free Lance," delivered his blows right and left on
municipal matters, etc., irrespective of politics. The first
number of this journal was issued on 30th October, 1880,
and the last in August, 1881—there were thus ten numbers
published. At number 5 of the issue, the size was altered
to a demy 4to of 16 pages, with some woodcuts thereafter
embodied in the text. The title was changed as follows:—
"The Invernessian: " An Independent Monthly Illustrated
Journal, Critical and Instructive. This number 5 bears no
imprint, but numbers 6 to 10 have the imprint—"Published
by A. & W. Mackenzie, 2 Ness Bank, Inverness." The
greater portion of the pages of Nos. 5 to 10 were sent from
London, and only pages 1, 8, 9, and 16, were printed locally
with northern articles and notes.

1881-88. "The Northern Chronicle and General Advertiser for

the North of Scotland." 8 pages double royal folio; price
1d. Inverness: printed and published by the Northern
Counties Newspaper and Printing and Publishing Co.
(Limited), at their office situated in Margaret Street, Inverness. This weekly newspaper was begun on the 5th of
January, 1881, in the interests of the Conservative party
in the northern counties. The "Chronicle" has been
edited by Mr. D. Campbell since its commencement. The
principles by which the "Chronicle" seeks to obtain the
object for which it was started are set forth in its first
number as follows:—"The 'Northern Chronicle' will
discuss ministerial home policy, and bills by whomsoever
laid before Parliament. . . . It will aim at creating
good feeling between class and class, promoting those just
relations between man and man which lie at the foundation
of commercial prosperity, and uphold patriotic and con-
stitutional views as the soundest guarantee for maintaining the integrity and developing the resources of the
Empire. The 'N.C.' will oppose disestablishment.
. . . In its columns prominence will be given to all
matters affecting the interests of farmers, the class upon
whose welfare all other classes in the northern counties
mainly depend."

1881-83. "The General Machinery Register, and Architectural
    Engineers' and Iron Merchants' Museum Circular:" A
    monthly periodical, 10 pages, royal 4to, with cover; price
    2d. Inverness: printed at the "Courier Office" for Messrs
    William Smith & Sons. The first number was issued on
    the 21st November, 1881, and the last number (19) is dated
    26th May, 1883. It was issued by a local firm of trades-
    men as a means of forwarding their business and disposing
    of many articles, machinery, etc., consigned to them for
    sale. It contained throughout all its numbers many
    articles on agriculture; criticisms practical and suggestive,
    on new patents; trade news; contracts taken in the district
    for buildings, etc., with results of the tenders and their
    amounts by the various tradesmen offering. The first
    seven numbers were printed at the "Courier Office," and
    bear imprint as above. From No. 8 to 19 they bear as

John MacLeod, Editor and Proprietor of

the " Highland News."

printed and published by George Wood, Museum Buildings, Dempster Gardens, Inverness.

1882-83. "The Inverness Frolic: A new Illustrated Journal for Highlanders at Home and Abroad." 12 pages demy 4to, with printed cover, price 2d. Printed at the "Courier" Office, Inverness. The first number of the "Frolic," and the first attempt to establish a comic journal in the Highland capital, was issued on Saturday, the 9th December, 1882. It was intended to be a monthly periodical and to appear on the second Saturday of each month. It, however, only had a life of three months—No. 2, dated 13th January, 1883, and the last number published, dated 10th Feb., 1883. The proprietor of the "Frolic" was Mr. A. H. Cruickshank, a designer and wood engraver, who came from London in 1881-1882 with the view of establishing himself in business in Inverness if encouragement was given. Mr. C. had some experience in the metropolis as an illustrator of serial works, having been engaged during his apprenticeship, and after, in designing and cutting for several of the publishers of the weekly penny periodicals. The illustrations of the "Frolic" were all designed and cut by himself, but, as depictions of Highland features and figure, they were not successful. There is a stilted sameness in all the faces, as may be seen in the every week issue of any of the London penny illustrated journals. It required more than the draping of the cockney figures in the tartan, the bonnet, and the sporran to hit the Celt, and his physiog, as is done so successfully by W. Ralston, an "artist to the very manner born," in his illustrations of "Sketches of Highland Character," "The Pugnacious Celt," and the plate "Chentlemen, since it is your pleasure I'll tell you aal apout it," as examples. In the literary department of the "Frolic," Mr Cruickshank was aided by several local contributors.

1883-88. "The Highland News: The Organ of the Highland Temperance League." Underneath the heading were views of Oban and Inverness, these places being the centres of the League's operations. The news was a sheet of 4 pages double demy. The first number was issued on 8th October, 1883, price one penny. The imprint bore as "Printed every Monday morning, by Lewis Munro, Dingwall, and published by him at 5 Castle Street, Inverness." The "News" was conducted by Mr. Munro, with occasional contributions from friends engaged in the temperance movement. On the 3rd November, 1884, there was a change in imprint to "Printed for, and published by, Philip Macleod, at Office of 'Highland News,' 11 Castle Wynd, Inverness." With this change, a portion of the paper began to be printed in Inverness, viz., the second and third pages, the other two continuing to be printed at Dingwall by Mr. Munro. On the 30th of May, 1885, the "News" ceased to be issued as the special organ of the Highland Temperance League, and its title changed to what it now is, "The Highland News," circulating in the Counties of Inverness, Nairn, Moray, Ross, Sutherland, Caithness, Argyle and Perth." It was first printed entirely in Inverness on the 14th June, 1886, as it still continues to be, with imprint as "Printed by the Northern Counties Newspaper and Printing and Publishing Coy., Ltd., and published by the proprietor, Philip Macleod." On the 5th March, 1887, the "News" was enlarged to its present size of 4 pages double royal. The editor is Mr. Philip Macleod. In politics, the paper supports advanced Liberalism, or rather Radical, as the term is now more frequently used, while, at the same time, it continues to make a feature of, as one of the leading objects, as set forth in its opening address in the first number issued, "To supply news gathered from all parts of the Highlands, and a modest endeavour to assist in advancing the moral and social well-being of the people."

1885-88.   "The Scottish Highlander:" Edited by Alexander Mackenzie. Price one penny. A weekly newspaper of 16 pages, crown folio, with imprint—Inverness: printed and published at the "Scottish Highlander" Office, Meal Market Close, High Street, Inverness, every Friday afternoon, by Mackenzie, Thomson & Co. The aims sought by its promoters are set forth in No. 1, issued 17th July, 1885, to be as follows:—"Stated broadly, the main object of the

'Scottish Highlander' will be a temperate, but bold and independent spirit to advocate the rights and promote the interests of the Highland people. It will be impossible to do this effectually without at the same time advocating very great alterations in the existing state of the law: but no changes will be urged except those based on the equitable principle that every man, whatever his position, be he landlord or tenant, employer or labourer, should be secured in the full enjoyment of the fruits of his labour, whether physical or mental." On the 4th March, 1886, the day of publication was changed to Thursday morning, and on the conclusion of the first year of publication, the size was altered to a double crown sheet of 8 pages. On 1st January, 1887, the property was formed into a limited liability company, under the name of "The Scottish Highlander" Printing Co., Ltd. There was a slight change, more recently introduced in the title to that of "The Scottish Highlander, and North of Scotland Advertiser." Many valuable antiquarian and literary contributions have appeared from time to time in the columns of the "Scottish Highlander." I may mention a series, entitled "Letters of Two Centuries," being original hitherto unpublished letters of northern celebrities—valuable as affording illustrations of social life and manners, economics, etc., of the seventeenth and eighteenth centuries. They are contributed with comments on, and notices of, the writers, by Charles Fraser Mackintosh, M.P., from his unique collection, formed and collected during the past thirty years. These letters will ultimately, I understand, be issued in a large volume, and will form an authentic picture of past life among the middle and upper classes in the Highlands, no longer existing. Mrs. Mary Mackellar, the Gaelic poetess, has also contributed papers on Highland superstitions and kindred subjects, while the editor's wife, Mrs. Mackenzie, under the nom de plume, M. A. Rose, has supplied tales and other papers. Of more recent literary papers are the unpublished poems in Gaelic and English of an hitherto unknown Highland poet, D. B. Macleod, a native of Brora, Sutherlandshire. The MSS. of these poems were preserved, after the death of the author, by Evan M'Coll, the bard of Lochfyne, who carried them with him to Canada on his emigrating there. The poems are of considerable merit, and worthy of the receptacle they have found in the pages of the "Scottish Highlander."

1885-88. "Transactions of the Inverness Scientific Society and Field Club." Vol I., 1875-1880. Edited by James Barron. 8vo. Inverness, printed at the "Courier" Office, 1885. A second volume, containing the transactions from 1880-1883, was issued this year 1888. No name of editor, or date of publication, appears on this latter title page, the preface alone, dated 1st May, 1888. I understand, however, that Mr. Barron, of "Inverness Courier," has also edited this, the latest volume of the Club's proceedings issued. Both of these volumes contain the papers read at the monthly meetings, also accounts of the various excursions and scientific expeditions of the Club, account of the annual meetings, etc. The papers contributed by the members contain a great mass of original facts, and information on the archæology, geology, folk-lore, antiquities, etc., of Inverness and the surrounding country. Several of the papers have engraved illustrations accompanying them. In Vol. I., there is a most valuable geological map of the district. It may be mentioned that previous to the Club undertaking the publication of these volumes, printed copies of papers, etc., were supplied to members, done up from the necessarily imperfect reports of local newspapers. These now are embodied and extended by their authors in the published volumes as above.

1887-88. "The Raining School Magazine:" 4 pages, post 4to. price $\frac{1}{2}$d. Printed and published for the proprietors by William Mackay, 27 High Street, Inverness. A bi-monthly periodical, got up by the senior pupils attending the Raining School, Inverness, under the editorship of Mr. G. A. Wilson. This educational institution, the oldest in Inverness, was founded in 1726 by John Raining, a merchant in Norwich —"A Scotsman, who, from love to his native country, bequeathed funds to plant a school," in which "fatherless and other poor children would receive instruction in English,

INVERNESS FIELD CLUB.

———

Some contributors to the " Transaction "
volumes :

Dr. Aitken.

William Jolly.

Thomas D. Wallace.

James Ross.

Joseph Melven.

James Melven.

(The latter two gentlemen being publishers of the
" Northern Evangelist.")

———

View of the River Ness at the Islands, and
reproduction of the Inverness Seals.

Latin, and arithmetic, as the said yearly income will maintain." An interesting account of the founder and the
institution is given by Mr. Alexander Macbain, the present
Headmaster, in the fifth and sixth numbers of the current
series of the "School Magazine." The first number of the
Rainingites' magazine that honoured the art discovered by
Guttenberg is dated 23rd September, 1887. The
"Magazine," however, had a pre-existent state—nay, three
—from its first original as a manuscript, "written on 12
sheets of foolscap paper, issued every week" (1884). It
came to an end in this state at the close of the school
session in June of that year, and was not resumed until
September, 1886, when it appeared "on a one page sheet
of medium, in a glazed (sic) frame and exhibited in the
school. Passing through this glacial period, a Cyclostyle
Copier was requisitioned, and 11 numbers of 4 pages each
and a Christmas number of 8 pages, post 4to, appeared.
"This," says the chronicler, "the third venture, ended
16th February, 1887." The writer possesses a complete
set of this Cyclostyle printed periodical, and places it among
the curiosities in his collection of local newspapers and
magazines. The imprint of this series bears as being
"printed at Culcabock, and published at the Raining
School, Inverness," most certainly the first print dated
from this rural village, so well known to school boys of
Inverness of a former generation by the more derogatory
name of Sraid na Leobaig—anglice, Fluke Street. As I
have mentioned, the aid of the invention of printing was
finally called in to help the efforts of the young Rainingites,
and the result is the 4 page magazine above duly chronicled,
which has run, during the session 1887-88, to 18 numbers
the latest, dated 21st June, being a "Special Double Number of 8 pages, and concluding Vol. I. in its present form.
On the fourth number is the Gaelic motto—"Imthigh, a
Dhuilleachan, gu dan"—"Go forth, leaflet, boldly"—
Kirke, 1684—the minister of Balquhidder, I presume, who
translated from Irish into Scottish Gaelic the first edition
of the Bible. The articles appearing in the "School
Magazine" are set forth by the editor as "Literary
Matters bearing on Highland History, Tradition, Lore,

Gaelic Literature, etc." These, in a small measure, have been attained.

1888. "Inverness Football Times. Published only during the season. Price ½d. Inverness: printed for "Athlete," by the "Scottish Highlander" Company, Limited, High Street, Inverness. The publication is a single leaf of demy folio, printed on both sides, and, as its title sets forth, only during the season when this now popular game is in fashion. The first number of the first season on which the "Times" was started is dated Saturday, 14th January, 1888 ; and it continued to be issued every Saturday afternoon thereafter till the close of the football season on 5th May. In all 17 numbers have appeared, the last with a Supplement containing a portrait and biographical sketch of a well known local player, Dr. John Macdonald. "The undertaking of ' Times ' is purely and simply to supply an enthusiastic, interested, and considerable portion of the community with faithful and impartial reports of the matches of the day immediately after these are completed." So states the editor of the "Athlete" (Mr J. Tulloch), is the purpose of the publication of the "Football Times."

In answer to a correspondent, Mr. Noble, in "Scottish Notes and Queries," of August, 1888, wrote :—There was no periodical entitled "Chronicles of the City by the Sea" published in Inverness "some twenty years ago." There was, however, three jeu d'esprits with this title issued at long intervals, with no intention of a serial or a continuation when the first was printed. The first of these was in 1864, viz., "Chronicles of the City by the Sea," Book I., in four chapters, a post 4to sheet of four printed pages. The second in 1865-66, Book II., in five chapters, uniform in size and pages with the preceding. The third of these in 1879-80, Book III., in six chapters, printed on five pages, uniform with the other two. None of these sheets were dated, hence the difficulty to fix the exact year ; but as they all are the chronicle of events that were well known, the dates I attach may be approximately fixed as now stated. Books I. and II. refer entirely to noted cases that troubled the usually peaceful waters of the local Ecclesiastical Court of the Auld Kirk. Book III. relates to a different atmosphere :—the financial crisis of 1878—the closing of the City of Glasgow Bank—the involvement of the Caledonian Bank, with interests so much intertwined with the prosperity of Inverness and the Highlands, and the successful efforts made for the resuscitation of this the most valued of our local commercial institutions. All of the "Chronicles" are written in imitation of the Biblical writers of the Old Testament, or rather more closely resembles that of the famous Chaldee MS. of "Blackwood's Magazine," which created a noise in Edinburgh in the early career of "Ebony." The authorship of Books I. and II. belongs to the late Mr. Ebenezer Forsyth, editor and proprietor of the "Inverness Advertiser." At the time of publication it was said that he had been aided by a well known town official recently deceased; but Mr. F. was far too clever a man to allow any intermeddling, or call in aid with his compositions. The official's concern with it would have gone no further than being probably its first auditor, and the last verse in Chapter V. of Book II., which may have given rise to the supposition of outsiders as to joint authorship, was likely added to gratify his hearer. The Third Book of the "Chronicle" I believe I am not doing injustice to any one in giving the credit of it to Mr. W. B. Forsyth, his father's successor in the editorship of the "Advertiser."

The Editor of "Scottish Notes and Queries," in a note to the writer, expresses his surprise to find "that nothing of the nature of a periodical was published in Inverness earlier than 1807." This is no cause for wonder if one considers the condition of the country north of the Grampians preceding the rising of "Forty-five," and the opinion held by the mass of the Highlanders in regard to education,—the scorn for those engaged in trade, and the accomplishments that were alone considered essential and worthy of a Highland gentleman. Sir Walter Scott was well within the mark when he places in the mouth of Rob Roy the contemptuous reply made by that cateran to the worthy Bailie Nicol Jarvie, on the latter's invitation to send his sons, Robert and Hamish, to Glasgow; or even the opinion of one of a later generation of Highlanders as to the acquirement of penmanship, "that he would rather plough a straight furrow for the length of a bow-rig, than draw a line half-an-inch long as he ought with a pen." With such opinions held by the mass literature would make but slow progress. It was not till 1778 that, according to the "Memorabilia of Inverness," a printing office was established in the town. The first bookseller's shop is said to have been opened in 1775—("History of Inverness," 1847)—but this is an error, for Dr. Johnson, on his way to the Hebrides in 1773, purchased a volume here, and was flattered by having an offer of his own "Rambler," which was for sale in the bookseller's shop. But there is still earlier data: A volume of "Meditations on Several Subjects," written by the Rev. Hugh Rose of Nairn, bears the imprint—"Edinburgh: Printed for William Sharp, Bookseller in Inverness, 1762." The earliest imprint I have seen attached to a local publication occurred in the Catalogue of my former assistant, Mr. D. Macdonald, the publisher of "Reminiscences of a Clachnacuddin Nonagenarian." It is only a small pamphlet, a "Letter addressed to the Burgesses" of the Burgh, by "Veritas," and bears the imprint of "Inverness, 6th July, 1784." Not, then, till thirty years after the first printing office was set up here is there any trace of a news-sheet or periodical, although many volumes and pamphlets were published in the interval, both in Gaelic and English—original works and reprints. These as specimens of typography would reflect credit on the metropolitan press.

The present effort at a Bibliography of Inverness Newspapers and Periodicals has not been the first attempt in this direction. More than forty years ago the compilation of a list of publications of the Inverness Press was contemplated by Mr. George Cameron, Wholesale Stationer, Glasgow—a native of the town —who, in 1847, published a small 12mo. volume, "History and Description of the Town of Inverness, etc." In this work he states that it was his intention to have given a Catalogue of all the Books, Pamphlets and other prints issued in the town, with the authors' and publishers' names and dates of publication: but having been unable to procure sufficient data for completing the List, he left it out rather than insert it imperfect. It is to be regretted that it was not given even in an imperfect condition; the list of pamphlets with names of authors would of itself have been of great importance. Many curious things were issued from 1828 to 1846, the very period over which Mr. C.'s knowledge of the subject would have been most accurate, having

acquired it while in the service of his relative, Mr. Kenneth
Douglas, one of the best known Booksellers in the North during
the greater portion of the first half of the present century.

The present Bibliography was not contemplated to extend beyond, as its title embraces, Newspapers and Periodicals, and I
believe the List, as it has appeared from time to time in these
pages, with the few additions to be given in this present article,
will form as complete a Catalogue as is possible to be made, if
indeed it does not contain all.   When I undertook this compilation a list had been furnished me of the bare titles of eleven
Newspapers and Magazines.   A look at it satisfied me that I
could add seven or eight more from memory, but I have now
finally extended these to thirty-three.   In the furnished list
made by Mr. Fraser-Mackintosh there was only one periodical
the name of which I had not previously known.   In a note to
Mr. M., I expressed some doubt if ever such a one had been
issued.   He wrote me immediately that he would put me right
as to its existence on his return to the North, as he had a note
with respect to it at Lochardill.   Mr. Fraser-Mackintosh has
done so, with the usual exactness that characterizes all the data
in his published volumes regarding his native town.   It here
follows:—"Excerpts from Papers lent me by Mr. D. A. Nicol,
late of Holm Tweed Mill, 21st December, 1866."

"1830. 'The Northern Mirror: or Inverness Magazine.'   A
    Magazine appeared at Inverness in September, 1830. Size of
    this sheet, post 8vo.   No name of Printer or Publisher.
    Called the 'Northern Mirror: or Inverness Magazine.'
    Two articles were contributed, it is believed, by Donald Mac-
    donald, afterwards of the 'Inverness Journal,' and two by
    one Andrew Fraser.   These are the most interesting.   It
    is not known if more than one number appeared.   The
    number of pages, 24.   Fraser was called Andrew
    'Goggan' * as mentioned to me by Mr. James Macpher-

* Andrew Fraser, "Goggan," a native of Inverness, a gardener. A short
notice of him appears in the "Recollections of Inverness, by an Invernessian"
(Robbie Munro). He was a contributor to newspapers and several periodicals.
Some tales of his appeared in "Wilson's Tales of the Borders." One,
"Donald Gorm," is specially mentioned by Munro. The Writer of these
Notes possesses two MSS. volumes of poems, with legendary and other notes,

son. * The best Article is ' The Floater '—Case of Simon Henderson, Bught, an old man living **30** years before (1800).† Told a story of his coming down the Ness on a Raft with James Urquhart, the Floater, and dashed to pieces on the two Carries nearly opposite to Torvean. Mr. D. A. Nicol has the copy C. F. M. saw. The name as sent to the late Dr. Nicol‡ is upon it thus, at the top of the outside, ' Mr. John Nicol.' ''

Since I received Mr. Mackintosh's note on the "Mirror" I have happily found one of the original contributors, who still survives, the last most certainly of all connected with this the first effort to establish a magazine in Inverness. Fresh from Aberdeen University at this date, he had to do with the publication, and knew who were the contributors. Mr. John Nicol, whose name appears on the copy Mr. Mackintosh took his notes from, was a son of Dr. Nicol, and himself a contributor.

1840-41. "The Clachnacuddin Record." Under the date 1839 I inserted this periodical. I wrote of it then from recollection, as stated. Since then I have found a number that was really at the time in my possession, but which I had forgotten. I found it in making search for another. The correct title is, "The Inverness Spectator, and Clachnacuddin Record." It was a monthly of four pages, crown folio, price 2d., and bears the imprint—Inverness, printed and published on the first Friday of every month, by John Maclean, No. 7 High Street. The "Spectator," while containing some local news paragraphs, is more of a literary journal, containing articles original and selected. I re-

by Fraser. They are beautiful specimens of his caligraphy. The poems are of considerable merit. I propose, at a future time, in another undertaking, to publish some specimens of his poetical genius.

* James Macpherson here mentioned was a well known Solicitor in Inverness, and senior partner in the legal firm *now* represented by Sir H. C. Macandrew.

† The correct name was William Henderson. His daughter became the second wife of Sir Hector Mackenzie of Gairloch, and the late Provost John Mackenzie of Eileanach was her son. William Henderson survived until about 1816, and died aged 97.

‡ Dr. Nicol—the leading man of his day in Inverness—acted as Chief Magistrate for some years—father of D. A. Nicol.

cognise, in one of the articles in the number in my possession, the hand of Finlay Maclean, the son of Old Maclean,
the Inverness Centenarian, who, himself a printer, was
also author of "Sketches of Highland Families," Dingwall,
1848. I believe also David (Davie) Macdonald, who
published a volume of Poems (English and Gaelic)—"The
Mountain Heath: consisting of Original Poems and Songs,"
Inverness, 1838, was a contributor to the "Spectator."
The No. of the "Spectator" in my possession is the 6th, and
dated 5th March, 1841.

1841-42. There was a monthly journal published in connection
with the temperance movement about this date. My recollection of it is but little, chiefly in connection with a
pamphlet reprinted from its columns of a controversy, in
which the editor and printer (Mr. Hutchison) laid a weighty
hand on the late Rev. A. Cook of Daviot, at that time the
minister of the now Free North Church. Mr. C. had
attacked the teetotal party in some address, and in return
received a severe handling. The reverend gentleman was
no match for the editor. The title of the periodical was
"The Northern Temperance Journal," or something akin
thereto—its size a foolscap or pott folio, of 8 pages.

1876. "Gathered Fragments:" a Monthly Magazine, with
motto, "That nothing be lost."—St. John vi. 12. 20
pages, crown 8vo, and printed cover. Inverness, 1876.
Under date of 1879 I noticed two privately printed
magazines that were issued in the neighbourhood of Inverness. My notice of the Rev. Mr. Parminter's little serial,
issued of that date, and notice of his printing press, has
brought to me a note, for which I am obliged, from Miss
Isabel H. Anderson, authoress of the delightfully pleasant
reminiscences of old times and characters of her native
town, embodied in the volume "Inverness before Rail-
ways," 1885, enclosing the only two numbers published of
the other periodical printed at Mr. Parminter's press.
"Gathered Leaves" seems, from a notice on the cover, to
have been intended for distribution among the congregation
of St. John's Episcopal Chapel, and "for its maintenance,"

26

on "voluntary contributions, both literary and pecuniary."
While circulating among members of St. John's, "extra
copies may be purchased at the rate of two-and-sixpence
for the half year, or sixpence the single number." It
seems not to have received the support expected, as only
two numbers were issued. The dates on these are—No. I.,
January 31, and No. 11., March 13, 1876. Miss Anderson
contributed a poem to the second number. In connection
with the other magazine printed at the private press at
Gollanfield House, by Miss Isobel Mackenzie, I have only
been able to ascertain that the title of it was "The Cabar-
feidh,"—from the stag's head in the crest of the Clan
Mackenzie. The size was a 16mo; date of publication,
circa 1877-78.

CONTINUATION AND NOTES BY THE PRESENT EDITOR.

1889. "The Highland Monthly." This serial was published by the proprietors of the "Northern Chronicle" as a literary Highland journal. Its editors during the whole period of its existence were Mr Duncan Campbell, editor of the "Northern Chronicle," and Dr. Alexander Macbain. Its contents, which were interesting and valuable, were chiefly in English, but it had also several highly competent Gaelic contributors. Its first number was issued in April, 1889, and fifty-one numbers were issued, the closing one being dated June, 1893.

1892. "The Academical," a monthly illustrated magazine in connection with the Royal Academy. Its editors were Mr. George T. Bruce, who was Rector of the Academy from 1888 to 1894, and is now Principal of the New Glenmoriston College, Inverness, and Mr. Pierre Delavault, Art Master. Its first number appeared in February, 1892, and it was continued till June, 1894. It consisted of contributions by the staff and pupils, past and present, of the Academy. The printers and publishers were the "Highland News" Printing and Publishing Co., Inverness, and its price 2d. monthly.

1893. "The Olde Normandie Fayre Daily Gazette." A 4-page demy sheet, price twopence, "registered as a newsance," and "printed for the 'Olde Normandie Fayre' Committee by the Northern Counties Newspaper and Printing and Publishing Company, Limited, Margaret Street, Inverness. Thursday, September 14, 1893." As may be inferred from the title, the "Daily Gazette" was issued in connection with the Olde Normandie Fayre held at Inverness in aid of the funds of the Northern Counties Cricket and Inverness Tennis Clubs. In the first number, it is announced in an editorial that "we shall last as long as the necessity for us lasts—and no paper lasts longer," with the further intimation that "this illustrated paper is by the help of the gods and several promising young people expected to live three days." This prophecy, unlike many that appear in the daily Press nowadays, was duly fulfilled, the paper ceasing to exist after a bright career extending over three days. The "Daily Gazette," as naturally it should, contained numerous articles, topically treated, on matters immediately associated with the Fayre, "Stray Notes," by Autumn Leaf, being most prominent, and running through the three issues; in addition, there were humorous articles—"Jules Fairan in the Highlands," "Jules Fairan Visits 'the Coonsil,'" "Notes on Natural History," "The Cheap Forest Commission"—successfully hitting off the local municipal and parliamentary situation. The "Daily Gazette" reflected the highest credit on the "promising young people" responsible for its publication.

1896. "The Highland Times." This journal was commenced as a weekly advanced Liberal paper on February 8th, 1896. Its proprietor is Mr. Philip Macleod, formerly of the "Highland News," and its first editor was Mr. John Whyte. During the first two years of its course it was published on Saturdays, but on the discontinuance of the "Scottish Highlander," in May, 1898, its day of publication was changed to Thursday, and it still continues to be issued on that day.

1896. "The Northern Evangelist." This is a mid-monthly record of Christian thought and work. Its conductor is Mr. Joseph T. Melven, of Melven Brothers, booksellers. It is exclusively, as its name imports, a religious magazine, one of its features being a Gaelic department. Its first number appeared in April, 1896. The uumber for February, 1902, contains an announcement that the sale of the "Evangelist" is not sufficient to encourage the publishers to continue its issue any longer.

1899. "New Glenmoriston College Magazine." This attractive and interesting Christmas Annual is now in its third year. It is issued in connection with the institution whose name it bears, and is edited by Mr G. T. Bruce, the Principal, the contributors being the staff and pupils. The illustrations, which evince considerable merit, are the work of the pupils. The first year's issue was printed at the office of the "Inverness Courier," the numbers for 1900, 1901 being produced at the printing office of the "Northern Chronicle."

1901. "The Ratepayers' Monthly." This is a monthly serial devoted chiefly to the chronicling of the sayings and doings of the Inverness Town Council, and critical notes on the town's affairs generally. Its proprietor and conductor is Mr. George Young, Bookseller. Its first number was issued in October, 1901, and it is still being conducted on the original lines. The first two issues were printed at the office of the "Highland Times." It is now printed at the office of the "Highland News."

Transactions of the Gaelic Society, Page 197.

These most important volumes still continue to be issued by the Gaelic Society, the last published being Vol. xxii.

The Celtic Magazine, Page 200.

Volume XIII. closed the career of "The Celtic Magazine." During the last four years its editor was Dr. Alexander Macbain, who was himself a large contributor to its pages.

The Highland News, Page 205.

In the beginning of the year 1895 this paper became the sole property of Mr. John Macleod, sometime M.P. for Sutherland-shire, who became its editor in 1887, and by whom it is still vigorously conducted as an advanced Liberal and Land Law Reform advocate. In December, 1901, the proprietors of the "Highland News" issued a "Christmas Annual," crown folio, which had a very extensive circulation. It is intended to issue similar special numbers in future years at the Christmas season.

The Scottish Highlander, Page 206.

Mr. Alexander Mackenzie, the editor of this paper, died in January, 1898, and the issue of the "Scottish Highlander" ceased in May of the same year.

Transactions of the Inverness Scientific Society and Field Club,
Page 208.

Four volumes of these valuable Transactions have now been issued under the editorship of Mr. Barron, editor of the "Inverness Courier."

Inverness Football Times, Page 210.

This periodical subsequently passed into the hands of the proprietors of the "Highland News," who issued it for a time as an evening edition of that paper. It is still continued, at the same office, with its original name resumed, and has a very large circulation.

The Northern Mirror, Page 213.

In a footnote to Mr. Noble's notice of this paper the authorship of "Donald Gorm," one of the "Tales of the Borders," is ascribed to Andrew Fraser, "Goggan." This is incorrect, the author of "Donald Gorm" being Alexander Campbell.

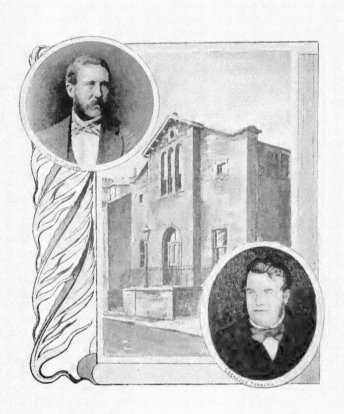

"INVERNESS ADVERTISER."

Editors :

Ebenezer Forsyth.

W. B. Forsyth.

View of Publishing Office.

APPENDIX.

The Agricultural Register.

The "Agricultural Register" was a monthly publication, started in 1873, and was chiefly devoted to agricultural affairs, with advertisements from all and sundry appealing to country customers. It was a small sheet—double-crown—got up by a new firm of agricultural agents—Messrs Fraser & Mactavish, of Lombard Street, Inverness—and was, while it was published, well patronized by advertisers, and promised success, and could ultimately have developed into a power; but the firm were so successful in the amount of their business, that they were unable to devote the necessary attention. Every month it had a re-sume of matters relating to country produce and affairs. One thousand copies were printed and gratuitously circulated each month through the country and the north. It was printed by Mr. William Mackay, Inverness.

The Inverness Advertiser.

The "Advertiser" was started in the year 1847, at a time when the animosities of the Disruption of 1843 had not subsided. A party of the Free Church, feeling that the "Courier" did them less than justice, brought out the paper on Liberal and Free Church principles. The first editor was Mr. James MacCosh—a gentleman of diminutive stature, but an able writer and a thorough journalist, under whose editorship the "Advertiser" was very successful, the circulation for those days being large— quite equal to that of the "Courier," then the leading journal and the largest circulation in the north. Mr. MacCosh, being of delicate physique, shortly afterwards succumbed, and lies interred in the now almost disused Greyfriars' Burying-ground. An interregnum followed, which was filled by the editorship of a visitor—Mr. Mullock, father of the more celebrated Miss Mullock or Mrs. Craik, author of "John Halifax, Gentleman," etc. Mr. Mullock was a ready and capable man and writer, but notorious for some extreme views socially. He conducted the "Advertiser" with much vigour, making it a sheet to be

reckoned with in these parts; but ultimately the "Witness,"
then edited by the famous Hugh Miller, denounced the incon-
gruous connection of Mr. Mullock and the Free Church paper,
exposing Mr. Mullock's erratic conduct and views of the marriage
laws, which, to say the least, were very advanced. The article
in the "Witness" was extremely bitter, quoting Byron in connection with Mr. Mullock, and the end of the matter was that
Mr. Mullock had to relinquish his connection with the "Advertiser," pithily remarking that Byron "was at least a gentleman"—inferring that Hugh Miller was no gentleman—which
was an opinion not generally accepted by the public of the
north.   Mr. France, of Wester Lovat, and latterly for many
years resident at Silverwells, Ness Bank, shortly afterwards
acquired the "Advertiser," and carried it on for some time,
Mr. Gossip, well-known afterwards as a journalist in Glasgow
and Edinburgh, being editor.   Mr Gillies, afterwards of the
"Daily Review," was also connected with the "Advertiser."
Mr. Gavin Tait, still in business as a printer in Inverness, printed
the paper until the late Mr. Ebenezer Forsyth purchased it.
Mr. Ebenezer Erskine Forsyth, the new editor and proprietor
of the "Advertiser," in whose family the paper remained for
many years, was a native of Langholm, Dumfriesshire, and for
several years acted as sub-editor and theatrical critic of the
"Scotsman," under the celebrated editor, Dr. Russell.   Later
Mr. Forsyth founded a weekly paper called the "Edinburgh
News," which ran with great success for several years under his
management, but having disposed of it he purchased the
"Inverness Advertiser" from Mr. France.   Mr. Forsyth was
conspicuous as editor for his independent Liberalism in politics
and his earnest advocacy of local reform in municipal affairs,
at that time in the hands of a burgh clique of a very exclusive
character.   Mr. Forsyth died in 1873 at the comparatively early
age of 57 years.   He was a free burgess of Edinburgh, and
reckoned amongst his intimate friends Russell of the "Scotsman," Hugh Miller of the "Witness," Dr. Carruthers of the
"Inverness Courier," and many other distinguished contemporaries.   While in failing health for several years before his death,
the "Advertiser" was edited and conducted by his son, Mr. W.
B. Forsyth, who for fifteen years afterwards continued—until
1889—to edit and manage the business, when, owing to an

" INVERNESS COURIER."

———

Editors and Contributors :

Dr. Robert Carruthers.

Robert Carruthers, jun.

Walter Carruthers.

James Barron.

Dr. Alexander Stewart
("Nether Lochaber").

Hugh Miller.

———

View of the "Courier" Office.

opposition newspaper being started in Inverness on Highland lines and keen opposition the "Advertiser" became financially a failure, and was ultimately amalgamated with its contemporary the "Courier." During the editorship of Mr. W. B. Forsyth, in pursuance of the character of the paper, he fought the old Whig clique, and ultimately got returned to Parliament the popular and patriotic Mr. Fraser-Mackintosh for the Inverness Burghs. Again the paper fought the Tory party in the county, though unsuccessfully at first, with Sir Kenneth Mackenzie as Liberal candidate, but succeeded ultimately with the burgh member—Mr. C. Fraser-Mackintosh—as county member.

We are glad to add that Mr W. B. Forsyth—the last editor of the "Advertiser"—is having a successful career in London, limiting himself to the quiet confines of trade journalism— editor of "Harper's Weekly" and London correspondence—and seeking to advance as far as in his power the interests of Scotch- men and Highlanders in the great metropolis. Mr. Forsyth has travelled in the United States and Canada in journalistic work, and during the last 12 years been over the wine countries of Europe—France, Spain, Portugal, and Germany—to report for a wine trade journal on the vintage crops at various seasons.

Inverness Courier.

On the 4th December, 1817, the first number of the "Inverness Courier" was issued. It was printed in the office situated at 22 High Street, above the shop at present occupied by Messrs. Fraser & Campbell, drapers; at that time occupied by a grocer, Mr. John Mackay. The "Courier" was started in opposition to an active local party of those days which created ill-feeling in the burgh. Its object was to provide news and avoid personalities. The paper was con- tinued as a weekly until August, 1880, when it was issued as a tri-weekly till the end of 1885, and since that date it has been published as a bi-weekly. Whether it was an im- provement to have departed from its weekly character—to the regret of many readers—its appearance on the Tuesday and Friday—the choicest days of the week—very effectively disposed of the "Inverness Advertiser," which was shortly

after extinguished, and merged or incorporated in the
"Courier." The "Courier" at first had a chequered enough
career, with many changes of editor in its early life. The
first editor, Mr. John Johnstone, was famous as the husband
of "Meg Dods," of cookery fame—"Meg Dods' Cookery Book"
—who was also the authoress of a novel, "Clan Albyn," and
who edited the "Edinburgh Tales." Mrs. Johnstone contributed to the columns of the "Courier" while under her
husband's management. After the withdrawal of the
Johnstones, a local gentleman—the late Mr. James Sutor,
Church Street—took charge, and wrote extensively for its
columns. Mr. Sutor was a ready and original writer, great
in figures, and many of the older Invernessians remember
the quaintness and singularity of his demeanour. Mr. Sutor
had a standing feud with the railway directors here, claiming
a large sum for projecting and proving the feasibility of the
Highland Railway. When offered an amount which the
railway directors considered fair, Mr. Sutor promptly rejected
the proffered sum, and most sarcastically descanted on the
idiosyncrasies of the individuals comprising the Board, to
the amusement and hilarity of Invernessians of those days
"Before the Railway." "The Memorabilia of Inverness" was
Mr. Sutor's work, a very curious production inserted by him
in the "Courier," and published in a separate form by Mr.
Donald Macdonald, at one time assistant to the late Mr.
John Noble, bookseller. Mr. Sutor used to tell a good story,
though rather against himself. An advertisement appeared,
requesting the heirs of a certain gentleman of the name of
Sutor to apply. The interim editor wrote stating that he
was a Sutor, and if there were no other applicant he might
possibly be the right one. The advertiser wrote in answer,
stating that "he thought all the Sutors from Land's End to
John o' Groats had applied, with the exception of the 'Sutors
of Cromarty,' from whom as yet there had been no communication."

The late Dr. Carruthers became editor of the "Courier"
in 1828, and some time afterwards proprietor as well as

editor. He continued to conduct the "Courier" for fifty years with remarkable ability and success, making the "Inverness Courier" a power—famous, widely known, and keenly appreciated. Dr. Carruthers—then Mr. Robert Carruthers—got the "Courier" with a circulation under 500 copies a week, but it speedily sprang up to 1000. The "Inverness Journal," then edited by Mr. Lachlan Mackintosh of Raigmore—grandfather of the present Raigmore—a man of prodigious powers, who delighted in castigating officials of the town and kirk, and others, when anything remiss was discovered, was then the only rival of the "Courier." With a view to angle for advertisements—"The 'Journal'" (said the editor) "has double the circulation of the 'Courier' in the parish of Moy and Delarossie." "We have made inquiries," said the "Courier" of next issue, "as to the respective circulations of the 'Courier' and 'Journal' in the said parish, and we are informed by the postmaster that the circulation of the 'Journal' in the parish is 2 copies per week, that of the 'Courier,' 1." The result was that a good deal of banter was indulged in, proving that the "Courier" was always ready for "him" of the "Journal," who usually made those of the opposition sharply feel "his" comments. In those days a good deal, if not all, business in the local parliament was perpetrated in secret conclave, and the press had to ferret out the doings of the Council, and often did so successfully. Both "Journal" and "Courier" had to act artfully. On one occasion, after Raigmore had rather roughly handled the Council, a meeting was being held, and when approaching a ticklish bit of the business, one of the bailies whispered, "Take care, take care; there is an *Achan* in the camp," referring to some member of the Council who was suspected of communicating the discussion of the Council to the press. In the next issue of the "Journal," in reference to the remark, it was put, "Bailie Achan said," &c. The bailie was known as "Bailie Achan" all his days, and the epithet sticks to this day to his worthy and respectable family. Several of them have acquitted themselves so well

that titles of honour, " Sir " this and " Dr." that, have fallen
on them. When required to distinguish them even now,
" Achan " is uttered as a distinguishing word to mark them
out from many other families of the same name. The influence of the press in those days was not small. The "Courier"
and its editor could, however, always hold its own in encounters with the " Journal," who, as we said, was a hard
hitter ; and in circulation the " Courier " exceeded all com-
petitors in the North. In 1846 the circulation of the
" Courier " was 1300 copies weekly, and the advertisements
numerous. It must be remembered that the price of the
paper was 4½d. per copy—a penny for the stamp which was
impressed on the sheet before printing, and that 1s. 6d. duty
had to be paid for each advertisement—a scandalous impost.
The reading circulation of the " Courier " would be at least
four times that number. One old decayed burgher—Tommie
Ross—used to buy some two dozen copies of the paper a
week, and let or lend each copy for one hour at one penny
each reader, enabling many of the inhabitants to know what
" he " (the editor) had to say : very important to them, for
those were the days " Before the Railway " and the daily
press. " What does ' he' say this morning ? "—equivalent to
" What news ? "—being frequently asked of the boys delivering their " Couriers " on the morning of publication. Even
in the remote from Inverness town of Stonehaven, an Invernessian long resident there in business, the late Mr. Robert
Ross, saddler, was the centre of a club who got the " Courier "
regularly for years before and after 1853. It was keenly
looked for, and passed round several shops and homes—not
all Highlanders—who much appreciated the style and trend
of the paper, which ultimately fell to one of the clique, who
usually sent it abroad. This points to the fact that, while
a penny or a halfpenny may now be paid for a newspaper
individually, the old and higher price shows a larger circulation than was apparent from the original issue. When it is
considered that the whole paper was read—religiously read—
advertisements and all, the reading public of those days was

not so far behind that of the present, when thousands are sold compared to hundreds in the old order. The "Courier" was the first in the North to discard the hand-press. Shortly after 1840, Dr. Carruthers introduced a machine —the "Belper"—fed and rolled from both sides by, of course, manual labour, a great improvement on the hand-press, printing some 400 or 500 per hour, one side at a time. The "Belper" was superseded shortly after by the "Kirk-caldy," which took three men to work it, till steam was introduced. The "Belper" went farther north, and did good work for many years in one of the "nightless" northern towns.

The "Courier" progressed so satisfactorily that by 1860 the circulation reached the very large number of nearly 4000 copies a week, and still sold at 4½d. per copy; was considerably enlarged, and was so well advertised that, with the abolition of the stamp and advertisement duty, advertisers became so numerous that Dr. Carruthers had to ask the favour (now almost incredible), on more than one occasion, of some advertisers to curtail or postpone their advertisements, that the "Courier" might present its usual interesting and readable character. There used to be a "Poet's Corner" in the "Courier," the editor's exquisite taste ensuring that nothing second-rate or trashy ever cumbered that corner.

The editor of the "Courier," Dr. Carruthers, being a Dumfries man, the land of big farms and a non-crofter district, doubtless had ideas of farming from his experience there, which led him to palliate or defend the evictions in Sutherland—a great mistake, which we are sure he regretted ever after, for we observed a change in the tone of the "Courier" on the occurrence of another eviction in Ross-shire many years afterwards. The charge of venality made in the Sutherland case was ungenerous, untrue, and we think was never really believed in. In controversy any "stick will do," and the charge was strongly urged, and sorely, though quietly, resented. Among those at this time who emerged to fame was the now famous Hugh Miller, whose centenary took place in October, 1902. Hugh, as he was familiarly and kindly styled, was frequently admitted to the " Poet's Corner," though the editor on one occasion enjoined Hugh to devote himself to prose, and when Hugh " came to his own," the editor of the " Courier " jocularly referred to this advice. The writer on one occasion saw Hugh Miller when visiting the editor of the " Courier," but, unfortunately, did not hear the conversation. Hugh Miller appeared to be a tall, strongly-built person, wrapped in the famous shepherd-tartan plaid. The editor of the " Courier " and the now famous Hugh Miller were great friends, and it was said the editor of the " Witness " refused to countenance the starting of the " Inverness Advertiser" in opposition to the "Courier" —Free Church though it was. Dr. Carruthers succeeded during his time in surrounding himself with a rather brilliant circle of friends with a literary turn, many of whom did good service in the colums of the " Courier." Among them were the late Mr. Kenneth Murray, Tain, whose agricultural articles were famous ; the late Dr. Macdonald, of the High Church ; Mr. Peter Scott, rector of the Royal Academy ; Mr. Thomas Falconer, solicitor, and the Rev. Mr. Clark, of the West Church ; and among the younger townsmen the late Sir Henry Macandrew must not be omitted, for he frequently contributed to the " Courier " excellent articles and reviews. Mr. Geo. G. Mackay was also a contributor on many occasions. The " Courier " was at its zenith when the late Dr. Macdonald, of the High Church, took umbrage at an occasional paragraph appearing in the " Courier," which he assumed to be maliciously aimed at the ministers of the Established Church, of which Dr. Carruthers was a member. The editor of the " Courier " was not responsible for these paragraphs, and they could fairly be written in reference to any church ; and none could be more severe than Dr. Macdonald himself, for on one notable occasion he told a clergyman of many years standing that he should be " sent back to the university." It was a most unfortunate quarrel, and divided attached friends, breaking friendship of years standing. The attack on both sides was very able ; but Dr. Macdonald's family, as well as that of Dr. Carruthers, were extremely pained by the exhibition of the rancour displayed by two gentlemen of unquestioned ability, and long friends. The quarrel did no good. Dr. Carruthers reminded Dr. Macdonald that he (Dr. Macdonald) had frequently urged Dr. Carruthers to become an elder of the High Church. " Yes," said the fiery doctor, " and I am willing that that should be so still." It was widely held that the making an elder of Dr. Carruthers would be a most desirable thing for the High Church, for a better man or elder never filled this office in the church. It was supposed at the time that Dr. Macdonald was irritated at a number of 'verts from the High Church to the Cathedral. That could hardly be, for in answer to a letter from a gentleman leaving the High Church, Dr. Macdonald wrote to the effect that he did not wish for any to attend on his ministrations who did not benefit from them—" You evidently have not done so, and I highly approve of your going elsewhere ! "

The " Courier's " London connection was wide and important, and embraced among others that of Thackeray, Shirley Brooks of " Punch," the two Reachs (father and son), Angus B. Reach, and other famous writers with whom Dr. Carruthers enjoyed friendship—Mr. A. B. Reach dedicating a novel to him. At the time Thackeray was touring with his famous lectures on " The Four Georges," and when at Inverness he was the guest of Dr. Carruthers at his residence at Silverwells, Ness Bank. It was stated that Thackeray and Dr. Carruthers greatly resembled each other, and that Dr. Carruthers on one occasion was taken by Thackeray's Irish servant to be Thackeray's brother—" And sure, sir," said he, "and ar'int you his brother ! " When entering the Northern Meeting Room to deliver his lecture, arm-in-arm with Dr. Carruthers, the resemblance was not so very striking. Thackeray was an extremely tall, loosely-got-up man, with a broken or very small nose, and a full, dull complexion; while Dr. Carruthers was well set up, tall, but several inches

Bailie Stuart, a frequent contributor to the Gaelic Society's " Transaction " volumes.

INDEX.

APPENDIX.

EXTRACT FROM "WILD EELIN" (CHAPTER VI), BY WILLIAM BLACK.

. . . " Down the gravelled walk, along the banks of the river, up the Castle Hill, and into Castle Street, and here she disappeared. For in this thoroughfare there was an Old Curiosity Shop,* the owner of which, an exceedingly good-natured gentleman, allowed Miss Eelin to ransack his stores at will; so that especially on wet days she would spend hour after hour poring over and examining books, medals, coins, engravings, armour, furniture, pottery and porcelain, and the like ; and in this way she had acquired a good deal of desultory knowledge. But on this occasion her quest was of a more definite character. She marched up to the counter, and said, indignantly :

" ' Mr. Edel,† have you seen this morning's " Observer ? " ' ‡

" The portly antiquarian beamed benevolently upon her from over his spectacles," &c.

---

* Mr. Noble's book shop.   † Mr. John Noble.   ‡ " Inverness Courier."

Pages 1 to 182 printed by JOHN NOBLE at his Printing Press, Castle Street,
Inverness; the remainder of letterpress, with accompanying blocks, by
MUNRO & JAMIESON, Stirling.

Lightning Source UK Ltd.
Milton Keynes UK
UKHW011020070223
416609UK00006B/1378

CONTENTS

COMPREHENSIVE INSIGHTS INTO FOLATE DEFICIENCY ANEMIA: FROM PATHOPHYSIOLOGY TO PERSONALIZED MANAGEMENT

Chapter 1: Introduction to Folate Deficiency Anemia

1.1 Overview of Anemia

1.2 Types of Anemia

1.3 Understanding Folate and its Importance

Chapter 2: Physiology and Biochemistry of Folate

2.1 Folate Metabolism in the Body

2.2 Role of Folate in DNA Synthesis and Cell Division

2.3 Absorption, Transport, and Storage of Folate

Chapter 3: Causes and Risk Factors
3.1 Dietary Causes of Folate Deficiency

3.2 Malabsorption Syndromes and Folate Deficiency

3.3 Medications and Conditions Leading to Folate Deficiency

Chapter 4: Clinical Manifestations of Folate Deficiency
4.1 Hematological Changes and Anemia

4.2 Neurological Symptoms and Cognitive Impairment

4.3 Other Systemic Effects of Folate Deficiency

Chapter 5: Diagnosis of Folate Deficiency Anemia
5.1 Laboratory Tests and Biomarkers for Folate Levels

5.2 Differential Diagnosis with Other Types of Anemia

5.3 Imaging and Additional Diagnostic Approaches

Chapter 6: Treatment and Management
6.1 Dietary Modifications and Nutritional Supplements

6.2 Pharmacological Interventions

6.3 Monitoring and Follow-Up in Treatment

Chapter 7: Prevention Strategies
7.1 Importance of Folate in Pregnancy and Birth Defect Prevention

7.2 Public Health Measures and Fortification Programs

7.3 Recommendations for Various Population Groups

Chapter 8: Holistic Approaches and Lifestyle Changes

8.1 Integrative Medicine and Folate Deficiency Management

8.2 Role of Exercise and Stress Management

8.3 Dietary and Lifestyle Changes for Folate Maintenance

Chapter 9: Research and Future Perspectives

9.1 Ongoing Research in Folate and Anemia

9.2 Potential Innovations in Folate Supplementation

9.3 Challenges and Future Directions

Chapter 10: Case Studies and Clinical Scenarios

10.1 Case Studies Illustrating Folate Deficiency Anemia

10.2 Clinical Scenarios and Treatment Outcomes

10.3 Lessons Learned and Recommendations

CHAPTER 1: INTRODUCTION TO FOLATE DEFICIENCY ANEMIA

Anemia, a condition characterized by a deficiency in red blood cells or hemoglobin, stands as a silent yet formidable health challenge worldwide. Among its multifaceted forms, folate deficiency anemia emerges as a significant subset, intricately linked to the body's intricate web of biochemical pathways, nutrition, and overall health.

This treatise endeavors to delve into the depths of folate deficiency anemia, unearthing its biochemical underpinnings, the orchestration of physiological mechanisms, and the wide-ranging impact on human health. Folate, an essential B-vitamin, assumes a pivotal role not only in hematopoiesis but also in fundamental cellular processes, including DNA synthesis, repair, and methylation.

In this exploration, we aim to navigate through the intricate pathways of folate metabolism, elucidate the intricate dance between folate and human physiology, and comprehend the repercussions when this delicate balance falters. Folate, acquired primarily through diet, undergoes a complex journey in the human body, from absorption in the intestines to utilization in various tissues, playing a key role in ensuring cellular integrity and optimal functioning.

Beyond the confines of hematological consequences, this treatise extends its purview to the diverse manifestations of folate deficiency, encompassing neurological manifestations, developmental anomalies, and systemic effects that transcend the confines of blood cell production.

Moreover, the treatise aims to offer a comprehensive view of diagnostic modalities, treatment modalities ranging from nutritional interventions to pharmaceutical strategies, and the far-reaching implications for preventive healthcare measures.

Beyond the conventional medical paradigm, this exploration touches upon holistic approaches, recognizing the interconnectedness of lifestyle, diet, and overall well-being in mitigating the risk and impact of folate deficiency anemia. It emphasizes the importance of integrative health, lifestyle modifications, and the potential role of exercise and stress management in bolstering the body's resilience against such deficiencies.

As this treatise unfolds, it endeavors to amalgamate the complexities of biochemistry, the intricacies of human physiology, and the broader landscape of public health strategies to present a comprehensive understanding of folate deficiency anemia. Through this collective exploration, we aspire to empower healthcare professionals, researchers, and individuals alike in their pursuit of knowledge, effective management, and prevention of this intricate yet modifiable health condition.

1.1 Overview of Anemia

Anemia, a pervasive hematologic disorder, represents a condition characterized by a reduction in the number of red blood cells (RBCs) or the concentration of hemoglobin in the blood, leading to a decreased oxygen-carrying capacity. This reduction impedes the efficient delivery of oxygen to tissues and organs, thereby affecting their normal functioning. It's a prevalent global health concern, affecting individuals across diverse age groups, geographic locations, and socioeconomic strata.

Understanding Blood and Red Blood Cells:

To appreciate anemia, one must first comprehend the crucial role of blood and its components. Blood, the life-sustaining fluid coursing through our bodies, comprises various cellular elements suspended in a liquid matrix called plasma. Among these cellular constituents, red blood cells (erythrocytes) reign supreme. These specialized cells, produced in the bone marrow, house hemoglobin —a protein responsible for binding and transporting oxygen.

Role of Red Blood Cells in Oxygen Transport:

The primary function of RBCs hinges on their ability to transport oxygen from the lungs to tissues and organs throughout the body. Hemoglobin within RBCs binds to inhaled oxygen in the lungs, creating oxyhemoglobin. This compound journeys through the bloodstream, releasing oxygen to tissues and retrieving carbon dioxide, a waste product, to be exhaled from the body.

Anemia's Impact on Oxygen Delivery:

When the RBC count or hemoglobin concentration falls below normal thresholds, as observed in anemia, the body's oxygen-carrying capacity diminishes. This deficiency in oxygen supply can manifest in a myriad of symptoms, including fatigue, weakness, shortness of breath, dizziness, and pallor. In severe cases, it can lead to complications affecting vital organs, hampering their optimal function.

Classification and Causes of Anemia:

Anemia isn't a singular entity but a spectrum of conditions with various causes, classifications, and manifestations. It can stem from diverse etiologies, broadly categorized into three primary mechanisms:

1. **Decreased Red Blood Cell Production:** This may result from nutritional deficiencies (e.g., iron, vitamin B12, or folate), bone marrow disorders, or chronic diseases hindering RBC formation.
2. **Increased Red Blood Cell Destruction:** Termed hemolytic anemia, this occurs when RBCs are destroyed at an accelerated rate due to inherited conditions, autoimmune disorders, infections, or certain medications.
3. **Blood Loss:** Acute or chronic blood loss, whether due to trauma, menstruation, gastrointestinal bleeding, or other sources, can deplete the body's RBC reserves, leading to anemia.

Anemia's Varieties and Impact:

Anemia isn't homogeneous; its presentation varies based on its underlying cause, severity, and duration. Some common types include iron-deficiency anemia, pernicious anemia (caused by vitamin B12 deficiency), aplastic anemia (stemming from bone marrow failure), and sickle cell anemia (a hereditary disorder altering RBC shape).

The impact of anemia stretches beyond physical symptoms, affecting an individual's quality of life, cognitive function, work capacity, and overall well-being. Additionally, certain populations, such as pregnant women and children, face heightened risks due to increased physiological demands or inadequate nutritional intake.

Diagnostic Approach to Anemia:

Accurate diagnosis of anemia involves a comprehensive evaluation, including medical history, physical examination, and laboratory tests. Blood tests assessing RBC count, hemoglobin levels, hematocrit, mean corpuscular volume (MCV), and other indices aid in determining the type and severity of anemia, guiding appropriate management strategies.

Conclusion:

In summation, anemia constitutes a multifaceted condition with diverse etiologies and manifestations, impacting millions worldwide. Its identification, rooted in understanding blood physiology and comprehensive diagnostic approaches, forms the cornerstone for tailored interventions aimed at ameliorating symptoms, preventing complications, and improving the quality of life for affected individuals. An in-depth exploration into anemia's intricacies enables healthcare providers to employ targeted strategies for effective management and underscores the importance of addressing underlying causes for optimal patient outcomes.

1.2 Types of Anemia

Exploring the diverse array of anemia types provides a nuanced understanding of this complex condition. Anemia isn't a singular entity but a spectrum of disorders, each with distinct causes, pathophysiology, and clinical presentations. Delving into the various types sheds light on their intricacies, aiding in accurate diagnosis, tailored management, and improved patient outcomes.

Iron-Deficiency Anemia:

One of the most prevalent forms globally, iron-deficiency anemia arises due to insufficient iron stores, impairing the body's ability to produce hemoglobin adequately. Causes include inadequate dietary intake, blood loss (from menstruation, gastrointestinal bleeding, or surgeries), or impaired absorption. Symptoms encompass fatigue, pale skin, weakness, and shortness of breath. Treatment involves iron supplementation and addressing underlying causes of blood loss.

Vitamin Deficiency-Related Anemias:

a. Pernicious Anemia (Vitamin B12 Deficiency):

Arising from inadequate absorption of vitamin B12, pernicious anemia often results from autoimmune destruction of gastric parietal cells or gastrointestinal surgeries affecting vitamin B12 absorption. Neurological symptoms, along with typical signs of anemia, may manifest. Treatment involves B12 supplementation, either through injections or oral forms.

b. Folate Deficiency Anemia:

Insufficient dietary intake, malabsorption syndromes, or medications impairing folate absorption can lead to folate deficiency anemia. Folate, crucial for DNA synthesis and cell division, deficiency manifests with symptoms mirroring other anemias, along with potential neurological complications. Treatment involves folate supplementation and addressing underlying causes.

Hemolytic Anemias:

a. Inherited Hemolytic Anemias:

Conditions like sickle cell anemia, thalassemia, and hereditary spherocytosis result from genetic defects impacting RBC structure or function. Sickle cell anemia, characterized by abnormal hemoglobin causing RBCs to assume a sickle shape, leads to hemolysis, vaso-occlusive crises, and chronic organ damage. Treatment focuses on symptom management and supportive care.

b. Acquired Hemolytic Anemias:

These emerge due to external factors triggering premature destruction of RBCs. Autoimmune hemolytic anemia occurs when the immune system attacks its RBCs, leading to their destruction. Other causes include infections, medications, or certain toxins. Management involves identifying and treating underlying triggers, along with medications to suppress the immune response if autoimmune in nature.

Anemias of Chronic Disease:

Chronic conditions like chronic kidney disease, inflammatory disorders, or cancer can induce anemia through various mechanisms, including reduced erythropoietin production, impaired iron utilization, or chronic inflammation hindering RBC production. Managing the underlying chronic disease and addressing contributory factors is key in managing this type of anemia.

Aplastic Anemia:

A rare but serious condition characterized by bone marrow failure, aplastic anemia results in decreased production of RBCs, white blood cells, and platelets. It may arise from autoimmune processes, exposure to toxins, certain medications, or viral infections. Treatment involves blood transfusions, immunosuppressive therapy, or stem cell transplantation in severe cases.

Other Rare Forms:

a. Hemoglobinopathies:

Conditions like thalassemia, an inherited disorder affecting hemoglobin production, result in abnormal RBCs and anemia. Management typically involves regular blood transfusions and supportive care.

b. Sideroblastic Anemias:

These rare anemias involve defective iron utilization within developing RBCs, leading to anemia. They may be inherited or acquired and are managed based on the underlying cause.

Conclusion:

The multitude of anemia types underscores the heterogeneity of this condition, each with its unique etiology, clinical manifestations, and management strategies. A comprehensive understanding of these variations facilitates accurate diagnosis, tailored treatments, and enhanced patient care. Healthcare providers, armed with knowledge about the diverse types of anemia, can employ targeted interventions to address specific deficiencies, underlying diseases, or genetic abnormalities, aiming for optimal outcomes and improved quality of life for individuals affected by anemia.

1.3 Understanding Folate and its Importance

Understanding folate, a pivotal B-vitamin, and its profound significance in human physiology unveils its intricate role in various biochemical pathways, emphasizing its critical importance for overall health and well-being.

Folate: An Essential B-Vitamin

1. Folate in Biochemical Pathways:

Folate, also known as vitamin B9, serves as a coenzyme in numerous essential metabolic reactions within the body. Its primary role lies in one-carbon metabolism, where it participates in the transfer of one-carbon units required for DNA synthesis, repair, and methylation processes. These functions are fundamental for cellular growth, proliferation, and overall tissue development.

2. Sources and Absorption:

Natural sources of folate include leafy green vegetables, legumes, fruits, and fortified cereals. Upon ingestion, folate undergoes absorption predominantly in the small intestine, where it is converted into its active form, tetrahydrofolate (THF), before being utilized in various cellular processes.

3. Folate and DNA Synthesis:

One of folate's primary roles involves facilitating the synthesis of purines and pyrimidines, the building blocks of DNA. By contributing methyl groups, folate aids in the synthesis of thymidine, a crucial component of DNA. Thus, adequate folate levels are vital for cell division, growth, and repair.

4. Methylation and Epigenetics:

Folate plays a pivotal role in methylation reactions, where it acts as a methyl donor in the conversion of homocysteine to methionine. Methionine, in turn, contributes methyl groups essential for DNA methylation and gene regulation, impacting cellular function and differentiation.

5. Folate in Red Blood Cell Formation:

Folate plays an indispensable role in erythropoiesis, the process of red blood cell production. It aids in the maturation of RBC precursors and the synthesis of DNA required for their proliferation, making it crucial for maintaining adequate RBC levels and preventing anemia.

Importance of Folate for Human Health

1. Folate Deficiency and Health Ramifications:

Inadequate folate levels can have profound health implications, leading to folate deficiency. Such deficiency can manifest in various ways, including anemia, where impaired RBC production results from inhibited DNA synthesis in bone marrow.

2. Neural Tube Defects and Pregnancy:

Adequate folate intake before and during pregnancy is crucial in preventing neural tube defects (NTDs) in infants. Folate plays a pivotal role in early fetal development, particularly in the closure of the neural tube, emphasizing its significance for maternal and child health.

3. Cardiovascular Health:

Folate, along with other B-vitamins, contributes to cardiovascular health by participating in homocysteine metabolism. Elevated levels of homocysteine, linked to cardiovascular disease, can be mitigated by adequate folate intake, reducing associated risks.

4. Neurological Function:

Folate deficiency can impact neurological health, leading to cognitive impairments, mood disturbances, and potentially contributing to conditions like depression and dementia. Adequate folate levels are essential for optimal brain function.

Factors Affecting Folate Status

1. Dietary Intake:

A balanced diet rich in folate-containing foods is critical for maintaining adequate folate levels. However, cooking methods and food processing can impact folate content, affecting overall intake.

2. Absorption and Metabolism:

Factors such as malabsorption syndromes, certain medications, alcohol consumption, and genetic variations can influence folate absorption and metabolism, potentially leading to deficiencies.

3. Age and Life Stages:

Different life stages, such as pregnancy, lactation, infancy, and aging, demand varying levels of folate. Adequate intake becomes crucial during these stages to support optimal growth, development, and health.

Conclusion

Folate stands as a pivotal player in myriad biochemical processes, influencing DNA synthesis, methylation, cellular proliferation, and overall health. Its indispensability in various physiological functions underscores the significance of maintaining adequate folate levels through dietary intake and supplementation when necessary. A comprehensive understanding of folate's intricate role in human biology allows for informed approaches in healthcare, emphasizing the importance of folate not just in preventing deficiencies but also in promoting overall well-being and health across diverse populations.

CHAPTER 2: PHYSIOLOGY AND BIOCHEMISTRY OF FOLATE

2.1 Folate Metabolism in the Body

Understanding the intricate pathways of folate metabolism within the human body unveils the complex journey this essential B-vitamin undergoes, elucidating its critical role in various biochemical processes essential for cellular function and overall health.

Folate Metabolism Pathways

1. Absorption and Cellular Uptake:

Folate, primarily in the form of polyglutamates within dietary sources, enters the body via the small intestine. In this form, it undergoes enzymatic cleavage to monoglutamates, allowing for absorption across the intestinal epithelium into the bloodstream.

2. Folate Circulation and Distribution:

Once absorbed, folate circulates in the bloodstream, primarily bound to carrier proteins. This circulation ensures its transport to various tissues and organs where folate serves as a coenzyme in crucial metabolic reactions.

3. Cellular Uptake and Activation:

Folate enters cells through specialized transporters present in cell membranes. Within the cell, folate undergoes polyglutamation via enzymatic processes, converting it into its active form, tetrahydrofolate (THF). This activation step is vital for folate's participation in subsequent metabolic reactions.

4. Folate as a One-Carbon Carrier:

As tetrahydrofolate (THF), folate serves as a carrier of one-carbon units, crucial for numerous biosynthetic pathways. Through a series of enzymatic reactions, THF facilitates the transfer of methyl groups (one-carbon units) required for the synthesis of nucleic acids, amino acids, and other vital molecules.

5. Role in DNA Synthesis and Repair:

Within the nucleus, folate plays a pivotal role in DNA synthesis, providing the necessary building blocks for purine and pyrimidine synthesis. Adequate folate levels are crucial for cell division and the repair of damaged DNA, ensuring genomic integrity.

6. Methylation and Epigenetic Regulation:

Folate's involvement in one-carbon metabolism extends to methylation reactions. By contributing methyl groups, folate influences DNA methylation, an epigenetic modification crucial for gene regulation, cellular differentiation, and overall genomic stability.

Enzymatic Pathways Involved in Folate Metabolism

1. Dihydrofolate Reductase (DHFR):

This enzyme catalyzes the conversion of dihydrofolate (DHF) to tetrahydrofolate (THF), a critical step in regenerating the active form of folate necessary for continued participation in metabolic pathways.

2. Methylenetetrahydrofolate Reductase (MTHFR):

MTHFR catalyzes the conversion of 5,10-methylenetetrahydrofolate to 5-methyltetrahydrofolate, a crucial step in providing methyl groups for DNA methylation and other methylation reactions.

3. Serine Hydroxymethyltransferase (SHMT):

SHMT facilitates the conversion of serine to glycine, generating 5,10-methylenetetrahydrofolate. This reaction serves as a pivotal step in serine-glycine interconversion and folate-mediated one-carbon metabolism.

4. Thymidylate Synthase:

Thymidylate synthase utilizes 5,10-methylenetetrahydrofolate to synthesize thymidine, a critical component of DNA. This enzyme ensures a steady supply of thymidine for DNA replication and repair processes.

Regulation of Folate Metabolism

1. Dietary Intake and Absorption:

Adequate dietary intake of folate-rich foods is essential for maintaining optimal folate levels in the body. Factors affecting absorption, such as gastrointestinal health and certain medications, can impact folate availability.

2. Enzymatic Regulation:

Enzymes involved in folate metabolism undergo intricate regulation, ensuring a balanced and controlled flow of folate-mediated one-carbon units for cellular processes. Dysregulation of these enzymes can lead to disruptions in folate metabolism and subsequent cellular functions.

3. Cellular Transport and Distribution:

Transporters facilitating folate uptake into cells and its distribution among various tissues play a crucial role in regulating folate levels within different cellular compartments, influencing its availability for metabolic reactions.

4. Genetic Variations:

Genetic polymorphisms in enzymes involved in folate metabolism, such as MTHFR, can impact folate utilization and metabolism, potentially influencing an individual's susceptibility to folate-related deficiencies or disorders.

Conclusion

Folate metabolism constitutes a complex network of enzymatic reactions and pathways essential for cellular function, DNA synthesis, methylation, and overall metabolic homeostasis. Understanding the intricate mechanisms governing folate metabolism allows for a deeper comprehension of its significance in human health and disease. Perturbations in folate metabolism, whether due to dietary inadequacies, enzymatic dysregulation, or genetic variations, can lead to disruptions in cellular processes, emphasizing the critical importance of maintaining optimal folate levels for overall health and well-being.

2.2 Role of Folate in DNA Synthesis and Cell Division

The role of folate in DNA synthesis and cell division is fundamental, exerting a profound influence on cellular growth, proliferation, and maintenance of genomic integrity. Understanding how folate contributes to these critical processes unveils its significance in ensuring proper cell function and overall physiological health.

Folate's Contribution to DNA Synthesis

1. Purine and Pyrimidine Synthesis:

Folate, in its active form as tetrahydrofolate (THF), plays a pivotal role in the synthesis of purines (adenine and guanine) and pyrimidines (thymine and cytosine), the fundamental building blocks of DNA. Through the donation of one-carbon units, folate provides the necessary precursors for these nucleotide bases, essential for assembling DNA strands during replication and repair.

2. Thymidylate Synthesis:

One of folate's crucial roles in DNA synthesis involves providing methyl groups for thymidylate synthesis. Thymidylate is a critical component necessary for the production of thymine, a pyrimidine base required for DNA replication. Thymidylate synthase utilizes 5,10-methylenetetrahydrofolate, a derivative of folate, in the conversion of deoxyuridine monophosphate (dUMP) to deoxythymidine monophosphate (dTMP), ensuring a steady supply of thymidine for DNA replication.

3. Maintenance of Genomic Integrity:

Adequate folate levels are crucial for maintaining genomic stability by facilitating proper DNA replication and repair mechanisms. Insufficient folate can lead to uracil misincorporation into DNA, compromising its integrity and potentially contributing to genomic instability.

Folate and Cell Division

1. Role in Cell Proliferation:

Folate's involvement in DNA synthesis is intricately linked to cell division. As cells replicate, DNA replication is a prerequisite for cell division, ensuring the accurate transmission of genetic material to daughter cells. Folate's provision of nucleotide precursors is vital for the replication of DNA strands during the cell cycle.

2. Influence on Mitosis and Meiosis:

In both mitosis (cell division for growth and tissue repair) and meiosis (cell division for reproductive purposes), folate's contribution to DNA synthesis is indispensable. Proper DNA replication and accurate distribution of chromosomes during cell division rely on adequate folate levels to ensure genetic fidelity in daughter cells.

3. Impact on Stem Cells and Tissue Regeneration:

Stem cells, possessing the ability to self-renew and differentiate into specialized cell types, rely on precise regulation of DNA synthesis and cell division. Folate's role in providing the necessary nucleotide precursors is vital for maintaining the integrity of stem cell populations and facilitating tissue regeneration and repair processes.

Folate Deficiency and Effects on DNA and Cell Division

1. Impaired DNA Synthesis and Repair:

Folate deficiency impedes DNA synthesis, leading to decreased availability of nucleotide precursors required for replication and repair. This deficiency can result in the accumulation of uracil in DNA, potentially compromising its integrity and stability.

2. Altered Cell Proliferation:

Insufficient folate levels can hinder proper cell division, leading to impaired proliferation and abnormal growth patterns. This disruption in cell division processes can impact tissues with high turnover rates, such as the bone marrow, where RBC production occurs, potentially contributing to anemia.

3. Developmental Consequences:

During embryonic development, folate deficiency can have profound effects due to impaired DNA synthesis and cell division. Neural tube defects, arising from disrupted cell proliferation during early embryogenesis, exemplify the critical role of folate in preventing developmental anomalies.

Conclusion

Folate's indispensable role in DNA synthesis and cell division underscores its significance in maintaining genomic stability, supporting proper growth, and ensuring cellular proliferation. The provision of nucleotide precursors, involvement in thymidylate synthesis, and influence on mitosis and meiosis highlight folate's multifaceted contributions to fundamental biological processes. Adequate folate levels are crucial for preserving genomic integrity, sustaining healthy cell division, and preventing developmental abnormalities, emphasizing the critical importance of maintaining optimal folate status for overall cellular health and physiological well-being.

2.3 Absorption, Transport, and Storage of Folate

Understanding the complex journey of folate from absorption in the intestines to its transportation, utilization, and storage throughout the body unveils the intricate mechanisms that ensure its availability for crucial metabolic processes. Delving into the absorption, transport, and storage of folate sheds light on the orchestrated processes vital for maintaining adequate folate levels and supporting cellular functions.

Absorption of Folate

1. Intestinal Absorption:

Folate, obtained from dietary sources primarily in the form of polyglutamates, undergoes enzymatic hydrolysis in the small intestine to monoglutamates before absorption. The reduced monoglutamate form facilitates its absorption across the intestinal epithelium into enterocytes, primarily in the duodenum and jejunum.

2. Folate Transporters:

Within enterocytes, specialized transporters—such as the reduced folate carrier (RFC) and the proton-coupled folate transporter (PCFT)—mediate the uptake of folate into the cells. These transporters play a crucial role in the efficient absorption of folate from the intestinal lumen into enterocytes.

3. Folate Polyglutamation:

Following absorption, folate undergoes polyglutamation, a process where glutamate residues are added to folate molecules within enterocytes. This polyglutamation enhances the retention of folate in cells and facilitates its subsequent utilization in various metabolic pathways.

Transport and Circulation of Folate

1. Binding to Carrier Proteins:

Once inside enterocytes, folate undergoes modifications, including the addition of a methyl group to form methylfolate, before being released into the bloodstream. In circulation, folate primarily binds to carrier proteins, including serum albumin and specific binding proteins like folate-binding protein (FBP).

2. Distribution Among Tissues:

Folate circulates in the bloodstream, bound to carrier proteins, ensuring its transport to various tissues and organs throughout the body. These tissues include the liver, bone marrow, brain, and others, where folate serves as a coenzyme in numerous essential metabolic reactions.

3. Cellular Uptake and Utilization:

Transporters present on cell membranes facilitate the uptake of folate into cells across various tissues. Inside the cells, folate is converted into its active form, tetrahydrofolate (THF), by enzymatic processes, allowing it to participate in one-carbon metabolism and various metabolic pathways.

Folate Utilization and Metabolic Pathways

1. Activation of Folate:

Tetrahydrofolate (THF), the active form of folate, undergoes various enzymatic reactions to become involved in one-carbon transfer reactions, essential for DNA synthesis, methylation, and nucleotide biosynthesis.

2. One-Carbon Metabolism:

Folate's primary role lies in serving as a carrier of one-carbon units required for various biosynthetic processes. Through a series of enzymatic reactions, THF shuttles one-carbon groups, contributing to the synthesis of nucleotides, amino acids, and other vital molecules.

3. Role in DNA Synthesis and Repair:

As a crucial participant in one-carbon metabolism, folate provides the necessary precursors for purine and pyrimidine synthesis, contributing to DNA replication and repair processes essential for maintaining genomic integrity.

Folate Storage and Excretion

1. Hepatic Storage:

The liver serves as a significant reservoir for folate storage, storing a substantial portion of the body's folate reserves. Folate accumulates in the liver as methylfolate and polyglutamated forms, ensuring a readily available supply for metabolic demands.

2. Biliary Excretion and Recycling:

Folate undergoes biliary excretion, where a portion is eliminated in the feces. However, the body also efficiently reabsorbs and recycles folate from the bile, contributing to its conservation and reuse within the body.

Factors Influencing Folate Absorption and Utilization

1. Dietary Factors:

Adequate dietary intake of folate-rich foods is crucial for ensuring optimal folate levels. Cooking methods and food processing can impact folate content, affecting overall absorption.

2. Genetic Variations:

Genetic polymorphisms in folate-related enzymes and transporters can influence folate metabolism, potentially impacting its absorption, utilization, and storage.

3. Medications and Health Conditions:

Certain medications and health conditions affecting gastrointestinal health, such as malabsorption syndromes or inflammatory bowel diseases, can hinder folate absorption and utilization.

Conclusion

The journey of folate, from intestinal absorption to circulation, cellular uptake, utilization, and storage, involves a meticulously orchestrated series of processes. Efficient absorption mechanisms, transportation via carrier proteins, cellular utilization, and hepatic storage ensure a steady supply of folate for essential metabolic pathways, including DNA synthesis, methylation, and nucleotide biosynthesis. Understanding these processes and the factors influencing folate absorption and utilization is crucial for maintaining optimal folate status, supporting cellular functions, and promoting overall health and well-being.

CHAPTER 3: CAUSES AND RISK FACTORS

3.1 Dietary Causes of Folate Deficiency

Importance of Dietary Folate

1. Folate-Rich Foods:

Folate, also known as vitamin B9, is abundant in various dietary sources, including:

- Leafy green vegetables (spinach, kale, broccoli)
- Legumes (beans, lentils, chickpeas)
- Fruits (citrus fruits, bananas, avocados)
- Fortified grains and cereals

2. Dietary Intake and Recommended Daily Allowance:

Adequate dietary intake of folate is critical for maintaining optimal levels in the body. The recommended dietary allowance (RDA) for folate varies by age, gender, and life stage, with higher requirements during pregnancy and infancy.

Causes of Folate Deficiency Due to Diet

1. Inadequate Dietary Intake:

Insufficient consumption of folate-rich foods, particularly among populations with limited access to diverse and nutrient-rich diets, contributes significantly to folate deficiency. Diets lacking in leafy greens, legumes, and fortified grains can lead to inadequate folate intake.

2. Food Processing and Cooking Methods:

Certain food processing methods, such as prolonged cooking or excessive heat, can lead to folate degradation. Loss of folate content during food preparation and cooking contributes to reduced folate intake.

3. Alcohol Consumption:

Excessive alcohol consumption can interfere with folate absorption and utilization in the body. Chronic alcoholism is associated with poor dietary habits and malnutrition, leading to folate deficiency.

4. Diet-Related Health Conditions:

Certain health conditions affecting the gastrointestinal tract, such as celiac disease, inflammatory bowel disease (IBD), or other malabsorption syndromes, can impair folate absorption, even with adequate dietary intake.

Impact of Dietary Folate Deficiency

1. Anemia:

Folate deficiency is a common cause of megaloblastic anemia, characterized by larger-than-normal red blood cells (macrocytes) due to impaired DNA synthesis in bone marrow. Insufficient folate affects erythropoiesis, hindering red blood cell production.

2. Neural Tube Defects:

Inadequate folate intake, particularly during early pregnancy, is linked to an increased risk of neural tube defects (NTDs) in infants. Folate plays a crucial role in neural tube closure, emphasizing its significance for maternal and fetal health.

3. Other Health Implications:

Besides anemia and NTDs, folate deficiency can contribute to a range of health issues, including:

- Cardiovascular diseases due to increased homocysteine levels
- Neurological disorders, such as cognitive impairment and depression

- Compromised immune function and increased susceptibility to infections

Addressing Dietary Folate Deficiency

1. Dietary Modifications:

Encouraging a diet rich in folate-containing foods is crucial for preventing folate deficiency. Promoting the consumption of leafy greens, legumes, fruits, and fortified grains helps increase folate intake.

2. Folate Supplementation:

In cases where dietary intake alone cannot meet the required folate levels, supplementation or fortified foods containing synthetic forms of folate (folic acid) might be recommended, especially in high-risk populations like pregnant women.

3. Public Health Initiatives:

Public health strategies include fortification programs where staple foods, such as grains and cereals, are fortified with folic acid to enhance folate intake across populations.

Conclusion

Dietary causes stand as significant contributors to folate deficiency, highlighting the critical role of adequate folate intake from various food sources in maintaining optimal health. Insufficient dietary intake, food processing methods, alcohol consumption, and underlying health conditions impacting nutrient absorption can lead to folate deficiency, resulting in various health complications. Emphasizing the importance of a folate-rich diet, supplementation when necessary, and public health initiatives aimed at fortification can mitigate the risk of folate deficiency, thereby promoting better health outcomes and reducing the associated health burdens.

3.2 Malabsorption Syndromes and Folate Deficiency

Malabsorption syndromes encompass a group of conditions characterized by impaired absorption of nutrients from the gastrointestinal tract. These disorders, affecting the absorption of various essential nutrients, can significantly contribute to folate deficiency, impacting overall health and leading to various complications due to insufficient folate levels.

Understanding Malabsorption Syndromes

1. Celiac Disease:

Celiac disease, an autoimmune disorder triggered by gluten ingestion, damages the lining of the small intestine, impairing nutrient absorption. The damage to intestinal villi reduces the absorptive surface area, affecting folate absorption among other nutrients.

2. Inflammatory Bowel Disease (IBD):

Conditions like Crohn's disease and ulcerative colitis, classified under IBD, lead to chronic inflammation and damage to the gastrointestinal tract. Inflammation disrupts the normal functioning of the intestines, impacting folate absorption.

3. Intestinal Resection or Surgery:

Surgical procedures involving resection or removal of parts of the intestine, often performed due to conditions like bowel obstructions or tumors, can reduce the absorptive surface area, affecting folate absorption.

4. Bacterial Overgrowth:

Small intestinal bacterial overgrowth (SIBO), where an abnormal increase in gut bacteria occurs in the small intestine, can interfere with folate absorption. These bacteria can consume folate, reducing its availability for absorption by the body.

Impact of Malabsorption Syndromes on Folate Absorption

1. Reduced Absorptive Surface Area:

Damage to the intestinal lining or surgical removal of portions of the intestine decreases the surface area available for nutrient absorption, including folate. This impairment leads to reduced uptake of folate from ingested foods.

2. Altered pH and Enzymatic Activity:

In conditions like SIBO or chronic inflammation, changes in intestinal pH levels and altered enzymatic activity can disrupt the breakdown and absorption of folate, further compromising its uptake.

3. Disrupted Transport Mechanisms:

Malabsorption syndromes can interfere with the function of folate transporters present on the intestinal epithelium, impacting the movement of folate into the bloodstream and reducing its availability for cellular utilization.

Consequences of Folate Deficiency due to Malabsorption Syndromes

1. Anemia and Hematological Complications:

Folate deficiency stemming from malabsorption syndromes contributes to megaloblastic anemia, characterized by larger-than-normal red blood cells due to impaired DNA synthesis. This anemia leads to fatigue, weakness, and other hematological complications.

2. Neurological Manifestations:

Inadequate folate levels due to malabsorption can result in neurological complications, including cognitive impairments, mood disturbances, and potential exacerbation of underlying neurological conditions.

3. Increased Risk in Pregnancy:

Women with malabsorption syndromes are at an increased risk of folate deficiency during pregnancy, potentially leading to neural tube defects and other developmental anomalies in the fetus.

Diagnosis and Management of Folate Deficiency in Malabsorption Syndromes

1. Diagnostic Evaluation:

Diagnosis involves assessing folate levels through blood tests to confirm deficiency. Further investigations may include assessing the underlying cause through imaging studies, endoscopy, or biopsy.

2. Treatment Approaches:

Treatment focuses on addressing the underlying malabsorption syndrome while managing folate deficiency. Strategies may include:

- Dietary modifications emphasizing folate-rich foods
- Folate supplementation or intramuscular injections in severe cases
- Treating the underlying condition, such as managing inflammation in IBD or SIBO with antibiotics

3. Monitoring and Follow-up:

Regular monitoring of folate levels and response to treatment is essential. Long-term management involves continuous monitoring, dietary adjustments, and potentially lifelong supplementation to prevent recurrent deficiencies.

Conclusion

Malabsorption syndromes pose a significant risk for folate deficiency due to impaired absorption of nutrients, including folate, from the gastrointestinal tract. These conditions, such as celiac disease, IBD, surgical interventions, and bacterial overgrowth, disrupt the normal absorptive mechanisms, leading to reduced folate uptake. Folate deficiency resulting from malabsorption syndromes can have profound consequences, impacting hematological, neurological, and developmental aspects of health. Timely diagnosis, addressing the underlying condition, folate supplementation, and ongoing monitoring are crucial in managing folate deficiency associated with malabsorption syndromes, aiming to mitigate complications and improve overall health outcomes.

3.3 Medications and Conditions Leading to Folate Deficiency

Medications and certain medical conditions can significantly impact folate levels in the body, leading to folate deficiency. Understanding how these medications and conditions interfere with folate absorption, utilization, or metabolism sheds light on their role in contributing to folate deficiency and its associated health implications.

Medications Leading to Folate Deficiency

1. Anticonvulsants:

Some anticonvulsant medications, such as phenytoin, carbamazepine, and valproic acid, can interfere with folate metabolism, leading to reduced folate levels. They may increase folate breakdown or hinder its absorption, contributing to deficiency.

2. Methotrexate:

Methotrexate, a medication used in chemotherapy and for certain autoimmune conditions like rheumatoid arthritis, inhibits dihydrofolate reductase, an enzyme involved in folate metabolism. Prolonged use can lead to folate depletion.

3. Sulfasalazine:

Sulfasalazine, prescribed for inflammatory conditions like ulcerative colitis and rheumatoid arthritis, can impair folate absorption, leading to reduced folate levels in the body.

4. Proton Pump Inhibitors (PPIs) and H2 Blockers:

Acid-suppressing medications like PPIs (omeprazole, esomeprazole) and H2 blockers (ranitidine, famotidine) used for managing gastrointestinal conditions can impact the absorption of dietary folate due to altered gastric pH.

5. Oral Contraceptives:

Long-term use of oral contraceptives, though controversial, has been associated with a slight reduction in serum folate levels in some individuals, potentially contributing to folate deficiency.

Medical Conditions Leading to Folate Deficiency

1. Alcoholism:

Chronic alcohol consumption can lead to poor dietary habits, malnutrition, and impaired absorption of folate, contributing to folate deficiency.

2. Hemolytic Anemias:

Conditions like sickle cell anemia or autoimmune hemolytic anemia increase the turnover of red blood cells, demanding higher folate levels. This increased demand, coupled with potential medications used to manage these conditions, can lead to folate depletion.

3. Chronic Kidney Disease (CKD):

Patients with CKD may experience folate deficiency due to altered metabolism and increased folate excretion, leading to reduced folate levels.

4. Liver Disease:

Liver diseases, such as cirrhosis, can impact folate metabolism and storage, potentially leading to folate deficiency.

Impact of Medications and Medical Conditions on Folate Levels

1. Impaired Absorption or Metabolism:

Medications and medical conditions can interfere with folate absorption, metabolism, or utilization within the body, leading to reduced availability of folate for essential metabolic processes.

2. Increased Demand or Loss:

Certain medical conditions, such as hemolytic anemias or chronic kidney disease, increase the body's demand for folate, potentially surpassing intake or absorption rates, leading to depletion.

3. Compromised Utilization:

Medications inhibiting folate-dependent enzymes or conditions affecting liver function can disrupt folate utilization, further contributing to deficiency and its associated complications.

Consequences of Folate Deficiency due to Medications and Medical Conditions

1. Anemia and Hematological Complications:

Reduced folate levels contribute to megaloblastic anemia, characterized by larger-than-normal red blood cells due to impaired DNA synthesis, leading to fatigue, weakness, and other hematological complications.

2. Neurological Manifestations:

Inadequate folate levels can lead to neurological complications, including cognitive impairments, mood disturbances, and potential exacerbation of underlying neurological conditions.

3. Developmental Risks:

Folate deficiency in pregnant individuals due to medications or medical conditions can increase the risk of neural tube defects and other developmental anomalies in the fetus.

Management Strategies for Folate Deficiency

1. Monitoring and Assessments:

Regular monitoring of folate levels through blood tests helps diagnose and manage folate deficiency associated with medications or medical conditions.

2. Supplementation:

Folate supplementation is often recommended to replenish depleted levels caused by medications or medical conditions. Physicians may prescribe specific doses tailored to individual needs.

3. Modification of Medications or Treatment Plans:

In some cases, altering medication regimens or treatment plans to minimize their impact on folate levels might be considered, if feasible and medically appropriate.

Conclusion

Medications and certain medical conditions can significantly affect folate levels in the body, contributing to folate deficiency and its associated health complications. Understanding how these medications interfere with folate absorption, utilization, or metabolism, as well as recognizing the impact of medical conditions on folate levels, is crucial in diagnosing, managing, and preventing folate deficiency. Timely monitoring, supplementation when necessary, and potential adjustments in treatment plans are essential strategies in addressing folate deficiency attributed to medications or medical conditions, aiming to mitigate complications and promote overall health and well-being.

CHAPTER 4: CLINICAL MANIFESTATIONS OF FOLATE DEFICIENCY

4.1 Hematological Changes and Anemia

Hematological changes and anemia associated with folate deficiency are intricate manifestations of altered blood cell production and function due to insufficient folate levels. Exploring these changes provides insight into the physiological impact of folate deficiency on hematopoiesis and the red blood cell lifecycle.

Understanding Hematological Changes

1. Megaloblastic Anemia:

Folate deficiency leads to megaloblastic anemia characterized by larger-than-normal red blood cells (macrocytes). Impaired DNA synthesis in bone marrow affects cell division, resulting in enlarged, immature red blood cell precursors (megaloblasts).

2. Hypersegmented Neutrophils:

Neutrophils, a type of white blood cell, display hypersegmentation in response to folate deficiency. An increase in the number of lobes in the nucleus of neutrophils (>5 lobes) reflects impaired cell division during granulopoiesis.

3. Pancytopenia:

Severe or prolonged folate deficiency can lead to pancytopenia, a reduction in the number of all types of blood cells (red blood cells, white blood cells, and platelets), impacting overall hematopoietic function.

Mechanisms Leading to Anemia

1. Impaired DNA Synthesis:

Folate deficiency hampers DNA synthesis, specifically affecting rapidly dividing cells, including those involved in hematopoiesis. Reduced folate levels hinder thymidylate and purine synthesis, crucial for DNA replication and cell division.

2. Ineffective Erythropoiesis:

Insufficient folate compromises the maturation process of red blood cells, leading to the production of large, immature cells with impaired functionality, contributing to anemia.

3. Shortened Red Blood Cell Lifespan:

Megaloblastic changes in red blood cell precursors can result in fragile cells with a shorter lifespan. These cells are more prone to premature destruction, contributing to anemia.

Clinical Features of Folate-Deficiency Anemia

1. Fatigue and Weakness:

Anemia leads to reduced oxygen-carrying capacity in the blood, causing fatigue, weakness, and reduced exercise tolerance due to tissue hypoxia.

2. Pallor and Shortness of Breath:

Reduced red blood cell count and oxygen-carrying capacity result in pallor (pale skin) and shortness of breath upon exertion due to inadequate oxygen supply to tissues.

3. Cardiovascular Manifestations:

Severe anemia might lead to palpitations, chest pain, and, in extreme cases, heart palpitations and heart failure due to the increased workload on the heart.

Diagnostic Evaluations for Folate-Deficiency Anemia

1. Complete Blood Count (CBC):

CBC reveals characteristic findings of megaloblastic anemia, such as macrocytosis (larger-than-normal red blood cells) and hypersegmented neutrophils.

2. Serum Folate Levels:

Measurement of serum folate levels helps confirm folate deficiency, providing insight into the cause of megaloblastic anemia.

3. Reticulocyte Count:

Low reticulocyte count signifies reduced red blood cell production, reflecting ineffective erythropoiesis in folate-deficiency anemia.

Management and Treatment Approaches

1. Folate Supplementation:

Oral folate supplementation is the primary treatment for folate-deficiency anemia. Physicians may prescribe folic acid supplements to replenish depleted folate levels.

2. Identification and Management of Underlying Causes:

Addressing underlying factors contributing to folate deficiency, such as dietary deficiencies or malabsorption syndromes, is crucial for long-term management.

3. Monitoring and Follow-Up:

Regular monitoring of hematological parameters and serum folate levels helps track the response to treatment and ensures adequate folate replenishment.

Prevention Strategies

1. Dietary Modifications:

Encouraging a diet rich in folate-containing foods, such as leafy greens, legumes, fruits, and fortified grains, aids in preventing folate deficiency.

2. Supplementation in High-Risk Groups:

Identifying high-risk populations, such as pregnant women, individuals with malabsorption syndromes, or chronic medication users, and providing targeted folate supplementation helps prevent deficiencies.

Conclusion

Folate-deficiency anemia manifests as megaloblastic changes in blood cells due to impaired DNA synthesis and ineffective erythropoiesis. Clinical features include fatigue, pallor, and cardiovascular manifestations resulting from reduced red blood cell functionality and oxygen-carrying capacity. Diagnostic evaluations, including CBC and serum folate levels, aid in confirming folate deficiency anemia. Management involves folate supplementation, addressing underlying causes, and continuous monitoring. Prevention strategies, such as dietary modifications and targeted supplementation, play a pivotal role in preventing folate-deficiency anemia, emphasizing the importance of adequate folate intake for optimal hematological health.

4.2 Neurological Symptoms and Cognitive Impairment

Neurological symptoms and cognitive impairment associated with folate deficiency encompass a spectrum of manifestations affecting the nervous system. Understanding these effects sheds light on the importance of folate in neurological health and the consequences of its deficiency.

Impact of Folate Deficiency on Neurological Health

1. Cognitive Impairment:

Folate plays a crucial role in various neurological processes, including neurotransmitter synthesis and methylation reactions. Deficiency can lead to cognitive dysfunction, affecting memory, concentration, and executive functions.

2. Neuropsychiatric Symptoms:

Folate deficiency is linked to neuropsychiatric manifestations, such as depression, irritability, anxiety, and changes in mood regulation, due to alterations in neurotransmitter synthesis and function.

3. Neural Tube Development:

Adequate folate levels during pregnancy are vital for proper neural tube development in the fetus. Folate deficiency increases the risk of neural tube defects, leading to severe neurological abnormalities in infants.

Mechanisms Underlying Neurological Manifestations

1. Methylation Reactions:

Folate participates in methylation reactions, crucial for the synthesis of neurotransmitters like dopamine, serotonin, and norepinephrine. Folate deficiency disrupts these processes, affecting mood and cognitive functions.

2. Homocysteine Accumulation:

Inadequate folate leads to elevated levels of homocysteine, impacting vascular health and contributing to neurological damage due to its neurotoxic effects.

3. DNA Methylation:

Folate deficiency affects DNA methylation, influencing gene expression patterns in the brain, potentially contributing to neurological disorders and cognitive impairments.

Clinical Presentation of Neurological Symptoms

1. Cognitive Dysfunction:

Folate deficiency may lead to cognitive impairment, including deficits in attention, memory, learning, and executive functions, impacting daily activities and quality of life.

2. Mood Disorders:

Neuropsychiatric symptoms, such as depression, anxiety, irritability, and mood swings, can manifest due to altered neurotransmitter levels resulting from folate deficiency.

3. Peripheral Neuropathy:

Severe and prolonged folate deficiency may cause peripheral nerve damage, leading to symptoms like tingling, numbness, or weakness in the extremities.

Diagnostic Evaluations for Neurological Manifestations

1. Serum Folate and Vitamin B12 Levels:

Assessing serum folate levels helps diagnose folate deficiency associated with neurological symptoms, distinguishing it from other potential causes.

2. Homocysteine and Methylmalonic Acid Levels:

Elevated homocysteine and methylmalonic acid levels, indicative of impaired methylation processes, might aid in confirming neurological manifestations due to folate deficiency.

3. Neuropsychological Testing:

Neuropsychological assessments evaluate cognitive functions, including memory, attention, and executive functions, providing insights into the extent of cognitive impairment.

Management Strategies for Neurological Manifestations

1. Folate Supplementation:

Oral folate supplementation is the primary treatment to replenish folate levels and address neurological symptoms. Physicians may prescribe folic acid supplements tailored to individual needs.

2. Vitamin B12 Supplementation:

Addressing potential coexisting vitamin B12 deficiency is crucial, as both folate and vitamin B12 deficiencies can present with similar neurological manifestations.

3. Behavioral Interventions and Therapy:

Cognitive rehabilitation, counseling, and behavioral interventions may help manage cognitive impairment and mood disturbances associated with folate deficiency.

Prevention and Long-Term Management

1. Education and Awareness:

Promoting awareness about the importance of folate-rich diets, especially during pregnancy, aids in preventing neurological complications in both mothers and infants.

2. Regular Monitoring:

Periodic monitoring of folate levels and neurological assessments in high-risk populations, such as the elderly or individuals with malabsorption syndromes, helps prevent neurological complications.

3. Lifestyle Modifications:

Encouraging a healthy lifestyle, including a balanced diet rich in folate, regular exercise, and stress management, supports neurological health and may mitigate the risk of deficiencies.

Conclusion

Folate deficiency profoundly affects neurological health, leading to cognitive impairment, mood disturbances, and potential neural tube defects in infants. Mechanisms involving disrupted neurotransmitter synthesis, altered methylation processes, and elevated homocysteine levels underlie neurological manifestations. Clinical presentations include cognitive dysfunction, mood disorders, and peripheral neuropathy. Diagnosis involves assessing serum folate levels, homocysteine levels, and conducting neuropsychological testing. Management strategies focus on folate supplementation, addressing vitamin B12 deficiency, and behavioral interventions. Prevention efforts emphasize education, regular monitoring, and lifestyle modifications. Recognizing the neurological impact of folate deficiency underscores the significance of maintaining adequate folate levels for optimal neurological health and cognitive function throughout life.

4.3 Other Systemic Effects of Folate Deficiency

Folate deficiency exerts a wide range of systemic effects beyond hematological and neurological manifestations, impacting various bodily systems. Understanding these systemic implications sheds light on the multifaceted consequences of inadequate folate levels throughout the body.

Impact on Cardiovascular Health

1. Increased Homocysteine Levels:

Folate deficiency contributes to elevated levels of homocysteine, an amino acid associated with cardiovascular risk. High homocysteine levels are linked to atherosclerosis, increasing the risk of cardiovascular diseases.

2. Cardiovascular Events:

Elevated homocysteine levels due to folate deficiency are associated with an increased risk of cardiovascular events such as heart attacks, strokes, and peripheral vascular diseases.

Effects on Gastrointestinal Health

1. Impaired Digestive Functions:

Folate deficiency can exacerbate gastrointestinal symptoms, potentially contributing to digestive issues like diarrhea, abdominal discomfort, and impaired nutrient absorption.

2. Gastrointestinal Mucosal Changes:

Chronic folate deficiency may lead to alterations in the gastrointestinal mucosa, affecting the health and integrity of the digestive tract.

Impact on Immune Function

1. Altered Immune Response:

Inadequate folate levels may compromise immune function, potentially leading to increased susceptibility to infections and impairing the body's ability to mount an effective immune response.

2. Impaired Wound Healing:

Folate deficiency can hinder the body's capacity for proper wound healing due to its role in cellular proliferation and tissue repair mechanisms.

Endocrine and Metabolic Effects

1. Insulin Resistance:

Folate deficiency has been associated with an increased risk of insulin resistance and metabolic disturbances, potentially contributing to conditions like diabetes.

2. Hormonal Imbalances:

In some cases, folate deficiency might influence hormonal imbalances, impacting various endocrine functions and potentially contributing to reproductive or thyroid-related issues.

Impact on Bone Health

1. Osteoporosis Risk:

Some studies suggest a possible association between folate deficiency and an increased risk of osteoporosis or bone-related issues, though the exact mechanisms remain under investigation.

2. Bone Marrow Suppression:

Severe and prolonged folate deficiency may affect bone marrow function, potentially contributing to decreased bone marrow activity and its impact on overall bone health.

Dermatological Manifestations

1. Skin Changes:

Folate deficiency might manifest in certain dermatological

changes, including pale skin, mucosal changes, or in rare cases, specific skin lesions.

2. Hair and Nail Health:

In some instances, folate deficiency might contribute to changes in hair texture, color, or nail health, though these manifestations are less common.

Impact on Reproductive Health

1. Fertility Issues:

Folate deficiency has been associated with fertility problems in both men and women, potentially affecting reproductive health and fertility outcomes.

2. Pregnancy Complications:

Inadequate folate levels during pregnancy increase the risk of neural tube defects and other developmental anomalies in the fetus, emphasizing its critical role in maternal and fetal health.

Management and Prevention Strategies

1. Dietary Modifications:

Promoting a balanced diet rich in folate-containing foods aids in preventing deficiencies and mitigating the risk of systemic effects across various bodily systems.

2. Supplementation:

Oral folate supplementation is a cornerstone in managing and preventing systemic effects of folate deficiency, especially in high-risk populations or individuals with malabsorption syndromes.

3. Routine Monitoring:

Regular monitoring of folate levels and clinical assessments in at-risk individuals allows for timely interventions and mitigates the risk of systemic consequences.

Conclusion

Folate deficiency manifests with diverse systemic effects

impacting cardiovascular, gastrointestinal, immune, endocrine, bone, dermatological, and reproductive health. Elevated homocysteine levels contribute to cardiovascular risks, while gastrointestinal symptoms and compromised immune function are common systemic manifestations. Furthermore, endocrine and metabolic disturbances, potential impact on bone health, dermatological changes, and reproductive issues underscore the widespread influence of folate deficiency. Implementing dietary modifications, supplementation when necessary, and routine monitoring are essential strategies in managing and preventing the systemic effects of folate deficiency, emphasizing the significance of maintaining optimal folate levels for overall health and well-being across various bodily systems.

CHAPTER 5:
DIAGNOSIS OF FOLATE
DEFICIENCY ANEMIA

5.1 Laboratory Tests and Biomarkers for Folate Levels

Laboratory tests and biomarkers play a crucial role in assessing folate levels, diagnosing folate deficiency, and monitoring treatment responses. Understanding these tests and biomarkers provides insights into the methods used to evaluate folate status in clinical settings.

Serum Folate Assay

1. Serum Folate Measurement:

Serum folate levels indicate the amount of folate circulating in the bloodstream. The test measures both the unmetabolized folic acid from supplements and the naturally occurring folate from dietary sources.

2. Normal Range:

The normal range for serum folate levels typically falls between 3-20 nanograms per milliliter (ng/mL) in adults, but reference ranges may vary among laboratories.

3. Diagnostic Value:

Low serum folate levels indicate potential folate deficiency, but they might not necessarily reflect tissue stores or provide insights into functional folate status.

Red Blood Cell (RBC) Folate Assay

1. RBC Folate Measurement:

RBC folate levels reflect the folate content within red blood cells, providing insights into long-term folate status and storage within cells.

2. Normal Range:

The reference range for RBC folate levels is typically between 140-628 ng/mL, serving as a better indicator of tissue stores compared to serum folate.

3. Diagnostic Significance:

RBC folate levels offer a more reliable assessment of long-term folate status, as red blood cells have a lifespan of about 120 days, reflecting folate intake over several months.

Homocysteine Levels

1. Homocysteine Measurement:

Elevated homocysteine levels in blood serve as an indirect marker for folate deficiency. Folate is crucial for converting homocysteine into methionine, and low folate levels can lead to increased homocysteine.

2. Normal Range:

Normal homocysteine levels typically range between 5-15 micromoles per liter (μmol/L), but levels above this range may indicate folate deficiency.

3. Diagnostic Value:

Elevated homocysteine levels, along with decreased folate levels, can indicate impaired folate metabolism and serve as an indirect marker for folate deficiency.

Methylmalonic Acid (MMA) Levels

1. MMA Measurement:

MMA levels serve as a specific marker for assessing vitamin B12 deficiency, but elevated MMA levels can also indicate functional folate deficiency due to impaired methionine synthesis.

2. Normal Range:

Normal MMA levels usually range below 0.4 micromoles per liter (μmol/L), with higher levels suggesting impaired folate metabolism or other deficiencies impacting methionine synthesis.

3. Diagnostic Significance:

Elevated MMA levels, in combination with other markers like low serum folate, can indicate functional folate deficiency, emphasizing its importance in assessing folate status.

DNA Methylation Assays

1. Methylation-Specific Biomarkers:

Assessing DNA methylation patterns provides insights into folate's role in epigenetic processes. Altered methylation patterns can indicate impaired folate metabolism.

2. Diagnostic Use:

DNA methylation assays are research tools and aren't commonly used in routine clinical settings. However, they contribute to understanding folate's impact on epigenetic mechanisms.

Functional Assays

1. Formiminoglutamic Acid (FIGLU) Test:

FIGLU tests assess folate metabolism by measuring urinary excretion of FIGLU, a metabolite formed during folate breakdown. Elevated levels suggest impaired folate metabolism.

2. Diagnostic Relevance:

While the FIGLU test provides insights into folate metabolism, it's not routinely used due to its complexity and limited availability in clinical settings.

Conclusion

Laboratory tests and biomarkers serve as valuable tools in assessing folate status, diagnosing deficiencies, and monitoring treatment responses. Serum folate and RBC folate assays offer insights into immediate and long-term folate status, respectively. Elevated homocysteine and MMA levels provide indirect markers for folate deficiency, indicating impaired folate metabolism. While DNA methylation assays and functional tests offer deeper insights into folate's impact on epigenetics and metabolism, they are more commonly utilized in research settings. Understanding the nuances and diagnostic significance of these laboratory tests and biomarkers aids clinicians in accurately evaluating folate levels and guiding appropriate interventions for individuals at risk of folate deficiency.

5.2 Differential Diagnosis with Other Types of Anemia

Differential diagnosis involving various types of anemia is crucial in distinguishing folate deficiency anemia from other forms of anemia, considering their distinct etiologies, clinical presentations, and laboratory findings. Understanding these differences aids in accurate diagnosis and appropriate management strategies.

Iron-Deficiency Anemia

Etiology:

Iron-deficiency anemia stems from insufficient iron levels needed for red blood cell production, leading to smaller and paler red blood cells (microcytic, hypochromic).

Differential Diagnosis:

Distinguishing iron-deficiency anemia from folate deficiency involves assessing red blood cell indices. Iron-deficiency anemia exhibits low mean corpuscular volume (MCV) and mean corpuscular hemoglobin (MCH), whereas folate deficiency typically presents with larger cells (macrocytic) due to impaired DNA synthesis.

Vitamin B12 Deficiency Anemia (Pernicious Anemia)

Etiology:

Vitamin B12 deficiency results from inadequate dietary intake or impaired absorption, leading to megaloblastic anemia similar to that seen in folate deficiency.

Differential Diagnosis:

Differentiating between B12 deficiency and folate deficiency often involves assessing serum levels of both vitamins. Both deficiencies cause macrocytic anemia, but B12 deficiency might additionally manifest with neurological symptoms due to its role in myelin synthesis.

Hemolytic Anemias

Etiology:

Hemolytic anemias involve increased red blood cell destruction, leading to decreased red blood cell lifespan and anemia. Conditions like autoimmune hemolytic anemia or hereditary disorders can cause hemolysis.

Differential Diagnosis:

Distinguishing hemolytic anemias from folate deficiency involves assessing reticulocyte count and markers of hemolysis (e.g., elevated bilirubin, lactate dehydrogenase). Additionally, folate deficiency is not associated with increased reticulocyte count, while hemolytic anemias typically exhibit a higher count as a compensatory response.

Anemia of Chronic Disease (ACD)

Etiology:

ACD results from chronic inflammatory conditions, malignancies, or chronic infections leading to reduced red blood cell production and impaired iron utilization.

Differential Diagnosis:

Anemia of chronic disease is normocytic or slightly microcytic and hypochromic. It's characterized by low iron levels despite adequate iron stores, unlike folate deficiency, which presents with macrocytic red blood cells.

Thalassemia

Etiology:

Thalassemia comprises a group of inherited hemoglobin disorders characterized by reduced or absent synthesis of globin chains, leading to abnormal hemoglobin production.

Differential Diagnosis:

Distinguishing thalassemia from folate deficiency involves assessing hemoglobin electrophoresis to identify abnormal hemoglobin variants in thalassemia. Thalassemia often presents with microcytic, hypochromic red blood cells, contrasting with the macrocytic cells seen in folate deficiency.

Sideroblastic Anemia

Etiology:

Sideroblastic anemia involves defective heme synthesis, leading to the accumulation of iron in mitochondria and ineffective erythropoiesis.

Differential Diagnosis:

Distinguishing sideroblastic anemia involves assessing bone marrow aspirate or biopsy, revealing ringed sideroblasts. This form of anemia can be microcytic or normocytic, differing from the macrocytic cells observed in folate deficiency.

Chronic Kidney Disease (CKD)-Related Anemia

Etiology:

Anemia associated with CKD results from decreased erythropoietin production and impaired red blood cell production due to kidney dysfunction.

Differential Diagnosis:

CKD-related anemia typically presents as normocytic or slightly microcytic. Differential diagnosis involves evaluating kidney function and identifying the underlying CKD, contrasting with the macrocytic anemia seen in folate deficiency.

Conclusion

Differential diagnosis involving various types of anemia focuses on distinguishing folate deficiency anemia from other forms based on distinct clinical and laboratory findings. Assessing red blood cell indices, serum levels of folate, vitamin B12, iron studies, reticulocyte count, and specific diagnostic tests aids in differentiating between these anemias. Understanding the specific etiologies, characteristic features, and underlying pathophysiological mechanisms of each type of anemia is essential for accurate diagnosis and tailored management strategies.

5.3 Imaging and Additional Diagnostic Approaches

While laboratory tests are crucial in diagnosing anemia and assessing folate levels, additional diagnostic approaches, including imaging studies and specific diagnostic techniques, provide valuable insights into underlying causes and complications associated with folate deficiency and anemia.

Bone Marrow Aspiration and Biopsy

Purpose:

Bone marrow examination helps evaluate cellularity, morphology, and proliferation of hematopoietic cells, aiding in diagnosing various hematological disorders.

Diagnostic Value:

Bone marrow aspiration and biopsy reveal changes in cell

morphology, such as megaloblastic changes, aiding in confirming folate deficiency anemia and ruling out other hematological conditions.

Upper Gastrointestinal Endoscopy

Purpose:

Upper GI endoscopy examines the upper digestive tract, including the esophagus, stomach, and duodenum, to identify gastrointestinal abnormalities impacting nutrient absorption.

Diagnostic Value:

Identifying gastric or duodenal pathologies, such as gastritis, ulcers, or malabsorption syndromes, helps understand potential causes of folate deficiency due to impaired absorption.

Neuroimaging (MRI, CT Scan)

Purpose:

Neuroimaging studies like MRI or CT scans evaluate the brain and spinal cord, aiding in identifying structural abnormalities, lesions, or changes impacting neurological function.

Diagnostic Value:

In cases of neurological symptoms associated with folate deficiency, neuroimaging helps rule out structural abnormalities and provides insights into the neurological manifestations.

Ultrasound Imaging

Purpose:

Ultrasound scans assess various organs and structures, aiding in identifying abnormalities, such as liver diseases impacting folate metabolism or reproductive issues in women.

Diagnostic Value:

Detecting liver pathologies or reproductive abnormalities provides insights into potential systemic effects or underlying causes contributing to folate deficiency.

Genetic Testing and Molecular Diagnostics

Purpose:

Genetic testing evaluates specific genetic mutations or variants associated with inherited disorders impacting folate metabolism or hemoglobin synthesis.

Diagnostic Value:

Identifying genetic mutations, such as MTHFR polymorphisms, aids in understanding individual susceptibility to folate deficiency or other related conditions.

Absorption Studies

Purpose:

Absorption studies assess the absorption capacity of the gastrointestinal tract, helping identify malabsorption syndromes impacting folate uptake.

Diagnostic Value:

Evaluating the absorption of folate or other nutrients provides insights into gastrointestinal disorders leading to folate deficiency.

Functional Tests for Neurological Assessment

Purpose:

Functional tests assess neurological functions, including cognitive, motor, and sensory abilities, aiding in evaluating neurological manifestations associated with folate deficiency.

Diagnostic Value:

Conducting functional tests provides a comprehensive assessment of neurological deficits and monitors the response to treatment in neurological complications.

Conclusion

Imaging studies, specific diagnostic techniques, and functional assessments complement laboratory tests in diagnosing and evaluating folate deficiency anemia and its associated complications. Bone marrow aspiration and biopsy help confirm hematological changes, while imaging modalities like MRI, CT scans, and ultrasounds provide insights into structural abnormalities impacting various organ systems. Upper GI endoscopy aids in identifying gastrointestinal disorders affecting folate absorption, and genetic testing unveils specific genetic predispositions. Incorporating these additional diagnostic approaches helps clinicians comprehensively assess underlying causes, systemic effects, and complications associated with folate deficiency, enabling tailored management and targeted interventions for individuals at risk.

CHAPTER 6:
TREATMENT AND
MANAGEMENT

6.1 Dietary Modifications and Nutritional Supplements

Dietary modifications and nutritional supplements play a pivotal role in managing and preventing folate deficiency anemia. Understanding the importance of a balanced diet rich in folate and the role of supplements is crucial in addressing deficiencies and supporting overall health.

Dietary Sources of Folate

1. Leafy Greens:

Vegetables like spinach, kale, collard greens, and broccoli are excellent sources of natural folate.

2. Legumes and Beans:

Lentils, chickpeas, black beans, and kidney beans are high in folate content, offering a plant-based source of this essential nutrient.

3. Fruits:

Avocado, oranges, papaya, and bananas are fruits containing notable amounts of folate.

4. Fortified Grains:

Many cereals, bread, pasta, and rice products are fortified with synthetic folic acid, enhancing their folate content.

Importance of Dietary Modifications

1. Increased Folate Intake:

Promoting a diet rich in folate-containing foods ensures adequate intake of this essential nutrient, reducing the risk of deficiencies.

2. Whole Foods Approach:

Encouraging consumption of whole, unprocessed foods ensures a natural intake of folate along with other essential nutrients, supporting overall health.

Role of Nutritional Supplements

1. Folic Acid Supplements:

Oral folic acid supplements are commonly prescribed to replenish folate levels, especially in cases of diagnosed deficiency or increased requirements, such as during pregnancy.

2. Dosage and Duration:

Supplement dosage varies based on individual needs and medical recommendations. For instance, pregnant women often require higher doses to prevent neural tube defects.

Prevention Strategies

1. Prenatal Care:

Adequate folate intake during pregnancy is crucial for fetal development, emphasizing the importance of prenatal supplements and fortified foods.

2. Supplementation in High-Risk Groups:

Identifying high-risk populations, such as individuals with malabsorption disorders or those on certain medications affecting folate metabolism, warrants targeted supplementation.

Dietary Modifications in Specific Population Groups

1. Children and Adolescents:

Encouraging a balanced diet rich in folate supports growth, development, and overall health in younger age groups.

2. Elderly Individuals:

Aging populations might have altered nutrient absorption, emphasizing the importance of a nutrient-dense diet or supplements to meet folate requirements.

Challenges and Considerations

1. Availability and Access:

Ensuring access to folate-rich foods or fortified products might be challenging in certain regions or socio-economic groups.

2. Cultural and Dietary Preferences:

Encouraging dietary changes must consider cultural preferences and dietary habits to effectively incorporate folate-rich foods.

Education and Awareness

1. Public Health Campaigns:

Public awareness campaigns educate communities about the importance of folate-rich diets, especially for pregnant women and individuals at risk of deficiencies.

2. Healthcare Provider Guidance:

Healthcare professionals play a crucial role in advising patients about dietary modifications and appropriate supplement use based on individual needs.

Conclusion

Dietary modifications emphasizing the consumption of folate-rich foods and the use of nutritional supplements are essential strategies in managing and preventing folate deficiency anemia. Encouraging a diverse diet comprising leafy greens, legumes, fruits, and fortified grains ensures adequate folate intake. Supplements, particularly folic acid, are instrumental in addressing deficiencies, especially in high-risk populations. Prevention strategies, such as prenatal care and targeted supplementation, are critical in mitigating the risks associated with folate deficiency, particularly in vulnerable groups. Overcoming challenges related to access, cultural preferences, and awareness through education and healthcare guidance is fundamental in promoting folate-rich diets and preventing deficiencies, contributing to improved overall health and well-being.

6.2 Pharmacological Interventions

Pharmacological interventions are essential in the management of folate deficiency anemia, involving the use of medications to address deficiencies, support red blood cell production, and correct underlying causes. Understanding these interventions and their mechanisms aids in effectively treating and preventing folate deficiency.

Folic Acid Supplementation

Purpose:

Folic acid supplements are the cornerstone of pharmacological intervention, replenishing folate levels in cases of deficiency.

Dosage:

Dosage varies based on individual needs, but typical supplementation for adults ranges from 400 to 800 micrograms daily. Pregnant women often require higher doses under medical supervision.

Mechanism:

Folic acid supplements provide a synthetic form of folate that the body converts into the active form, supporting DNA synthesis and red blood cell production.

Prenatal Vitamins

Purpose:

Prenatal vitamins contain higher doses of folic acid, specifically designed to support fetal development and prevent neural tube defects during pregnancy.

Composition:

Prenatal supplements typically contain folic acid alongside other vitamins and minerals essential for maternal and fetal health.

Dosage:

Pregnant women are often advised to take prenatal vitamins with higher folic acid content, usually 600 to 1000 micrograms or more, based on individual requirements.

Vitamin B12 Supplementation

Purpose:

Addressing coexisting vitamin B12 deficiency is crucial, as deficiencies in both B12 and folate can present similarly and lead to megaloblastic anemia.

Dosage:

Vitamin B12 supplements vary in dosage and form, often administered orally or via intramuscular injections based on the severity of deficiency.

Mechanism:

Correcting vitamin B12 deficiency aids in supporting red blood cell production and prevents neurological complications often associated with B12 deficiency.

Combination Therapy

Purpose:

In cases of concurrent folate and vitamin B12 deficiencies, combination therapy with both folic acid and vitamin B12 supplements is necessary for comprehensive treatment.

Dosage and Administration:

Adjusting dosage and mode of administration, whether oral or injectable, is determined by the severity of deficiencies and individual patient needs.

Mechanism:

Combined supplementation supports the synthesis of DNA, red blood cell maturation, and prevents neurological complications associated with both deficiencies.

Antacids and Medications Impacting Absorption

Purpose:

Addressing conditions or medications that hinder folate absorption or utilization, such as antacids or certain drugs affecting gastrointestinal absorption.

Management:

Adjusting medication regimens or using alternative formulations to mitigate interference with folate absorption is essential in preventing deficiencies.

Mechanism:

Minimizing interference with folate absorption ensures optimal utilization of dietary folate and supplements, preventing deficiencies.

Management of Malabsorption Syndromes

Purpose:

Addressing underlying malabsorption disorders, such as celiac disease or inflammatory bowel disease, which can impair folate absorption.

Treatment Approach:

Managing the underlying condition involves dietary modifications, medications, and therapies tailored to specific malabsorption syndromes.

Mechanism:

Correcting malabsorption disorders ensures adequate nutrient absorption, including folate, reducing the risk of deficiencies.

Conclusion

Pharmacological interventions in folate deficiency anemia

primarily involve folic acid supplementation, prenatal vitamins during pregnancy, and addressing coexisting vitamin B12 deficiencies. The use of supplements and medications aims to replenish folate levels, support red blood cell production, and correct underlying causes such as malabsorption syndromes or medications impacting absorption. Combination therapy with folate and vitamin B12 supplements is crucial when deficiencies coexist, ensuring comprehensive treatment and preventing complications. Managing conditions affecting folate absorption or utilization is also vital in preventing deficiencies. Tailored interventions and appropriate dosages based on individual needs and underlying conditions are key in effectively managing folate deficiency anemia, contributing to improved hematological health and overall well-being.

6.3 Monitoring and Follow-Up in Treatment

Monitoring and follow-up in the treatment of folate deficiency anemia are critical aspects of ensuring the effectiveness of interventions, tracking progress, and preventing recurrence. Establishing regular assessments and follow-up protocols are essential in managing and maintaining optimal folate levels and overall health.

Initial Assessment

1. Diagnostic Evaluation:

Conducting a comprehensive diagnostic workup, including laboratory tests, clinical evaluation, and medical history, aids in confirming folate deficiency anemia and identifying underlying causes.

2. Identifying Risk Factors:

Determining risk factors such as dietary habits, medical conditions, medications, and lifestyle factors influencing folate levels guides tailored management strategies.

Monitoring Parameters

1. Serum Folate Levels:

Regular measurement of serum folate levels helps assess the response to treatment and ensures adequate supplementation.

2. Red Blood Cell Indices:

Monitoring changes in red blood cell indices, particularly mean corpuscular volume (MCV) and mean corpuscular hemoglobin (MCH), reflects the impact of treatment on red blood cell size and hemoglobin content.

3. Hemoglobin and Hematocrit:

Tracking hemoglobin and hematocrit levels helps evaluate improvements in red blood cell production and overall oxygen-carrying capacity.

Follow-Up Frequency

1. Short-Term Follow-Up:

Initially, more frequent follow-ups, such as every few weeks to months, are advisable to assess response to treatment and adjust supplementation if needed.

2. Long-Term Monitoring:

After the initial phase, regular but less frequent follow-ups, typically every three to six months, help ensure sustained improvement and prevent recurrence.

Adjusting Treatment

1. Supplement Titration:

Adjusting supplement dosages based on response and serum folate levels is crucial in achieving optimal folate levels without excessive supplementation.

2. Addressing Underlying Causes:

Continuously evaluating and managing underlying conditions

impacting folate levels, such as malabsorption syndromes or medication changes, is essential for long-term management.

Evaluation of Complications

1. Neurological Assessments:

Monitoring and assessing neurological symptoms, cognitive functions, and peripheral neuropathy help detect and manage neurological complications associated with folate deficiency.

2. Other Systemic Effects:

Evaluating for other systemic effects, such as cardiovascular, gastrointestinal, or reproductive complications, aids in comprehensive management and timely interventions.

Patient Education and Compliance

1. Understanding Treatment Plan:

Educating patients about the importance of adherence to supplementation, dietary modifications, and lifestyle changes supports successful management.

2. Reinforcing Follow-Up:

Encouraging patients to attend scheduled follow-up visits and emphasizing the importance of regular monitoring helps maintain continuity of care.

Prevention Strategies

1. Lifestyle Modifications:

Promoting a balanced diet rich in folate and healthy habits supports prevention and reduces the risk of recurrent deficiencies.

2. High-Risk Population Management:

Ensuring targeted monitoring and interventions in high-risk populations, such as pregnant women or individuals with malabsorption disorders, prevents recurrences.

Long-Term Care

1. Continuity of Care:

Establishing a long-term care plan involving regular follow-ups, continued monitoring, and addressing evolving patient needs ensures sustained management.

2. Multidisciplinary Approach:

Collaborating with healthcare professionals, including primary care physicians, hematologists, dietitians, and specialists, supports comprehensive care and tailored interventions.

Conclusion

Monitoring and follow-up in the treatment of folate deficiency anemia are integral components of successful management. Regular assessments of serum folate levels, red blood cell indices, and hemoglobin concentrations guide treatment adjustments and ensure optimal responses. Tailoring follow-up frequency, adjusting treatment protocols, evaluating complications, and promoting patient education and compliance contribute to effective management and prevention of recurrences. Long-term care plans, preventive strategies, and a multidisciplinary approach are essential in maintaining optimal folate levels, addressing underlying causes, and promoting overall health and well-being for individuals affected by folate deficiency anemia.

CHAPTER 7: PREVENTION STRATEGIES

7.1 Importance of Folate in Pregnancy and Birth Defect Prevention

Folate plays a pivotal role in pregnancy, supporting maternal health and significantly impacting fetal development. Understanding the importance of folate in pregnancy and birth defect prevention underscores the necessity of adequate folate intake, especially during the early stages of pregnancy.

Role of Folate in Pregnancy

1. Neural Tube Development:

Folate is crucial for neural tube formation in the early stages of pregnancy, preventing neural tube defects (NTDs) like spina bifida and anencephaly.

2. DNA Synthesis and Cell Division:

Folate supports DNA synthesis and cell division, critical processes for fetal growth and development, particularly during organogenesis in the first trimester.

3. Red Blood Cell Production:

Adequate folate levels prevent maternal anemia, supporting the increased demands for red blood cell production during pregnancy.

Prevention of Neural Tube Defects

1. Timing of Supplementation:

Adequate folate intake before conception and in the early weeks of pregnancy is crucial in reducing the risk of neural tube defects.

2. Recommended Folate Intake:

Health organizations recommend supplementing with 400 to 800 micrograms of folic acid daily before conception and throughout the first trimester.

3. Impact on Birth Defects:

Studies demonstrate a significant reduction in the incidence of neural tube defects when mothers consume sufficient folate before and during early pregnancy.

Maternal Health and Red Blood Cell Formation

1. Prevention of Maternal Anemia:

Folate supports red blood cell production, reducing the risk of maternal anemia, which can affect pregnancy outcomes and maternal well-being.

2. Prevention of Preeclampsia:

Adequate folate levels may contribute to lowering the risk of developing preeclampsia, a serious complication in pregnancy.

Other Developmental Benefits

1. Brain and Spinal Cord Development:

Beyond preventing neural tube defects, folate supports overall brain and spinal cord development, influencing cognitive function and overall health in offspring.

2. Reduced Risk of Other Birth Defects:

Folate intake during pregnancy may reduce the risk of other congenital abnormalities, though more research is ongoing in this area.

Importance of Preconception Folate Intake

1. Early Pregnancy Preparation:

Adequate folate intake before conception ensures optimal levels during the critical early weeks when fetal development begins.

2. Unplanned Pregnancies:

As many pregnancies are unplanned, maintaining adequate folate levels through a balanced diet or supplements is vital for all women of childbearing age.

Challenges and Considerations

1. Awareness and Education:

Ensuring widespread awareness about the importance of folate supplementation before and during pregnancy remains crucial for birth defect prevention.

2. Access to Healthcare and Supplements:

Addressing disparities in access to healthcare and supplements is essential to ensure all women have the means to maintain adequate folate levels.

Public Health Interventions

1. Fortification Programs:

Implementing food fortification programs with folic acid helps increase folate intake, reducing the risk of deficiencies and birth defects in populations.

2. Healthcare Provider Guidance:

Healthcare professionals play a pivotal role in educating and advising women about the significance of folate intake, guiding them on supplementation and dietary modifications.

Conclusion

Folate's role in pregnancy is paramount, influencing critical aspects of fetal development and maternal health. Adequate folate intake, especially in the early stages of pregnancy, significantly reduces the risk of neural tube defects and supports overall fetal development. Preconception folate supplementation and a balanced diet rich in folate-containing foods are key in birth defect prevention. Ensuring widespread awareness, addressing access barriers, implementing fortification programs, and healthcare provider guidance are crucial in promoting optimal folate intake, safeguarding maternal health, and ensuring healthy pregnancies with reduced risks of birth defects. Prioritizing folate intake before and during pregnancy is a fundamental step towards ensuring the well-being of both mothers and their developing babies.

7.2 Public Health Measures and Fortification Programs

Public health measures and fortification programs play a pivotal role in addressing folate deficiency on a population level, aiming to improve folate intake, prevent deficiencies, and reduce the incidence of neural tube defects and other related conditions.

Importance of Public Health Measures

1. Addressing Deficiencies on a Population Level:

Public health initiatives target broad segments of the population, addressing deficiencies that impact maternal and fetal health.

2. Preventive Approach:

These measures adopt a proactive stance, focusing on prevention through education, fortification, and access to supplements.

Fortification Programs

1. Purpose:

Fortification involves adding folic acid to staple foods, such as grains, cereals, or flour, to increase their folate content.

2. Effectiveness:

Fortification programs have shown substantial success in increasing folate intake, reducing neural tube defects, and improving overall population health.

3. Examples of Successful Fortification:

Countries like the United States, Canada, and others have implemented mandatory fortification of certain food products, leading to significant reductions in neural tube defects.

Benefits of Fortification Programs

1. Wide Reach:

Fortification reaches a large portion of the population, irrespective of socioeconomic status or access to healthcare, benefiting diverse groups.

2. Cost-Effectiveness:

Fortification is a cost-effective strategy, requiring minimal individual effort while producing substantial public health benefits.

3. Long-Term Impact:

These programs offer sustained benefits, as fortified foods remain available and contribute to improved folate intake over time.

Challenges and Considerations

1. Monitoring and Evaluation:

Continuous monitoring is essential to ensure adequate fortification levels and assess the program's effectiveness in reducing deficiencies and birth defects.

2. Overconsumption Risk:

Balancing fortification levels to prevent excessive folate intake, which could have adverse effects, requires careful consideration.

3. Access and Equity:

Ensuring equitable access to fortified foods among various populations, including marginalized communities, is crucial to prevent disparities in folate intake.

Global Efforts and Guidelines

1. World Health Organization (WHO) Recommendations:

WHO encourages fortification as a key strategy to reduce neural tube defects, providing guidance on optimal folate levels in fortified foods.

2. National Guidelines:

Many countries have developed national guidelines for fortification, setting standards for folate levels and the types of foods to be fortified.

Implementation Strategies

1. Collaboration with Food Industry:

Collaborating with the food industry facilitates the incorporation of folic acid into various staple foods, ensuring compliance with fortification standards.

2. Education and Awareness Campaigns:

Public education campaigns raise awareness about the importance of folate intake, fortification programs, and the benefits of consuming fortified foods.

Success Stories and Impact

1. Reduction in Neural Tube Defects:

Countries with successful fortification programs have reported significant reductions in the incidence of neural tube defects, demonstrating the program's impact.

2. Health and Economic Benefits:

The success of fortification programs translates into improved health outcomes, reduced healthcare costs, and enhanced quality of life.

Future Directions

1. Continuous Improvement:

Ongoing research aims to refine fortification strategies, considering optimal folate levels, additional fortified foods, and monitoring techniques.

2. Addressing Global Disparities:

Efforts are directed towards addressing disparities in access to fortified foods, especially in low-income regions or countries with limited resources.

Conclusion

Public health measures, particularly fortification programs, are instrumental in addressing folate deficiency and preventing related birth defects on a population level. These initiatives effectively increase folate intake across diverse populations, demonstrating significant reductions in neural tube defects and improving overall health outcomes. Successful implementation requires careful monitoring, collaboration with the food industry, and robust education campaigns to ensure awareness and compliance. Despite challenges like monitoring, potential overconsumption, and equitable access, fortification programs remain a cost-effective and impactful strategy to improve folate intake and prevent birth defects globally. Continued efforts, collaborations, and refinements in fortification strategies pave the way for a healthier future, reducing the burden of folate deficiency-related conditions and promoting better maternal and fetal health worldwide.

7.3 Recommendations for Various Population Groups

Recommendations for various population groups regarding folate intake and strategies to prevent folate deficiency aim to address specific needs based on age, gender, health conditions, and life stages. Tailoring recommendations ensures adequate folate intake and mitigates the risk of deficiencies and related complications.

Women of Childbearing Age

1. Preconception Planning:

Encouraging women planning pregnancy to maintain adequate folate levels through a balanced diet and supplementation to reduce the risk of neural tube defects.

2. Folic Acid Supplementation:

Recommending daily folic acid supplementation (400 to 800 micrograms) before conception and during the early weeks of pregnancy to support fetal development.

Pregnant Women

1. Prenatal Supplements:

Advising pregnant women to continue folic acid supplementation, preferably through prenatal vitamins, to ensure sufficient folate intake for fetal development.

2. Diet Rich in Folate:

Encouraging a diet rich in folate-containing foods to supplement folic acid intake and support overall maternal and fetal health.

Infants and Young Children

1. Breastfeeding Recommendations:

Encouraging breastfeeding mothers to maintain a balanced diet rich in folate to provide sufficient nutrients to their infants.

2. Introduction of Solid Foods:

Recommending the introduction of folate-rich foods as part of solid food introduction for infants, supporting their nutritional needs.

Adolescents

1. Education on Dietary Habits:

Providing education on healthy dietary habits and the importance of folate-rich foods to support growth and development during adolescence.

2. Addressing Menstrual Health:

Addressing menstrual health and iron needs, which may impact folate absorption, to ensure overall nutritional well-being.

Elderly Population

1. Nutritional Needs:

Emphasizing the importance of a balanced diet, including folate-rich foods, to meet the nutritional needs of aging individuals.

2. Monitoring Absorption:

Addressing potential issues with nutrient absorption due to age-related changes and medication use that may affect folate utilization.

Individuals with Chronic Diseases

1. Chronic Conditions and Nutritional Support:

Tailoring recommendations for individuals with chronic diseases affecting nutrient absorption, ensuring adequate folate intake through supplements or specific dietary modifications.

2. Collaboration with Healthcare Providers:

Collaborating with healthcare providers to manage chronic conditions and optimize nutritional support, including folate intake.

Vegetarians and Vegans

1. Plant-Based Folate Sources:

Educating individuals following vegetarian or vegan diets about plant-based folate sources to ensure adequate intake without animal products.

2. Supplements if Necessary:

Advising supplementation if dietary intake alone doesn't meet folate requirements, ensuring they receive sufficient amounts.

Individuals with Malabsorption Disorders

1. Medical Management:

Providing targeted interventions and medical management for individuals with malabsorption disorders impacting folate absorption.

2. Individualized Treatment:

Tailoring treatment strategies based on specific conditions to ensure optimal folate intake and prevent deficiencies.

Conclusion

Recommendations for various population groups regarding folate intake focus on tailored approaches to address specific needs and life stages. These recommendations encompass preconception planning for women of childbearing age, prenatal supplementation for pregnant women, education on dietary habits for adolescents, addressing nutritional needs for the elderly, and addressing individual needs for those with chronic diseases or malabsorption disorders. Emphasizing the importance of a balanced diet rich in folate-containing foods and, if necessary, supplementation ensures adequate intake and reduces the risk of folate deficiency-related complications across diverse population groups. Collaborative efforts between healthcare providers, public health initiatives, and educational campaigns contribute to promoting better folate intake and overall health outcomes among different segments of the population.

CHAPTER 8: HOLISTIC APPROACHES AND LIFESTYLE CHANGES

8.1 Integrative Medicine and Folate Deficiency Management

Integrative medicine, combining conventional medical approaches with complementary and alternative therapies, offers a comprehensive perspective on managing folate deficiency. This holistic approach focuses on optimizing overall health while addressing the specific needs related to folate levels and deficiency complications.

Understanding Integrative Medicine

1. Holistic Approach:

Integrative medicine considers the whole person—mind, body, and spirit—to promote overall well-being and health.

2. Combination of Modalities:

It combines conventional medicine with evidence-based complementary therapies, including nutrition, supplements, mind-body practices, and lifestyle modifications.

Nutritional Interventions

1. Dietary Counseling:

Providing guidance on a balanced diet rich in folate-containing foods to support natural folate intake and promote overall health.

2. Personalized Nutrition Plans:

Tailoring nutrition plans based on individual needs, considering dietary preferences, health conditions, and optimizing folate intake.

Nutritional Supplements

1. Folate Supplements:

Integrating appropriate folate supplements, including folic acid or methylfolate, based on individual requirements and absorption capabilities.

2. Co-factors and Synergistic Nutrients:

Including co-factors like vitamin B12, B6, and other nutrients essential for optimal folate metabolism and utilization.

Herbal and Botanical Support

1. Herbal Remedies:

Exploring herbal supplements like shatavari, nettle leaf, or dandelion root, known for their potential support in folate metabolism.

2. Herbalist Guidance:

Collaboration with trained herbalists to explore the potential benefits of herbal remedies while considering safety and efficacy.

Mind-Body Practices

1. Stress Management:

Incorporating stress-reduction techniques such as meditation, yoga, or mindfulness to support overall health and immune function.

2. Mindfulness-Based Nutrition:

Cultivating mindful eating practices to enhance the absorption and utilization of nutrients, including folate.

Acupuncture and Traditional Chinese Medicine (TCM)

1. Acupuncture Sessions:

Exploring acupuncture sessions, which in some studies have

shown potential benefits in addressing underlying conditions affecting nutrient absorption.

2. TCM Approaches:

Utilizing TCM perspectives to address imbalances that might contribute to folate deficiency, considering energy flow and balance.

Lifestyle Modifications

1. Exercise and Movement:

Encouraging regular physical activity and movement, which supports overall health and may indirectly impact nutrient absorption and utilization.

2. Sleep and Restorative Practices:

Emphasizing the importance of adequate sleep and rest, as restorative sleep positively influences overall health and immune function.

Collaborative Care

1. Integrative Healthcare Teams:

Collaboration between conventional healthcare providers, nutritionists, herbalists, acupuncturists, and other integrative practitioners for comprehensive care.

2. Individualized Treatment Plans:

Developing individualized treatment plans, considering patient preferences and the integration of various modalities.

Evidence-Based Approach

1. Research and Clinical Studies:

Utilizing evidence-based research and clinical studies to guide the integration of complementary therapies into folate deficiency management.

2. Patient Education:

Empowering patients with knowledge about integrative

approaches, ensuring informed decisions and active participation in their healthcare.

Conclusion

Integrative medicine offers a multifaceted approach to managing folate deficiency, encompassing nutritional interventions, herbal support, mind-body practices, and lifestyle modifications. This approach focuses on optimizing overall health while addressing specific nutrient needs. Collaborative care involving various healthcare practitioners ensures a tailored and holistic treatment plan, integrating conventional and complementary modalities. Patient education and evidence-based practices form the foundation of integrative medicine, providing individuals with comprehensive tools to address folate deficiency and promote holistic well-being. Integrating various modalities within the framework of evidence-based medicine offers a personalized and holistic approach to manage folate deficiency effectively.

8.2 Role of Exercise and Stress Management

The role of exercise and stress management in managing folate deficiency extends beyond physical well-being, encompassing mental health and overall physiological balance. Understanding how these factors influence folate levels and incorporating appropriate strategies can significantly impact folate absorption and utilization.

Exercise and Folate Metabolism

1. Impact on Circulation:

Regular exercise enhances blood circulation, potentially aiding in the transportation and absorption of nutrients like folate.

2. Metabolic Rate and Nutrient Absorption:

Exercise influences metabolic rate, potentially affecting nutrient absorption and utilization, including folate.

Exercise Recommendations

1. Aerobic Exercises:

Engaging in aerobic activities like brisk walking, jogging, or cycling promotes cardiovascular health, potentially supporting nutrient circulation.

2. Strength Training:

Incorporating strength training exercises helps maintain overall fitness and may indirectly influence nutrient metabolism.

Stress, Cortisol, and Folate

1. Cortisol's Impact:

Prolonged stress can elevate cortisol levels, potentially impacting folate absorption and utilization.

2. Immune Function:

Chronic stress may compromise immune function, affecting overall health and potentially influencing nutrient uptake.

Stress Management Techniques

1. Mindfulness Meditation:

Practicing mindfulness meditation can help reduce stress levels, positively influencing immune function and potentially supporting nutrient absorption.

2. Yoga and Relaxation Techniques:

Yoga and relaxation practices promote relaxation responses, potentially mitigating stress's impact on nutrient metabolism.

Exercise and Mental Health

1. Mood Regulation:

Regular exercise is associated with improved mood and mental well-being, indirectly impacting stress levels and overall health.

2. Cognitive Function:

Physical activity influences cognitive function, potentially supporting mental clarity and focus, factors that contribute to overall health and nutrient utilization.

Strategies for Stress Management

1. Breathing Exercises:

Deep breathing exercises and diaphragmatic breathing techniques promote relaxation and may positively impact stress hormone levels.

2. Time Management and Prioritization:

Organizing tasks and setting priorities can reduce stress, allowing for better focus on health-promoting activities, including adequate nutrition.

Exercise, Stress, and Folate Deficiency Prevention

1. Balancing Stress Levels:

Managing stress through exercise and stress-reduction techniques may indirectly support overall health, potentially impacting folate levels.

2. Enhancing Immune Function:

Stress management practices contribute to improved immune function, indirectly supporting the body's ability to absorb and utilize nutrients like folate.

Lifestyle Integration

1. Consistent Exercise Routine:

Incorporating regular exercise into daily routines promotes a healthy lifestyle and may positively impact nutrient absorption.

2. Stress-Reducing Activities:

Integrating stress-reduction practices into daily life supports overall well-being, potentially influencing nutrient metabolism and utilization.

Psychological Well-being and Nutrient Absorption

1. Mind-Body Connection:

Acknowledging the mind-body connection emphasizes the importance of mental health in optimizing physiological functions, including nutrient absorption.

2. Holistic Health Approach:

A holistic view of health considers both physical and mental well-being as integral components of overall health and nutrient metabolism.

Conclusion

Exercise and stress management are integral aspects of folate deficiency management, influencing nutrient absorption, utilization, and overall health. Regular exercise supports circulation and metabolic functions, potentially aiding nutrient uptake like folate. Stress management techniques, such as mindfulness, breathing exercises, and relaxation practices, contribute to reducing stress levels, indirectly impacting nutrient metabolism and immune function. Integrating exercise and stress reduction into daily routines promotes a holistic approach to health, supporting mental well-being and potentially enhancing folate absorption and utilization. Recognizing the interplay between physical activity, stress, and folate metabolism underscores the importance of a balanced lifestyle for optimal nutrient absorption and overall health.

8.3 Dietary and Lifestyle Changes for Folate Maintenance

Making dietary and lifestyle changes is fundamental in maintaining adequate folate levels and preventing deficiencies. These changes involve incorporating folate-rich foods, adopting healthy eating habits, and embracing lifestyle modifications that support optimal folate intake and absorption.

Importance of Dietary Changes

1. Folate-Rich Foods:

Emphasizing the consumption of foods naturally abundant in folate supports optimal nutrient intake.

2. Balanced Nutrition:

Encouraging a balanced diet rich in various nutrients, alongside folate, contributes to overall health and well-being.

Folate-Rich Foods

1. Leafy Greens:

Incorporating spinach, kale, and other leafy greens provides a significant source of natural folate.

2. Legumes and Beans:

Including lentils, chickpeas, and black beans boosts folate intake and adds variety to the diet.

3. Citrus Fruits:

Adding citrus fruits like oranges and grapefruits provides not only vitamin C but also folate.

4. Avocado and Asparagus:

Including avocado and asparagus diversifies folate sources in the diet.

Dietary Recommendations

1. Increased Vegetable Intake:

Encouraging a higher intake of folate-rich vegetables contributes to overall folate intake.

2. Balanced Protein Sources:

Combining folate-rich legumes with other protein sources promotes a balanced diet.

Cooking and Food Preparation

1. Minimal Processing:

Opting for fresh, minimally processed foods retains folate content better than heavily processed alternatives.

2. Cooking Techniques:

Choosing cooking methods that preserve folate, such as steaming or microwaving, maintains nutrient content.

Lifestyle Changes

1. Alcohol Moderation:

Reducing alcohol intake supports folate absorption, as excessive alcohol can interfere with its utilization.

2. Smoking Cessation:

Quitting smoking benefits overall health, including better folate utilization and absorption.

Meal Planning Strategies

1. Balanced Meal Composition:

Designing meals that include a variety of folate-rich foods ensures consistent nutrient intake.

2. Snack Choices:

Opting for folate-rich snacks like nuts, seeds, or fruits supports continuous nutrient intake throughout the day.

Reading Food Labels

1. Folate-Fortified Foods:

Identifying and incorporating folate-fortified foods, such as fortified cereals or bread, contributes to folate maintenance.

2. Understanding Labels:

Reading food labels helps identify sources of folate and make informed dietary choices.

Education and Awareness

1. Nutritional Education:

Providing information about folate-rich foods and their benefits fosters better dietary choices.

2. Public Awareness Campaigns:

Raising awareness about folate's importance and sources through public health campaigns encourages better dietary habits.

Dietary Supplements

1. Folate Supplements:

Considering supplementation, especially for individuals with increased requirements or difficulty meeting dietary folate needs.

2. Prenatal Vitamins:

For pregnant women or those planning pregnancy, prenatal vitamins containing folic acid aid in meeting increased folate demands.

Collaboration with Healthcare Providers

1. Nutritional Counseling:

Seeking guidance from registered dietitians or nutritionists for personalized dietary plans supports optimal folate intake.

2. Regular Health Check-ups:

Routine health assessments monitor folate levels and support timely interventions if deficiencies arise.

Conclusion

Implementing dietary and lifestyle changes is crucial in maintaining adequate folate levels and preventing deficiencies. Incorporating folate-rich foods, balanced meal planning, understanding food labels, and adopting healthy lifestyle habits, such as alcohol moderation and smoking cessation, contribute to optimal folate intake. Public awareness, education, and collaboration with healthcare providers further support informed dietary choices and supplementation when necessary. These changes promote overall health and well-being while specifically targeting the maintenance of adequate folate levels, ensuring optimal physiological function and reducing the risk of folate deficiency-related complications.

CHAPTER 9: RESEARCH AND FUTURE PERSPECTIVES

9.1 Ongoing Research in Folate and Anemia

Ongoing research in the field of folate and anemia continues to unravel the intricate connections between folate metabolism, its role in red blood cell production, and the multifaceted implications of folate deficiency in causing anemia. These investigations aim to enhance our understanding of the mechanisms involved, explore novel therapeutic approaches, and identify emerging trends in folate-related research.

Folate's Role in Anemia

1. Red Blood Cell Production:

Research delves into folate's indispensable role in erythropoiesis, the process of red blood cell formation, emphasizing its impact on preventing megaloblastic anemia.

2. Hemoglobin Synthesis:

Investigating how folate influences hemoglobin synthesis provides insights into its pivotal role in sustaining normal red blood cell function.

Folate Metabolism Studies

1. Genetic Factors:

Research explores genetic variations influencing folate metabolism enzymes, shedding light on individual susceptibility to folate deficiency-related anemia.

2. Pathways and Enzymatic Processes:

Detailed studies on folate metabolism pathways and enzymatic processes deepen our understanding of how disruptions lead to anemia.

Clinical Trials and Treatment Approaches

1. Therapeutic Interventions:

Ongoing clinical trials assess the efficacy of different forms of folate supplementation and combinations in managing folate deficiency anemia.

2. Novel Drug Development:

Investigating novel drugs targeting folate metabolism pathways presents potential alternatives for treating anemia and associated conditions.

Folate Deficiency and Disease Associations

1. Neurological Disorders:

Research explores the link between folate deficiency and neurological disorders, investigating potential preventive strategies and treatment modalities.

2. Cardiovascular Health:

Studies scrutinize the relationship between folate levels and cardiovascular health, assessing the impact of folate supplementation in reducing associated risks.

Emerging Trends in Research

1. Epigenetic Modifications:

Exploring how folate influences epigenetic modifications and gene expression patterns offers insights into its broader implications in health and disease.

2. Gut Microbiota and Folate Production:

Investigations into the interplay between gut microbiota and folate production unravel potential strategies to optimize folate absorption and utilization.

Nutritional Strategies and Population Studies

1. Dietary Patterns:

Research on diverse dietary patterns and their influence on folate intake and anemia prevalence contributes to tailored nutritional recommendations.

2. Population-Based Studies:

Large-scale studies analyze folate status across populations, identifying vulnerable groups and informing public health interventions.

Advanced Diagnostic Approaches

1. Biomarkers and Diagnostic Tools:

Advancements in identifying accurate biomarkers and diagnostic tools aid in early detection and precise management of folate deficiency anemia.

2. Imaging Techniques:

Innovative imaging techniques help visualize folate distribution and absorption patterns, contributing to a deeper understanding of folate metabolism.

Maternal and Child Health

1. Pregnancy Outcomes:

Investigating the impact of maternal folate status on pregnancy outcomes, including birth defects and long-term health implications in offspring.

2. Childhood Anemia:

Studies focus on childhood anemia, exploring preventive strategies and interventions to mitigate the long-term effects of folate deficiency.

Conclusion

Ongoing research in folate and anemia spans various domains, from fundamental biochemical pathways to clinical trials and population-based studies. Continual exploration of folate's role in red blood cell production, its metabolism, genetic influences, and disease associations forms the cornerstone of current investigations. Emerging trends in epigenetics, gut microbiota interactions, and advanced diagnostic tools offer promising avenues for understanding folate-related disorders. Integrating findings from these diverse areas contributes to refining therapeutic interventions, guiding public health policies, and improving outcomes for individuals affected by folate deficiency anemia and its associated complications. This persistent quest for knowledge fuels advancements aimed at better managing anemia, optimizing folate status, and promoting overall health across diverse populations.

9.2 Potential Innovations in Folate Supplementation

The field of folate supplementation continues to evolve, driven by ongoing research and innovative approaches aimed at enhancing the efficacy, accessibility, and personalized nature of folate interventions. These potential innovations span various realms, from novel delivery systems to tailored supplementation strategies, promising to address challenges and optimize folate intake.

Targeted Delivery Systems

1. Nanotechnology:

Nanoparticle-based delivery systems offer precise and controlled release of folate supplements, enhancing absorption and bioavailability.

2. Encapsulation Techniques:

Innovative encapsulation methods protect folate from

degradation, ensuring sustained release and improved absorption.

Enhanced Bioavailability

1. Methylated Folate Forms:

Utilizing methylated forms of folate, such as L-methylfolate, improves absorption for individuals with certain genetic variations impacting folate metabolism.

2. Liposomal Folate:

Liposomal formulations improve folate stability and absorption, potentially enhancing its utilization within the body.

Personalized Supplementation

1. Genetic Profiling:

Tailoring supplementation based on individual genetic profiles identifies optimal folate forms and dosages, maximizing efficacy.

2. Nutrigenomics:

Integrating nutrigenomic data enables personalized recommendations, considering an individual's unique response to folate supplements.

Fortification Innovations

1. Targeted Food Fortification:

Implementing targeted fortification programs in specific food groups based on consumption patterns improves folate intake in at-risk populations.

2. Biofortification:

Enhancing folate levels in staple crops through biofortification techniques addresses deficiencies at the source of dietary intake.

Combined Nutrient Approaches

1. Folate and Vitamin B12 Combination:

Formulating supplements combining folate and vitamin B12 improves their synergistic effects on red blood cell production.

2. Multivitamin Combinations:

Integrating folate within comprehensive multivitamin formulations ensures a balanced nutrient intake, benefiting overall health.

Novel Administration Methods

1. Transdermal Patches:

Exploring transdermal delivery systems for folate supplementation offers non-invasive and convenient options for absorption.

2. Sublingual Formulations:

Sublingual administration enhances folate absorption through the mucous membranes, bypassing digestive issues.

Technology Integration

1. Smartphone Applications:

Developing apps for personalized dosing reminders and tracking folate intake facilitates adherence and monitoring.

2. Wearable Devices:

Incorporating wearable devices for real-time monitoring of nutrient levels aids in personalized supplementation adjustments.

Natural Source Exploration

1. Phytochemical Extraction:

Extracting folate from natural sources like plants or algae provides bioactive forms for supplementation.

2. Fermentation Methods:

Utilizing fermentation processes to produce folate-rich supplements from microbial sources ensures natural and easily absorbed forms.

Sustainability and Accessibility

1. Cost-Effective Formulations:

Developing cost-effective formulations enables wider accessibility, ensuring affordability for diverse populations.

2. Global Health Initiatives:

Collaborative efforts focus on providing fortified foods or supplements in regions with limited access to folate-rich foods.

Regulatory and Safety Measures

1. Quality Control Standards:

Implementing stringent quality control measures ensures the safety and efficacy of folate supplements.

2. Regulatory Guidelines:

Continual refinement of regulatory guidelines addresses dosage recommendations and safety parameters for folate supplementation.

Conclusion

The potential innovations in folate supplementation encompass a wide spectrum of approaches, from advanced delivery systems and enhanced bioavailability to personalized and technology-integrated solutions. These innovations aim to address challenges in absorption, accessibility, and adherence while catering to individual needs and preferences. Novel fortification methods, combined nutrient approaches, and exploration of natural sources present promising avenues to optimize folate intake. Integrating technological advancements, sustainability considerations, and regulatory measures ensures safe, effective, and globally accessible folate supplementation strategies. These innovations herald a future where folate supplementation becomes more tailored, efficient, and impactful in addressing deficiencies and promoting overall health across diverse populations.

9.3 Challenges and Future Directions

The landscape of folate deficiency and its management presents multifaceted challenges and promising avenues for future exploration. Addressing these challenges while focusing on innovative directions can pave the way for improved prevention, diagnosis, and treatment strategies, enhancing overall health outcomes.

Challenges in Folate Deficiency Management

1. Access Disparities:

Disparities in access to folate-rich foods, supplements, and healthcare services contribute to varying prevalence rates of folate deficiency globally.

2. Awareness and Education:

Insufficient awareness about the importance of folate, particularly among at-risk populations, hampers timely interventions and preventive measures.

3. Genetic Variability:

Individual genetic variations impacting folate metabolism complicate supplementation strategies, requiring personalized approaches for optimal efficacy.

4. Compliance and Adherence:

Ensuring consistent compliance with supplementation regimens poses a challenge, impacting the effectiveness of interventions.

5. Diagnostic Accuracy:

Limited accuracy of diagnostic tools and biomarkers for assessing folate status presents challenges in precise identification of deficiencies.

Future Directions in Folate Deficiency Management

1. Targeted Interventions:

Developing targeted interventions that consider individual genetic profiles and nutritional needs for personalized folate supplementation.

2. Early-Life Interventions:

Focusing on maternal and childhood interventions to mitigate long-term consequences of folate deficiency, emphasizing prenatal care and childhood nutrition.

3. Technology Integration:

Leveraging technology for precision medicine, incorporating genetic testing, and digital health solutions for personalized folate supplementation guidance.

4. Public Health Initiatives:

Strengthening public health campaigns to raise awareness, educate communities, and promote accessible folate-rich foods and fortified products.

5. Holistic Approaches:

Embracing integrative approaches that combine nutrition, lifestyle modifications, and alternative therapies for comprehensive folate deficiency management.

6. Research Advancements:

Continual research into novel delivery systems, biofortification, and biomarkers to refine diagnostic accuracy and optimize folate interventions.

7. Global Collaboration:

Encouraging collaborative efforts among healthcare providers, researchers, policymakers, and international organizations to address global folate deficiency challenges.

8. Sustainable Strategies:

Developing sustainable fortification and supplementation

strategies to ensure long-term access and affordability, especially in resource-limited regions.

9. Regulatory Measures:

Strengthening regulatory frameworks to standardize folate fortification, supplementation guidelines, and safety parameters for optimal health outcomes.

Emerging Trends and Opportunities

1. Gut Microbiome Research:

Exploring the interplay between gut microbiota and folate production for innovative interventions and improved absorption.

2. Precision Nutrition:

Advancing precision nutrition models that integrate genetic, dietary, and lifestyle factors to tailor folate interventions.

3. Epigenetics and Folate:

Investigating epigenetic mechanisms influenced by folate, offering insights into disease prevention and personalized interventions.

4. Artificial Intelligence (AI) in Healthcare:

Harnessing AI-driven algorithms for predictive modeling and personalized folate supplementation guidance based on individual data.

5. Nutritional Genomics:

Expanding nutrigenomic research to decipher how genetic variations influence folate metabolism and guide personalized interventions.

Conclusion

Folate deficiency management faces challenges rooted in access, awareness, individual variability, and diagnostic limitations. However, promising future directions aim to address these challenges through targeted interventions, technology integration, holistic approaches, and global collaboration. Emerging trends in gut microbiome research, precision nutrition, epigenetics, AI in healthcare, and nutritional genomics offer opportunities for innovative strategies to combat folate deficiency. Embracing these directions and fostering interdisciplinary collaborations can pave the way for more effective, personalized, and accessible folate interventions, ultimately improving health outcomes and reducing the burden of folate deficiency-related conditions on a global scale.

CHAPTER 10: CASE STUDIES AND CLINICAL SCENARIOS

10.1 Case Studies Illustrating Folate Deficiency Anemia

Case studies serve as valuable tools in understanding the clinical manifestations, diagnostic challenges, and treatment approaches in individuals affected by folate deficiency anemia. Here are illustrative case studies showcasing the diverse presentations and management of this condition.

Case Study 1: Prenatal Folate Deficiency

Patient Profile:

Mrs. A, a 32-year-old pregnant woman in her second trimester, presented with fatigue, shortness of breath, and pale skin.

Clinical Presentation:

She reported adherence to a vegetarian diet with limited folate-rich foods. Blood tests revealed low hemoglobin levels and decreased serum folate levels.

Diagnosis and Treatment:

A diagnosis of folate deficiency anemia was made. Mrs. A was prescribed folic acid supplementation (800 mcg/day) and counseled on dietary modifications to increase folate intake. Regular follow-ups showed improvement in hemoglobin levels and overall well-being.

Case Study 2: Chronic Malabsorption and Anemia

Patient Profile:

Mr. B, a 45-year-old man with a history of Crohn's disease, presented with chronic diarrhea, weight loss, and fatigue.

Clinical Presentation:

Despite nutritional support and dietary adjustments, Mr. B showed persistent anemia. Blood tests revealed low serum folate and vitamin B12 levels.

Diagnosis and Treatment:

Extensive investigations confirmed chronic malabsorption contributing to folate and vitamin B12 deficiency anemia. Treatment included intramuscular vitamin B12 injections and high-dose oral folic acid supplementation (5 mg/day). Multidisciplinary care involving gastroenterologists and nutritionists was crucial in managing his condition.

Case Study 3: Alcoholism and Severe Anemia

Patient Profile:

Mr. C, a 50-year-old chronic alcoholic, presented with weakness, dizziness, and jaundice.

Clinical Presentation:

Blood tests indicated severe anemia, with macrocytic red blood cells and low serum folate levels. Liver function tests showed signs of alcoholic liver disease.

Diagnosis and Treatment:

A diagnosis of folate deficiency anemia secondary to chronic alcoholism was established. Mr. C received intravenous folate supplementation alongside nutritional support and addiction counseling. Collaboration between hematologists and addiction specialists facilitated his recovery and abstinence from alcohol, leading to gradual improvement in his anemia.

Case Study 4: Pediatric Folate Deficiency

Patient Profile:

Sarah, a 6-year-old girl, presented with recurrent infections, fatigue, and poor growth.

Clinical Presentation:

Blood tests revealed anemia, and further investigations identified inadequate dietary intake due to Sarah's selective eating habits, avoiding folate-rich foods.

Diagnosis and Treatment:

Sarah was diagnosed with folate deficiency anemia, emphasizing the importance of nutritional counseling and parental education. She received folic acid supplementation and was guided to incorporate folate-rich foods into her diet. Regular monitoring showed improvement in her growth and overall health.

Case Study 5: Elderly Patient with Dietary Restrictions

Patient Profile:

Mrs. D, an 80-year-old woman living in a nursing home, presented with weakness and confusion.

Clinical Presentation:

Blood tests revealed megaloblastic anemia with low serum folate levels. Mrs. D had dietary restrictions due to denture-related issues, leading to reduced intake of folate-containing foods.

Diagnosis and Treatment:

Folate deficiency anemia was diagnosed, and Mrs. D received folic acid supplementation along with dietary modifications. Collaborative care involving dietitians and dentists addressed her dietary limitations, leading to improved folate intake and resolution of her anemia.

Conclusion

These case studies underscore the diverse etiologies and

presentations of folate deficiency anemia across different demographics. They highlight the importance of timely diagnosis, personalized interventions, and multidisciplinary care involving healthcare professionals such as hematologists, gastroenterologists, nutritionists, and addiction specialists. Through these cases, the significance of nutritional education, targeted supplementation, and addressing underlying conditions contributing to folate deficiency becomes evident, emphasizing the need for holistic approaches in managing this condition across various patient populations.

10.2 Clinical Scenarios and Treatment Outcomes

Exploring clinical scenarios and treatment outcomes in the context of folate deficiency anemia provides insights into the diverse presentations, diagnostic challenges, and varying responses to interventions. Here are illustrative clinical scenarios highlighting different presentations and the corresponding treatment outcomes:

Clinical Scenario 1: Adolescent with Dietary Insufficiency

Patient Profile:

A 16-year-old adolescent presented with fatigue, pallor, and decreased exercise tolerance.

Clinical Presentation:

Blood tests revealed low hemoglobin and serum folate levels. Further evaluation indicated a diet lacking in folate-rich foods due to dietary preferences.

Treatment and Outcome:

The patient was prescribed folic acid supplementation and received nutritional counseling to incorporate folate-rich foods. Over the course of several months, improvement in hemoglobin levels and resolution of symptoms were observed with adherence to the dietary recommendations.

Clinical Scenario 2: Elderly Patient with Malabsorption

Patient Profile:

An 70-year-old individual with a history of celiac disease presented with anemia and neurological symptoms.

Clinical Presentation:

Blood tests showed macrocytic anemia and low serum folate levels despite a gluten-free diet. Malabsorption secondary to celiac disease was identified as the cause.

Treatment and Outcome:

Supplementation with high-dose oral folic acid was initiated alongside management of celiac disease. Gradual improvement in anemia and neurological symptoms was observed, emphasizing the need for addressing underlying malabsorption issues in treatment.

Clinical Scenario 3: Pregnancy Complicated by Folate Deficiency

Patient Profile:

A 30-year-old pregnant woman presented with weakness and preeclampsia during her second trimester.

Clinical Presentation:

Laboratory investigations revealed folate deficiency anemia, contributing to the pregnancy-related complications.

Treatment and Outcome:

Immediate supplementation with folic acid was initiated along with comprehensive prenatal care. Prompt intervention led to the resolution of anemia and improvement in pregnancy outcomes, underscoring the critical role of folate in maternal and fetal health.

Clinical Scenario 4: Chronic Alcoholism and Severe Anemia

Patient Profile:

A 45-year-old chronic alcoholic presented with lethargy, jaundice, and severe anemia.

Clinical Presentation:

Blood tests showed macrocytic anemia with markedly decreased serum folate levels, indicating alcohol-induced folate deficiency.

Treatment and Outcome:

Intravenous folate supplementation and alcohol cessation support were provided. Despite challenges in compliance, gradual improvement in anemia was observed with sustained abstinence and continued folate supplementation.

Clinical Scenario 5: Bariatric Surgery Complications
Patient Profile:

A 35-year-old woman who underwent bariatric surgery presented with weakness and anemia.

Clinical Presentation:

Postoperative complications led to malabsorption, causing folate deficiency anemia despite vitamin supplementation.

Treatment and Outcome:

Adjustment in folate supplementation dosage and supportive therapy for malabsorption were initiated. With tailored interventions, the patient showed improvement in anemia and related symptoms, emphasizing the importance of individualized post-bariatric care.

Clinical Scenario 6: Pediatric Case with Dietary Restrictions
Patient Profile:

A 8-year-old child presented with fatigue and developmental delays.

Clinical Presentation:

Laboratory investigations revealed folate deficiency anemia due to the child's restrictive diet and aversion to folate-rich foods.

Treatment and Outcome:

Supplementation with folic acid was coupled with behavioral interventions and parental education on nutrition. Over time, improvement in the child's symptoms and developmental progress was observed with adherence to dietary recommendations.

Conclusion

These clinical scenarios highlight the diverse etiologies, presentations, and treatment outcomes associated with folate deficiency anemia. They underscore the importance of personalized interventions tailored to address underlying causes, whether dietary insufficiency, malabsorption, pregnancy-related complications, or lifestyle factors like chronic alcoholism or bariatric surgery. Successful outcomes were achieved through a combination of targeted supplementation, dietary modifications, and management of underlying conditions, emphasizing the need for individualized care and comprehensive approaches in managing folate deficiency anemia across various patient populations.

10.3 Lessons Learned and Recommendations

Reflecting on lessons learned from clinical experiences with folate deficiency anemia offers valuable insights and informs recommendations for better management and prevention strategies. Here are key lessons learned and corresponding recommendations:

Lessons Learned

1. Importance of Early Diagnosis:

Timely recognition of folate deficiency anemia through comprehensive evaluations, including serum folate levels and blood counts, is crucial for prompt intervention.

2. Diverse Etiologies:

Acknowledging the various causes, from dietary insufficiency to malabsorption and underlying medical conditions, underscores the need for thorough assessments tailored to individual patient profiles.

3. Impact of Lifestyle Factors:

Lifestyle choices, such as dietary preferences, chronic alcoholism, or post-bariatric complications, significantly influence folate status, necessitating targeted interventions.

4. Role of Multidisciplinary Care:

Collaboration among hematologists, gastroenterologists, nutritionists, obstetricians, and addiction specialists facilitates holistic management, addressing underlying issues and improving outcomes.

5. Significance of Patient Education:

Educating patients and caregivers about the importance of folate-rich diets, supplementation adherence, and addressing lifestyle factors is critical for long-term management.

6. Effectiveness of Personalized Interventions:

Tailoring interventions based on individual needs, including genetic factors and dietary preferences, leads to better outcomes and improved patient compliance.

7. Maternal-Fetal Health Considerations:

Recognizing the impact of folate deficiency on pregnancy outcomes emphasizes the importance of early intervention and comprehensive prenatal care.

Recommendations

1. Enhanced Screening Protocols:

Implementing comprehensive screening protocols for at-risk populations, including pregnant women, individuals with malabsorption disorders, and chronic alcoholics, can aid in early detection.

2. Individualized Treatment Approaches:

Customizing treatment plans based on the underlying cause, patient demographics, and lifestyle factors is pivotal for optimizing outcomes.

3. Nutritional Counseling and Education:

Incorporating nutritional counseling and educational programs to promote folate-rich diets, especially in pediatric and pregnant populations, is crucial.

4. Integration of Technology:

Leveraging digital health platforms for patient education, monitoring supplementation adherence, and facilitating remote consultations improves patient engagement and follow-ups.

5. Interdisciplinary Collaboration:

Encouraging collaborative care among various specialties ensures comprehensive management, addressing both medical and lifestyle aspects contributing to folate deficiency.

6. Public Health Initiatives:

Strengthening public health campaigns to raise awareness about folate's importance, fortification programs, and accessible healthcare services promotes preventive measures.

7. Continuous Research and Innovation:

Encouraging ongoing research into advanced diagnostic tools, innovative supplementation approaches, and personalized interventions drives advancements in folate deficiency management.

8. Addressing Healthcare Disparities:

Focusing on addressing healthcare disparities, especially in underserved populations with limited access to folate-rich foods or healthcare services, is crucial for equitable care.

9. Long-Term Follow-Up:

Emphasizing the need for regular monitoring and long-term follow-ups post-treatment ensures sustained adherence to dietary modifications or supplementation regimens.

Conclusion

Lessons gleaned from clinical experiences underscore the multifaceted nature of folate deficiency anemia and its management. The recommendations outlined above aim to improve diagnosis, treatment, and preventive strategies by advocating for early screening, personalized care, patient education, interdisciplinary collaboration, and continued research efforts. Implementing these recommendations can significantly impact patient outcomes, enhance public health initiatives, and mitigate the burden of folate deficiency anemia, ensuring better health and well-being across diverse populations.

Printed in Great Britain
by Amazon

41686516R10059